Microsoft

Team Collaboration

Using Microsoft® Office for
More Effective Teamwork

JOHN PIERCE

PUBLISHED BY
Microsoft Press
A Division of Microsoft Corporation
One Microsoft Way
Redmond, Washington 98052-6399

Copyright © 2012 by John Pierce

Library of Congress Control Number: 2012950443
ISBN: 978-0-7356-6962-8

Printed and bound in the United States of America.

First Printing

Microsoft Press books are available through booksellers and distributors worldwide. If you need support related to this book, email Microsoft Press Book Support at mspinput@microsoft.com. Please tell us what you think of this book at http://www.microsoft.com/learning/booksurvey.

Acquisitions Editor: Rosemary Caperton
Developmental Editor: Rosemary Caperton
Project Editor: Valerie Woolley
Editorial Production: Megan Smith-Creed
Technical Reviewer: Jorge Diaz; Technical Review services provided by Content Master, a member of CM Group, Ltd.
Copyeditor: Megan Smith-Creed
Indexer: Perri Weinberg Schenker
Cover: Twist Creative · Seattle

Contents

What do you think of this book? We want to hear from you!

Microsoft is interested in hearing your feedback so we can continually improve our
books and learning resources for you. To participate in a brief online survey, please visit:

microsoft.com/learning/booksurvey

What do you think of this book? We want to hear from you!

Microsoft is interested in hearing your feedback so we can continually improve our books and learning resources for you. To participate in a brief online survey, please visit:

microsoft.com/learning/booksurvey

Introduction

THE EXPERIENCE OF working on a team can be deeply rewarding and deeply frustrating—and sometimes both at the same time. Team members can leave a meeting feeling good about themselves when they've solved a particularly difficult issue or seen the results of a new process that alleviated redundant work or reduced the number of errors. On the other hand, the imperative of getting work done on schedule can lead to miscommunications and misunderstandings, undocumented shortcuts, abbreviated reviews, or just sloppy preparation—experiences that can damage a team's spirit and its reputation. In these cases, team members need to have a system in place that allows them to do more than promise to avoid similar mistakes in the future.

On its own, Microsoft Office can't ensure that a team works together effectively. Team dynamics, leadership, clarity of goals, and other mostly intangible factors play a large role in that. But having a tool such as Office at the center of how a team produces its work does provide support for important needs, including access to information, ease of communication, and content management (such as document versions, reviews, workflows, and approved publishing).

In *Team Collaboration: Using Microsoft Office for More Effective Teamwork*, you'll learn about these and other capabilities in Office—and also receive some advice about the nature and goals of teamwork.

The nature of work in general has changed as the result of worker mobility, the use of mobile computing devices, cloud computing and services, and the predominance of teamwork of all sorts. To meet these needs, the programs in Office have steadily evolved to facilitate collaboration. As you'll see as you read this book, Office is no longer designed with the assumption that you'll use it all on your own—at least for very long. At times, of course, you'll be at your PC, typing a document, preparing a presentation, or crunching numbers. But in most cases, the results of these activities will soon be shared with your coworkers, not to mention with managers, partners, vendors, and others.

And sharing work is often just the beginning of effective collaboration. What I hope you gain from this book is an understanding of how the capabilities in Office let teams share work in context—to help gather opinions, set goals, manage time, and facilitate decisions.

Who this book is for

Team Collaboration: Using Microsoft Office for More Effective Teamwork is intended for individuals and groups who want to know how to use Office to facilitate the work they do as a team. In this context, "team" could mean a small business (say, 5 to 12 people), a department within a larger organization, a project team made up of individuals from several different departments, or a group of independent contractors working together on one or more projects.

I use the term "project" frequently in this book to refer to the work teams do together. In many cases, this might be a true project (an activity with a defined set of goals and with specific start and end dates), but I also intend "project" to refer to the ongoing work of a team—work that is structured by tasks and the creation, review, and approval of documents and information.

And, of course, this book is intended for teams that create content in Office as one of their principal activities. This covers a broad spectrum of job roles and industries, including (but not limited to) sales, marketing, legal work, insurance, publishing, retail, engineering, government and public policy, nonprofits, and education.

Assumptions

This book contains both descriptive information that highlights capabilities in Office and some step-by-step procedures that lead you through a series of commands to execute a particular task. I've written this book assuming that readers are familiar with the general Office user interface or are learning it by consulting another source. You should at a minimum understand the structure of the Office ribbon and how it is organized in tabs and groups of commands.

Advanced users of Office will likely already work with many of the features described in the book. This book also does not cover any Office administration tasks. It does not describe how to centrally administer a SharePoint site collection, for example, or how to configure Lync Server or Exchange Server. Readers who need this information should turn to Microsoft TechNet (*www.microsoft.com/technet*) or other books from Microsoft Press.

How this book is organized

This book is organized in two parts. Part 1, "Concepts and basic tools," includes the book's first four chapters. It provides background information about how people work as a team and describes steps teams can take in Office to set up the tools they use to manage their work over time.

- Chapter 1, "Collaboration basics," describes factors that influence team dynamics, how teams can avoid groupthink, the use of brainstorming techniques, and other aspects of working as a group. This chapter also introduces some of the collaboration capabilities in Office.

- Chapter 2, "Building a SharePoint team site," covers details of how a team site can facilitate collaborative work, including how to work with a document library, how to track and manage tasks, and how to conduct a team discussion in SharePoint. This chapter also covers how to set up a workflow to manage document approval as well as other capabilities in SharePoint.

- Chapter 3, "Managing access and preserving history," details why and how teams need to control access to at least some of the information and content that they produce. You'll learn about the digital rights service in Office, document passwords, and how you can inspect a document to detect information that is best not to share. Chapter 3 also returns to the discussion of SharePoint to cover how to implement versions and approved publishing on a team site.

- Chapter 4, "Building team templates," explains why templates are useful in coordinating the work a team does. It covers how to find and work with the templates that come with Office; describes elements and features that make up templates in Excel, PowerPoint, and Word; and offers examples of how to build templates from scratch.

Part 2, "Working day to day as a team," includes Chapters 5 through 11. The majority of these chapters examine how teams can use specific programs in Office to collaborate. They also describe how the programs work together—for example, how you can manage a SharePoint task list from Outlook (Chapter 5, "An integrated Outlook"), make a PowerPoint presentation in Microsoft Lync (Chapter 6, "Working together in Lync"), or link notes in a OneNote notebook to a document in Word (Chapter 7, "Keeping track of discussions and ideas"). Chapters 8 through 10, respectively, cover collaborative features in Word, Excel, and PowerPoint. In these chapters you'll learn about coauthoring, a feature that enables more than one person to work on a file at the same time, in addition to more conventional collaborative features such as comments, revision marks, and combining and comparing files.

Chapter 11, "Working with Office Web Apps on SkyDrive," provides an overview of the capabilities available on SkyDrive, Microsoft's cloud service that provides storage, versioning, e-mail (under most circumstances), a calendar, and a contact list. You'll also learn more about Office Web Apps, which are web-based versions of the desktop programs that let you work with documents in a web browser.

Reading this book in chapter order is not necessary, but the book is designed (especially in Part 1) to add layers to the descriptions of features and capabilities as chapters progress. Readers just starting out working on a team will benefit from reading and working through the examples in the chapters in Part 1 before moving on to the specific program features covered in Part 2.

Office versions and requirements

The screen shots and procedures in this book are based on the Office 2013 Preview available during the summer and early fall of 2012. Keep in mind that the appearance of Office and the steps you follow to complete a task might be different in the final version that is released.

Some of the programs discussed in this book require server systems to run. These include SharePoint and Lync. In addition, some of the features described for Outlook are tied to using Outlook on Exchange Server. You can find information about online hosting services for SharePoint and Lync on Microsoft's website. You can also find information about third-party hosting solutions on the web.

Acknowledgments

Thanks to Rosemary Caperton, Valerie Woolley, Megan Smith-Creed, and Jorge Diaz for their help organizing, editing, and producing this book. Thanks also to Charles Schwenk for his conversations over the years, especially regarding the nature of groups and organizations, and to Lucinda Rowley, who exemplifies a collaborative spirit. On the home front, gratitude to MC, Fox, and Holly.

How to get support & provide feedback

The following sections provide information on errata, book support, feedback, and contact information.

Errata & book support

We've made every effort to ensure the accuracy of this book and its companion content. Any errors that have been reported since this book was published are listed on our Microsoft Press site at oreilly.com:

> *http://go.microsoft.com/FWLink/?Linkid=263537*

If you find an error that is not already listed, you can report it to us through the same page.

If you need additional support, e-mail Microsoft Press Book Support at

> *mspinput@microsoft.com*

Please note that product support for Microsoft software is not offered through the addresses above.

We want to hear from you

At Microsoft Press, your satisfaction is our top priority and your feedback our most valuable asset. Please tell us what you think of this book at

> *http://www.microsoft.com/learning/booksurvey*

The survey is short, and we read every one of your comments and ideas. Thanks in advance for your input!

Stay in touch

Let's keep the conversation going! We're on Twitter:

> *http://twitter.com/MicrosoftPress*

1 Concepts and basic tools

CHAPTER 1

Collaboration basics

WHAT DOES IT MEAN to work in collaboration as a team? Sometimes, it's as simple as sharing resources and information, but complex concepts are also involved. For example, collaboration depends on relationships that team members build and maintain, and at the foundation of these relationships lies the need for each team member to act accountably toward his or her own responsibilities. The pursuit of group goals and objectives that depend on individual responsibilities is a dynamic that's always active, and how teams understand and remain aware of this context is part of how they remain effective.

In this chapter, I'll describe aspects of how teams work together. Many books are written on this topic, and you can find lots of information and a range of opinions by searching the web. This chapter won't cover the topic in full depth, of course. As a way of introducing ideas about the nature of collaboration, I've selected areas that in my experience are most relevant to the teams I've worked on. I'll briefly describe team dynamics, the perils of groupthink, types of group tasks, and a few other topics. In the last major section of this chapter, I'll relate some of these concepts to specific programs and features in Microsoft Office. The aims are to provide some ideas you can consider as you work as a team and to introduce how you can apply these ideas when you work together and on your own in Office.

<table>
<tr><td>NOTE</td><td>In preparing this chapter, I've relied on information from the following sources: "Virtual teamwork— nature's four collaboration methods" (http://www.bioteams.com/2005/06/04/virtual_teamwork.html) and "Ten rules that govern groups" (http://www.spring.org.uk/2009/07/10-rules-that-govern-groups.php).</td></tr>
</table>

Team dynamics and leadership

The groups and teams we're a part of can provide an important measure of our social and professional identity. We want to be identified with success and not with dysfunction, and we derive satisfaction from being a member of a team that projects values we agree with—an openness to new ideas, for example—and follows cohesive, well-designed processes and plans.

Who leads your team and your role on a team make a significant difference as to how your team operates. Are you in a role that is accountable for budgets and schedules? If something goes wrong, are you one of the team members who share the blame, or is your role more functional and operational—a role involved less with strategy and more with implementation?

Team dynamics—which involves how teams exchange ideas, make decisions, and resolve conflicts—are influenced by the composition and hierarchy of a team. Some teams have no specific reporting structure—no shared manager and no one member with overall responsibility for the success of the team. These might be teams of peers from different departments or groups. Each team member might report to a different group manager, who in turn reports to a division manager, which provides some common leadership. But lines of authority might be more diffuse than this. A team might consist of coworkers from different divisions, for example, or a team can be "virtual" and made up of people who work together as independent contractors on discreet projects.

Some teams aren't at all democratic. These teams have specific leaders as a result of a member's role (a designated project manager, for example) or organizational hierarchy. Team members can also assume positions of leadership through their experience and by example. On teams like this, collaboration still involves building consensus by adapting and expanding a point of view or a plan of action so that a team works collectively toward specific goals.

Whether a team is led by example, by committee, or by appointment, effective teams and those who lead them should strive to do the following:

- Encourage participation in discussions and the expression of ideas. How much fun is it to attend a team meeting every week where only the manager speaks or you hear from just the same few talkative individuals? Effective teams especially need good processes to orient new members. Documentation helps in this regard, but you can also use mentors and peers to introduce and coach new team members about common processes and practices.

- Find ways to let team members learn and apply new skills, which can be a tricky goal to implement. People have experience and expertise that make it imperative that they be the ones assigned to do certain tasks. You might work in an organizational environment that provides training and professional development, which can offer formal paths to gaining new skills. If not, more initiative is needed to acquire, enhance, and adapt skills that give you the versatility to take on different, more challenging opportunities within a team.

- Point to accomplishments. Most everyone likes to be praised and to receive recognition. You can do this in lots of different ways, both formal and informal.

- Share information. This sounds simple and straightforward, and it often is, especially for information that's related solely to the activities of the team. Teams need to set up mechanisms for regular feedback on the status of group work, which ensures that team members are all working with the latest information. But teams (especially those within larger organizations) don't work in vacuums. Sometimes rumors in the mill have a direct bearing on the composition of a team, its long-term plans, and its immediate work. Some team members might have information that others don't and might not be at liberty to reveal it. That can cause tension or ill will from time to time. Teamwork isn't a conflict-free zone, so . . .

- Discuss issues and conflicts and seek timely resolutions. Team members (and team leaders) need to be sensitive to the scope and effect of issues that cause controversy. Conversations that focus on gathering facts and opinions and on understanding whatever's been misunderstood might involve only one or two team members. If possible, a resolution that affects the entire team should be presented impartially (without pointing fingers, that is) and the reasons behind the decision explained. Some issues affect the whole team from the start (scheduling or resource conflicts are often among these topics), so taking on these issues in a full team meeting can help identify specific points that need attention and—with good luck—lead to a resolution the full team accepts. Keep in mind that impulsive actions aren't the same as timely actions. A desire to act quickly can sometimes make a situation worse, especially if the action isn't informed by all the facts and is taken without consulting everyone with a stake in the outcome.

That's some of what you want from a team leader. Team members play their part as well in creating a team dynamic that's effective:

- Do what you say you're going to do. Fulfilling the responsibilities you've been assigned generates confidence in other team members. Of course, forces are always at play that can hinder the performance of your work, so you can add "to the best of your abilities" here. It's a simple case of team members being able to depend on each other. Conscientious effort also builds a sense that you've made a contribution.

- In discussions with other team members, try not to personalize issues. Describe how an issue affects the completion of a task or delays the schedule or adds to the budget—in other words, try to focus your discussion on the situation and not on the team members involved, even when you believe a team member's performance is at the root of the issue. This approach is intended to maintain healthy lines of communication and respect. It's possible you don't have all the facts, and you want to avoid accusations that aren't grounded in the true nature of a situation.

- Do your work with the attitude you want other team members to display. Volunteer and show initiative, but be mindful of the role each team member has. In other words, initiative is great, but don't usurp responsibilities. Show respect for the experience and expertise of other team members, and offer suggestions for improvement openly.

The importance of dissent

Day to day, team members perform their work in the context of many different decisions. Some decisions are routine and straightforward and are made by team leaders, team members with specific expertise, or team members responsible for specific aspects of a team's work. But even with decisions that affect routine work, teams can sometimes turn a blind eye toward alternatives. A new team member, for example, with experience in another organization or with different tools, suggests a change to a process and is met only with a chorus of "That's not how we do it" or "That won't work because." Those types of answers are one way teams can become stale and gloomy places.

Teams should collect and welcome a wide range of opinions to remain effective in their decision making. Essentially, teams need to avoid groupthink, the phenomenon where everyone on a team agrees for the sake of agreeing and simply goes along. Structured work environments can provide plenty of incentives to agree for the sake of agreeing. Team members operate within a context of performance reviews, the prospect of pro-motions, and the desire to maintain positive relationships with team members and others within a larger group. Teams are often assembled with common values in mind. Team leaders and managers look for people who "fit," who will be good team players. And cohesiveness has an important role in making a team productive. If every action a team undertakes is subject to second guessing, little actual work can take place, or at least that's often the perception.

Sometimes, speaking up isn't easy, especially on teams where you might be new or on teams with a couple of members who tend to control and dominate conversations. If you disagree with the majority of your team members, even for reasons you find important and can document, your disagreement can be taken as a sign of disrespect. You don't want to be considered a troublemaker. Team members who do offer contrary opinions should offer them without attacking anyone else personally and generally focus only on issues that are truly important. Just as you don't want to agree only to agree, there's little value in a team member who always says the team is doing the wrong thing. That starts to sound more like whining than constructive dissent.

But team members should not simply dismiss opinions that aren't aligned with how the majority views an issue. It might seem like you are saving time by making a decision without pausing to take account of alternative views, but a team that doesn't cultivate the ability to consider and investigate alternatives runs the risk of missing opportuni-ties for productive change and can perpetuate inefficiencies by clinging to processes and procedures only because that's the way things have always been done. And there's another advantage to listening to all points of view: having listened openly to contrary views, if a team sticks with a time-honored process or decides to follow what the major-ity of team members think is the best approach, it's more likely that the decision will be carried out with a high degree of motivation.

Teams can put in place some practices to help lessen the ill effects of groupthink. Have a team member play devil's advocate (the team member asked to be the devil's advocate is generally not the team's leader). To do this, someone in the group has to be critical—to bring up weaknesses and poke holes in the viewpoints that currently prevail. The aim of devil's advocacy is to come up with a number of solutions and to lessen the bias that the team as a whole might have toward the current point of view. Remember that having someone on the team play the devil's advocate might not be enough. If someone is only playing a role, that person might not be taken seriously. Make room on your team for truly contrary opinions. This keeps the environment open to a broader range of possible solutions to the problem being discussed.

Team leaders play a crucial role in how well dissent is tolerated and used. It's nice to work on a team on which leaders facilitate conversation and encourage participation without pushing the conversation in one direction. Of course, when someone needs to make a decision, you want that aspect of leadership to be evident too.

Generating and evaluating ideas

Collaborative work is often facilitated through approaches that don't enforce rigorous structures. Brainstorming sessions can serve this purpose, where some or all of a team's members gather to generate ideas about future work, exchange ideas about what processes can be improved, or outline solutions to particularly difficult problems that keep coming up.

Brainstorming has been used for many years as a way for teams and groups to generate ideas. Brainstorming can be creative and help offset groupthink, for example, by letting team members offer ideas, share information, and outline suggestions in an environment that postpones evaluation and encourages a relaxed exchange. The idea is to generate idea after idea for further consideration, not to mull over the pros and cons of any particular idea on the spot.

Team brainstorming sessions can produce good results, but for a variety of reasons (listed next), these meetings can end up not being that effective:

- It can be hard to get everyone to participate in a group meeting. Because the environment is intended to be relaxed, some team members might decide they only need to show up; they don't need to come with ideas.

- Even though the goal of a brainstorming meeting is to generate ideas without evaluating them, team members will often be hesitant to speak up for fear that their ideas are being judged.

- The conversation becomes too detailed. Someone announces an idea that sparks further conversation, which is great, but the conversation can become bogged down. Team members waiting their turn to offer ideas might not get the chance if the meeting runs too long or won't speak up when it's time because they think their idea won't receive the same level of reception.

If your team does hold a brainstorming meeting, apply some or all of the ideas in the following list to run the meeting more effectively:

■ Let people know the topic of the brainstorming session ahead of time, and ask team members to prepare their ideas in advance.

■ Keep track of how many ideas each team member offers. Sounds sort of silly, but don't let one or two team members offer a dozen ideas, while other team members offer only a few.

■ Keep the scope of the issue you're brainstorming about manageable. If you are looking for feedback on large-scale concepts, break down the concept into questions that address specific aspects of the issue. You could even have the team meet in smaller groups and have each group brainstorm about one of the related questions.

■ Come away with as many ideas as possible. Tell the team at the outset that you want to list twenty or thirty or whatever number of good-quality ideas that the team can then consider and evaluate later in more detail.

Teams should not restrict themselves to brainstorming meetings as a way to generate ideas. You might get better results following a couple of different approaches. For example, some research has concluded that people working by themselves often come up with more and better ideas, and conducting brainstorming sessions online has been shown to produce good results. Teams might use e-mail to brainstorm, asking everyone to send ideas to a team member who collects the ideas in a single document. The team can then meet to review and discuss the ideas. At the meeting, team members might be inspired to come forward with additional ideas.

TIP   As you'll see in Chapter 2, "Building a SharePoint team site," you can set up a discussion board in Microsoft SharePoint. A discussion board lets people offer new ideas and also see ideas others have offered, which they can then start to build on.

Without diminishing the benefits of holding a brainstorming meeting, a team might be better off letting its members generate ideas on their own and come together later for discussion and evaluation. Evaluating ideas as a group has the added advantage that the team can begin to come to a consensus about the ideas they want to develop. Each member of the team participates in the evaluation process, and when agreement is reached on the course to take, the team should have a broad level of participation.

ARE WE BETTER WHEN WE WORK WITH OTHERS?

Does being part of a team inspire an individual to do better work? When you read about teams and the nature of teamwork, sports and animals inevitably come up as examples that point to the advantages of teamwork. For example, one ant building a nest works slowly, but when that ant is joined by others, work quickens significantly. Here, maybe the ants working together is the point, or maybe it's at least partly the competition.

Researchers have noted this trend in sports and in simple social situations. One experiment concluded that bicyclists ride faster when they're competing as part of a team. And, long ago (1898), a researcher interested in this topic had children wind thread onto a reel both on their own and in competition with others. The children wound more thread in the competitive context.

Like ants, do human beings achieve more simply because others are around? Over the years, research suggests that being engaged in an activity with other people does improve performance, and this concept seems particularly true when individuals in a group are working on tasks that are generally distinct, so that an individual performance can be recognized and not just the effort of the group. In situations when the contribution of a particular individual in the group is hard to determine, people have a tendency to make less effort. Researchers use a tug of war as an example of this kind of work.

Researchers have taken this one step further to study whether the element of competition is necessary to improve an individual's performance in a group or whether the simple presence of the group is enough. In one of the experiments designed to test this concept, people were asked to write down as many words as they could that were related to a given target word. They were given three one-minute periods and told they were not in competition with each other. More often than not, participants produced more words when others were present than when they were alone. Later research showed that for tasks that are harder than writing down words, performance of individuals didn't improve but got worse.

In the 1960s, some research on individual performance in groups focused on an approach called "drive theory." The idea here is that in front of other people, individuals are more alert and excited. In a state of greater awareness, we respond well if our habits and skills fit the situation but not if our habits and skills don't apply.

Later research developed a theory that centered on distraction and conflict. This theory asserted that a group can serve essentially as a distraction. In this context, a conflict arises between an individual's attention to a task at hand and the presence of the group. This conflict doesn't impede progress on generally simply tasks, but it can cause work on complex tasks to suffer.

Put into practice, the history of this and other research suggests that when teams are involved in work in which the effort of individual members is clear, the individuals perform better, which should carry over to the team as a whole. In situations where it's hard for individuals to distinguish themselves—in other words, where it's easy for team members to hide—being in a group makes an individual's performance worse.

The needs of virtual teams

I hope this book will appeal to teams of all sorts—small businesses, departments in larger organizations, as well as virtual teams made up of freelance workers or workers from several different companies. I'm not alone in the experience of having worked regularly with someone for years without ever meeting him face to face. I work in a home office most days, but when I need to, I work in coffee shops. People with full-time jobs in organizations large and small have similar experiences—working with partners and vendors across the globe, working on the road, catching up at home in the evening.

Given the nature of work these days—a highly mobile workforce, flexible work hours, lots of people working independently, companies with offices in different locations—I wanted to devote this section to some of the characteristics of virtual teams. Technology (including Microsoft Office, and especially the collaboration features Office provides) enables virtual teams to a large degree. Instant communications, social networks, shared storage, mobile computing—these and other features provide the kind of support virtual teams need. Virtual teams might also have technological challenges because they don't have a single platform they use and don't always have access to shared storage. It would be great if a virtual team could spend time to make sure all their tools are in sync, but time is often of the essence, so this isn't always a reality.

Some teams have a fairly long history and remain relatively stable in membership (in today's terms, at least). Virtual teams (collections of freelancers or a group of employees from different companies) are more likely to change their composition frequently. Being a member of a team like this—or being someone who depends on work a virtual team is producing—creates specific challenges. Because there's little cohesion, there's little history on which to base trust or reliance. And because members of teams might not be working for the same organization, there is no or little line of authority, which means decision making might be harder to facilitate.

This lack of common structure can make being part of a virtual team more difficult. It also makes it more difficult to manage them. If you are part of a virtual team, or are given the task of managing one, here are three qualities to cultivate to make the team's work more effective:

- **Self-management** Even if you are the manager of a virtual team, keep in mind that in many cases, you won't need to do much managing of the team's personnel. You should expect team members to more or less manage themselves. Keep your eye on overarching issues such as schedule, budget, specs, and so on. Independent contractors won't succeed without a healthy measure of initiative and discipline, so you probably don't need to spend a lot of time developing your skills as a motivational speaker.

- **Frequent communication in various forms** Virtual teams don't—and in many cases can't—meet face to face. Most of a virtual team's communication takes place outside scheduled events such as meetings. Communication is often frequent and outside regular business hours as well. A virtual team's manager might want to set up some standards for reporting status, especially if the manager needs to report to a client on a regular basis in turn.

- **Shoot first** Because virtual teams don't always have a rigorous structure and aren't subject to organizational needs for common processes and procedures, you can expect lots of experimentation and change. Members can pursue approaches that simply "work," without having to fully document an idea and have others review it before it is implemented. If an approach doesn't work, work quickly to pursue another path that might. This level of flexibility is an advantage of virtual teams, and anyone managing one should strive to nurture it.

Working alone and together

As you'll see, one of the refrains in this book is how the collaborative features of Office support the effort that team members need to make when they work on their own and when they work on tasks as a group. As part of a team, you'll find yourself engaged in work that involves or doesn't involve other team members to a varying degree:

- Individual tasks are those that can be finished by a single team member without help from others. Sometimes this is the best way to get work done, even in an environment that's set up for collaboration. Writing the first draft of a report or a schedule might fall in this category. That doesn't mean the document won't be reviewed later.

- Group tasks require more than one team member to do the same activity concurrently. Review meetings and brainstorming sessions are group tasks. Teams should be sure that group tasks don't waste resources. Does everyone who wants to participate truly need to, for example? Do you need two designers present or three engineers? If each team member is needed to represent a different point of view, probably so, but if they speak in unison from a shared role, you might not be gaining an advantage.

- Team tasks require more than one team member to perform different tasks concurrently. Different individuals must do different things at the same time. There is both division of labor and concurrent execution. These types of tasks require the highest degree of coordination between team members.

An important step in managing team resources and skills is to understand how these different types of tasks are implemented in a team's work. When your team is creating a report or developing a presentation (or any type of collaborative document), you often gain the best use of resources by assigning one team member to write at least the first draft and then make that draft available to other team members to review. This involves an individual task and a group task.

Another step you might take is to divide the report or presentation into sections that individual team members develop on their own. One team member then takes the individual sections and pulls them together into a cohesive document. Here again, this approach involves individual tasks and group tasks.

You can take this example one more step into the realm of team tasks by coauthoring the document, whereby more than one team member can author and develop a document at the same time. You'll learn how Office enables this approach in several chapters in Part 2 of this book. In a coauthoring approach such as this, one team member might work on several different sections, be solely responsible for another section, and also be involved in reviews.

Collaborative tools in Microsoft Office

In this section, I'll introduce how the remaining chapters in this book talk about collaboration, teamwork, and Microsoft Office together.

One point to make at the outset is that the difference between using Office and using Office collaboratively as part of a team becomes less distinct with each release of the programs. Office 2013 Preview makes that fact pretty clear. Figure 1-1 shows the Open page in Backstage view in Microsoft PowerPoint. When you click Open, you no longer see the Open dialog box, set by default to display your Documents library on your C drive. In fact, your local computer appears next to last in the list of places you go to open files. Ahead of it are locations such as your SharePoint team site (Flyingspress in Figure 1-1), SkyDrive, and the general entry Other Web Locations.

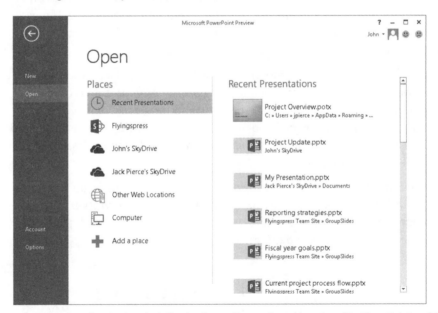

FIGURE 1-1 Opening (and saving) files leads you first to shared locations like SharePoint and SkyDrive.

Providing such prominent access to a SharePoint site and SkyDrive will make team collaboration a step or two easier, but it also recognizes the degree to which mobility goes hand in hand with personal computing these days. Mobility and sharing aren't the same as collaboration, but they are important aspects of it.

Many users work with Office files from different devices—a desktop PC at the office, a tablet or laptop when they aren't at the office, and (perhaps) a smartphone as well. People whose work requires them to be connected most of the time will find that they can access files and information with far less trouble with the way Office is now configured.

The prominence of SharePoint and SkyDrive is also about sharing files. Sharing a file—saving the file where it's accessible to everyone who needs it—is one of the first steps for any team involved in developing content collaboratively. Figure 1-2 shows the Save As page in Backstage view. Notice the similarity with the Open page shown earlier in Figure 1-2.

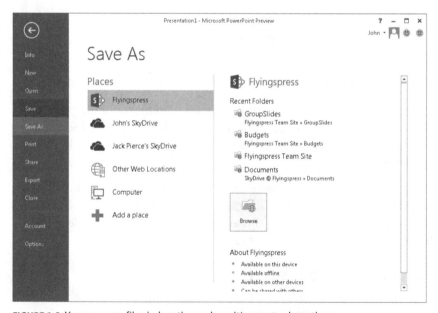

FIGURE 1-2 You can save files in locations where it's easy to share them.

After you save a file to SkyDrive, for example, switch to the Share page in Backstage view to see a variety of options for sharing the file. Figure 1-3 shows the options related to the Invite People command. Fill in fields provided to invite other people to work on the file with you.

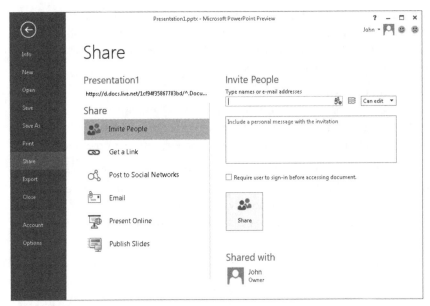

FIGURE 1-3 Office provides an array of options for sharing a file.

The options you see on the Share page will vary from program to program. Figure 1-3 again uses PowerPoint as an example, but Microsoft Word, Microsoft Excel, and Microsoft OneNote have similar options. You'll see examples of other sharing scenarios in later chapters in this book.

The ease with which you can work with files in shared locations is an important aspect of how Office facilitates the work of a team. Other features build on the capabilities Office provides. The following sections offer a brief preview of these features. You'll learn how to work with them in detail as you progress through the book.

Managing content and history

Teams working in Office need procedures and controls to manage content. Some of this control can be gained by using a SharePoint site, where teams can track versions, for example, or set up a publishing mechanism through which only approved users can make content available to every member of the team. Teams can also set up a permissions scheme in SharePoint that allows read access to some team members and full control access to others. The idea of applying "controls" isn't intended to exclude team members but to ensure that errors and omissions don't occur. You don't want to send a proposal to a client before it's complete. Teams can take simple steps like controlling access to documents via passwords. For the most sensitive information, teams can apply Information Rights Management in programs such as Word and Excel. This step lets you match users with specific levels of access and also lets you set expiration dates for specific documents.

These types of restrictions help protect not only sensitive information, but information that's potentially valuable.

Using templates

Work of any type often involves repetition. The hope is to set up processes through which some of the repetitious work can take care of itself—formatting, for example, or having in place the headings for the major sections of a PowerPoint presentation. By using and creating templates in Office, your goal is to emphasize and structure what needs to be repeated, and therefore avoid the effort (often redundant) of having to do that work each time yourself.

Office 2013 Preview is full of templates of all sorts, and teams will likely find many useful templates they can use as starting points for the documents they need to create in their work.

Communication and sharing

As described in earlier sections of this chapter, teams need both formal and informal communication tools. They also need capabilities to access shared content when they are involved in group tasks. In addition, virtual teams need software tools that enable them to work effectively without the benefit of working in a shared space. In Office, Microsoft Lync can fill many of these roles. In many respects, Lync should become the Office program teams use most often. You can use it to make a call, send an instant message or e-mail, or to set up a whiteboard for a brainstorming session. (That's just some of what you can do in Lync.) One of the most interesting new developments in Office 2013 Preview is how deeply Lync is now integrated with the rest of the Office programs. It's not an overstatement to say that Office now assumes that most users will turn to Lync frequently as a mechanism for sharing files, making online presentations, and staying in touch with colleagues.

Keeping records

In teamwork, there's a fine balance between collecting information, formalizing it, culling it for insights, and archiving it for future reference. Teams need a record of their activities, but gathering information can begin to show a diminishing return when you don't know what information you have, what project or event it's related to, or what someone said when discussing it. OneNote is a multifaceted program that teams can use to keep records straight. The notebook structure in OneNote is widely familiar as an organizational device, and the program's capacity to store an array of data types (text, images, tables, printouts, and so on), link the information together, and locate information via searching facilitates how teams can capture, maintain, and find information.

Document collaboration

As mentioned earlier in this chapter in the section "Working alone and together," teams can take a number of different approaches to developing documents collaboratively. Office supports all the approaches described earlier—single authorship and team review, multiple authors whose work is merged or combined into a master document, and coauthoring sessions in which more than one team member works on a document simultaneously.

Mobility and flexibility

Office Web Apps are web-based versions of the Office programs (Word, Excel, Power-Point, and OneNote) that render documents in your browser, where you can view and edit the documents using many of the same commands and features you use in the desktop version of Office. The Office Web Apps are available on SkyDrive, so team members with urgent work to do can gain access to a file and make changes to it from almost any computer that's connected to the web. In addition, SkyDrive itself provides a number of features that are helpful to teams, including storing files in a shared repository, sharing calendars, applying permissions, and restoring a previous version.

A real example

It's always fun to experience firsthand what you write about. For several months earlier this year (2012), I managed a series of content projects for a group at Microsoft. A new version of a software product related to the work was about a day from being released. I was working at home, some 50 miles from Microsoft's campus. In an Excel workbook stored on a SharePoint site, I was tracking the status of web articles that described how to use the new version, noting which had been updated and were ready to be published. In Word, I was opening older versions of the articles to grab images that needed to be copied to the updated ones. I began to notice some distortion in the images and sent an e-mail message to my contact at Microsoft. A minute later Lync rang, and my contact was on the line, sharing her desktop so that we could confer about settings that affected the sizes of the images. After a brief conversation, we'd agreed about what adjustments we needed to make, and then carried on with our work.

This scene is like a thousand others that team members using Office go through everyday—with hardly ever a wrinkle. Technology doesn't ensure that teams operate effectively—there's lots of personality and psychology involved. By using a tool like Office, teams can worry less about the technical side and just concentrate on getting along.

CHAPTER 2

Building a SharePoint team site

TEAMS CAN CREATE and develop many different types of sites in Microsoft SharePoint—sites designed for organizing and documenting meetings, for managing contacts, or for hosting blogs. This chapter focuses on the SharePoint team site, which is designed to facilitate collaboration. Teams and workgroups that rely on Microsoft Office to create content can make a team site the focal point of the team's activities, using the site to store and manage documents, maintain task and event lists, follow workflows, and more. As you'll see later in this chapter and in other chapters in this book, SharePoint is well integrated with other Office programs. This integration provides a platform from which team members can manage most every aspect of their work together.

The operations that team members can do on a team site are managed by site permissions. It's likely that only a few team members need to manage site users and the permissions they have, and it's possible, depending on the type of SharePoint deployment you are using, that permissions will be handled entirely by network administrators who aren't members of the immediate team.

In this chapter, after reviewing how to get started with a team site, I'll describe the use of site groups and permissions in more detail. You'll then learn how to work with some of the features of a team site and how to develop a team site beyond its basic elements. You'll also learn how to manage specific aspects of a site's operations.

Virtual teams, such as a group of independent contractors working together on a project, might use a SharePoint site that's provided by a third-party hosting company. Microsoft also offers access to SharePoint sites through a subscription to Microsoft Office 365 or the SharePoint Online service. The site I used for writing this chapter is part of an Office 365 subscription through the Office 2013 Preview program available in the summer and fall of 2012.

Getting started on the home page

When you first view a basic team site, you'll see a page something like the one shown in Figure 2-1. This figure shows the home page for a team site that's part of an Office 365 subscription to Office 2013 Preview. A couple of features I added to the site—the document libraries named Proposals and Department Budgets—are listed in the navigation pane at the left under the heading Recent.

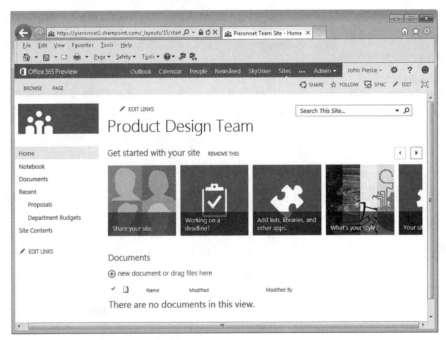

FIGURE 2-1 A basic team site.

The home page displays several tiles (not all of them are shown in the figure) that you can use to start adding features and apps to your site and to change your site's appearance. You can also click Remove This to remove the Getting Started tiles and start building your site from options available on the Settings menu. To display this menu, click the Settings button (just to the right of your name). If at some point you want to work with the Getting Started tiles after removing them, choose Getting Started from the Settings menu to display them again.

The following list describes what you can do with the Getting Started tiles. You can also access many of the settings and options the tiles provide from the Settings menu, using commands such as Add An App and Site Settings.

- **Share Your Site**   Use this tile to send an invitation to others to join your site. Figure 2-2 shows the dialog box you use to address the invitation. If you are a site owner, you can specify the level of permission the people you invite will have by using the list at the bottom of the dialog box. You'll learn more about the permission levels in the next section.

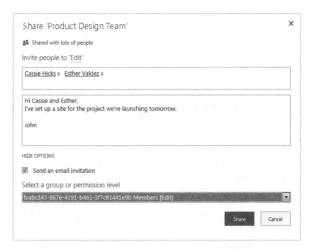

FIGURE 2-2 As one step in setting up your site, invite other team members by using the Share Your Site tile. You can also specify a permission level in the invitation.

- **Working On A Deadline**   Use this tile to turn your site's home page into a site for tracking a project. When you click this tile, SharePoint prompts you to add a project summary, a task list, and a calendar to your site. You can use the project summary to add tasks to a project timeline. The calendar and the task list are added to the navigation pane at the left. You'll see more details about working with a calendar and tasks later in the chapter.

- **Add Lists, Libraries, And Other Apps**   From this tile, you can choose from an assortment of lists and libraries (called apps in the latest version of SharePoint) to add features to your site. The types of apps you can add include a document library, a slide library, a discussion board, and many others. You'll see examples of these apps, including a slide library, later in this chapter.

- **What's Your Style**   Use this tile to select one of several themes to change the look of your site. Themes in SharePoint (as in other Office programs) define color and font schemes among other attributes.

- **Your Site. Your Brand**   You can use this tile to add a logo to your site and to change the site's title. The logo appears above the navigation pane in the upper-left corner of the site. It also works as a link to the site's home page.

- **Keep Email In Context**   From this tile, you can add a Site Mailbox app to your site. A Site Mailbox connects your site to a mailbox hosted on Microsoft Exchange (such as many Microsoft Outlook mailboxes). The Site Mailbox app lets you read e-mail on your site and view site documents in Outlook. (You can find other examples of how to integrate Outlook and SharePoint in Chapter 5, "An integrated Outlook.")

Working with the pages, settings, and options you access through these tiles, you can modify the site to give it a look and feel that identifies your team and provides access to the information and apps your team uses to conduct its work.

EDITING THE HOME PAGE

The building blocks of SharePoint pages are web parts and app parts. An example of a web part is the project summary you can add from the Getting Started tiles. App parts include document libraries and lists. In addition to using the Getting Started tiles to add features and change the appearance of your site, you can edit the home page (and other site pages) directly and add and format apps and web parts.

Start by clicking Edit in the group of commands at the right side of the home page. (You can also click Edit Page on the Settings menu.) Once a page is in editing mode, click the Page tab on the ribbon to display two contextual tabs with commands you use to customize the page. Use the Insert tab to add web parts, tables, pictures, video and audio, and other types of content to the page. To add text to your site, click on the page in an area outside a web part, and then type the text you want—which might describe the use of a web part or an app you've added. Then use the Format Text tab to apply formatting and styles to the text. Click Save & Close at the top right of the page when you finish editing.

Working with groups and permissions

As I mentioned earlier, SharePoint uses groups to manage access to a site and to control the scope of operations that members of a particular group (or an individual) can perform. Team members with responsibility for managing site access work with three main groups: Owners, Members, and Visitors.

By default, site owners have full control over a site. Members can contribute to the site, meaning they can upload and edit documents and add and edit list items, among other tasks. Users in the Visitors group have read access to the site. (You can also assign users of your site to the Viewers group, which grants them only the ability to view the site but not work with any of the site's content.)

■ **IMPORTANT**   **The procedures in this section are most relevant to team members who administer the team site—for example, a team member who signed up for Office 365. Readers who know they are not responsible for site administration may find the information useful but might not be able to perform all the steps described.**

Adding users to the site or a group

In the section "Getting started on the home page," you saw how you can use the Share Your Site tile (part of the Getting Started tiles) to invite users to share your site. If you are a site owner, you can select a permission level in the invitation to assign users to the Owners, Members, Visitors, or Viewers group.

After you remove the Getting Started tiles from you site, you can use the Share button (located in the group of commands at the top right of the site) to invite more users, or you can manage users and permissions directly from the People And Groups page.

Follow these steps:

1. Click the **Settings** button, and then click **Site Settings**.

2. Under Users And Permissions, click **People And Groups**.

   By default, the People And Groups page opens to display the list of users in the Members group.

3. On the People And Groups page, click **New**, and then click **Add Users**.

4. In the Share dialog box (see Figure 2-2 earlier), add names or e-mail addresses and type a welcoming message.

   By default, the users you add in this step receive an e-mail message notifying them that they've been added to the site. To not send a message, click Show Options and then clear the check box for Send An Email Invitation.

To add a user to a different group—for example, to add a team member to the Owners group—select the group in the pane at the left of the window, choose Add Users from the New menu, and then fill in the Share dialog box. If you need to remove a user from a group, select the user in the group list, click Actions, and then click Remove Users From Group.

TIP   You can also use the Actions menu to send an e-mail message to selected users or to contact selected users via Microsoft Lync. For more information about Lync, see Chapter 6, "Working together in Lync."

Managing permissions for users and groups

Placing users in groups and assigning permissions to the group (rather than to the individual users) saves time because you can change the permissions assigned to the group when necessary instead of changing permissions for each individual. You can, however, assign specific permissions to one or more individual users of the site. To manage permissions for an individual, follow these steps:

1. On the Settings menu, click **Site Settings**.

2. On the Site Settings page, under Users And Permissions, click **Site Permissions**.

   The groups defined for the site are listed along with the permission level each group has, as shown in the following screen shot. You can click a group name to see a list of the current members of that group.

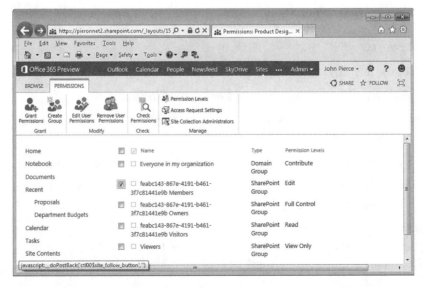

3. Click **Grant Permissions**.

   Once again, you'll see the Share dialog box.

4. In the Share dialog box, enter the names of users whose permission you want to change.

5. Click **Show Options**, and then use the Select A Group Or Permission Level list to specify the permission level you want to apply. In addition to the permission groups set up for the site, you'll see the following specific levels of permission:

   - **Full Control**   The user has full control of the site. This is the default level granted to site owners.

   - **Design**   The user can view, add, update, delete, approve, and customize items in the site.

   - **Contribute**   The user can view, add, update, and delete list items and documents.

   - **Edit**   In addition to the permissions granted to users with the Contribute and Read levels, users with the Edit level can manage lists on the site. This is the default level granted to the Members group.

   - **Read**   The user can view pages and list items and download documents. This is the default level granted to the Visitors group.

   - **View Only**   The user can view pages, list items, and documents. Document types that can be rendered in a browser can be viewed but not downloaded.

6. Type a message that accompanies the e-mail that SharePoint sends to users you've added. (You can forego the message by clearing the check box for Send An Email Invitation.)

To change the permission level assigned to a specific group, select the group and then click Edit User Permissions. In the page SharePoint displays, select the new permission level you want to assign to this group. The options are the same as the specific permissions described in the preceding procedure.

TIP   To see the permission level granted to a specific user or group, click Check Permissions, type the name of the user or group, and then click Check Now. The Check Permissions dialog box lists the group the user is a member of and the user's permission level.

Defining a permission level

The built-in permission levels and SharePoint groups will cover the needs for most team sites. You can define your own group (see the next section, "Creating a group") and, if necessary, define your own permission level. SharePoint provides a long list of specific permissions, organized under the headings List Permissions, Site Permissions, and Personal Permissions. Figure 2-3 shows some of the specific list permissions. By defining a permission level, you can fine-tune the tasks that a site member who's granted the permission level can perform.

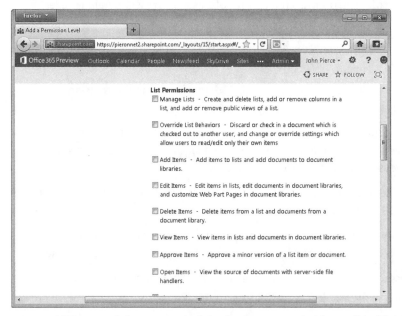

FIGURE 2-3 When you define a new permission level, you can select from a list of detailed options.

To create a permission level, follow these steps:

1. Open the Settings menu, and then click **Site Settings**.

2. Under Users And Permissions, click **Site Permissions**.

3. On the Permissions tab, click **Permission Levels**, and then select **Add A Permission Level**.

4. Type a name and description, and then work through the list of permissions and select those you want to apply to this level.

Creating a group

As you develop your team site, you might find that access to some lists and libraries will be better managed if you create a custom group. You can follow the steps in the previous section to define a custom permission level, for example, and then create a custom group you assign that level to. This gives you a better degree of control over the operations that members of the group can perform in that list or library, and you also preserve the default settings for the built-in groups.

If you want to create your own group for managing user permissions, click the Create Group button on the Permissions tab. On the Create Group page, you work with the following fields and options:

- **Name And About Me Description**   Enter a name for the group and describe the purpose of the group.

- **Owner**   By default, the person who creates the group is designated a group owner, but you can add other owners as need be.

- **Group Settings**   The options in this area control who can view group members and who can edit group membership. By default, only group members can see who is in the group, but you can choose Everyone for wider visibility. For editing group membership, the default setting is Group Owner, but you can choose to let group members manage membership as well.

- **Membership Requests**   In this area, choose options for managing requests to join or leave the group. By default, requests to join or leave are not allowed. To ease administration when conditions permit it, you can select Yes to allow requests and also select Yes to automatically accept requests. If you allow requests, provide the e-mail address where requests should be sent.

- **Give Group Permission To This Site**   The settings in this area grant the level of permission the new group will have. See the earlier section, "Managing permissions for users and groups" for a description of these options.

When you click Create on the Create Group page, SharePoint displays a page you use to add members to the group. See "Adding users to the site or a group" for more information.

INHERITING PERMISSIONS

By default, lists and libraries that are part of the team site inherit permissions from the site (the parent). This means that, by default, users in the Members group have the same level of permission for each list or library included in the site. You can tailor the permissions certain groups or users have for specific lists and libraries by breaking inheritance. For additional details, see the section "Breaking permission inheritance" later in this chapter.

■ Working on the team site

In this section, I'll describe details of how you work with a few of the lists and libraries that are part of many team sites. As you'll see, even a few features and apps on your site provide a range of capabilities that facilitate how teams manage their content, communicate, and plan.

Adding a slide library

In Chapter 10, "Preparing a presentation as a group," you'll see how to work with a slide library, a SharePoint app designed for storing and managing Microsoft PowerPoint slides that are used in more than one presentation. The following steps show you how to add a slide library to your team site, but you can adapt this procedure to add a different type of library (a picture library, for example) depending on the type of content you manage on your site.

■ **IMPORTANT**   You need Full Control permissions to add a library to the team site.

1. On the Settings menu, click **Add An App**.

2. In the search box, type **_Slide Library_**, and then press **Enter**. (You can also scroll through the page or pages of apps to find the Slide Library app—you might need to navigate to the next page to find it.)

3. Click **Slide Library**. (You can click **App Details** to see a page with a brief description that also lets you add the app).

4. In the Adding Slide Library dialog box, type a name.

    If you want to add a description of the library and enable versioning, click Advanced Options. On the Advanced Options page, fill in the description, and select

Yes to enable versioning. (You'll learn more about the versioning feature in Share-Point in Chapter 3, "Managing access and preserving history.")

5. Click **Create**.

You'll learn more about working with a slide library in Chapter 10.

TYPES OF LIBRARIES

Libraries are defined in part by the columns used to identify and manage content. For example, a report library includes the columns Report Status and Report Category. In a picture library, you can see information such as the file size and the dimensions of the picture. Libraries are also associated with specific content types. A forms library is set up to create a Microsoft InfoPath form, for example. A report library provides commands to create a Microsoft Excel workbook or a webpage on which you can display summarized information.

In addition to a document library and a slide library, the following list describes other types of libraries you can add to your team site:

- **Form Library** To store business forms that you create with a program such as InfoPath, add a form library to your team site. The New Document menu item in a form library is set up to create an InfoPath form.

- **Picture Library** This library is designed for storing and sharing pictures. You can view thumbnail images in the library. Double-click a thumbnail and then click Edit Item on the ribbon to add information about the picture.

- **Wiki Page Library** This library provides pages that are designed for quick collaboration. The welcome page that SharePoint displays when you create a wiki describes how you might use the library—for brainstorming or gathering research notes, for example. Click the Page tab, click Edit, and then use the commands on the Editing Tools tabs to add content and objects to the wiki pages. You can find more details about setting up a wiki library later in this chapter.

- **Asset Library** Use an asset library to store large media files, including image, video, and audio files. When you add an item to an asset library, you can choose the type of item from the New Document menu. SharePoint provides a dialog box in which you can provide a name and title, enter keywords for the item (which are used in searches), provide comments, identify the author, add a date and time stamp, and specify a copyright date.

- **Data Connection Library** A data connection library is used to store connection files that let you connect to applications outside the team site and SharePoint. In this library, you can store an Office Data Connection (ODC) file or a Universal Data Connection (UDC) file. InfoPath can use a UDC file for connections. An ODC file can be used with a server application such as Microsoft SQL Server to help generate reports.

- **Report Library** A report library is designed for documents related to goals, business intelligence, and organizational metrics. In a report library, you can assign a report to a category, for example, and specify the status of a report.

Adding list apps

Like libraries, SharePoint lists are designed for specific purposes—posting announcements, tracking appointments and events, holding discussions, assigning and monitoring group tasks, conducting surveys, and many others.

To add a list, follow these steps:

1. On the Settings menu, choose **Add An App**.

2. On the Your Apps page, scroll to find the list app you want to add (or use the search box), and then click the tile to add it to your site.

3. In the Adding dialog box, type a name for the list. (Use the Advance Options link to provide a description and choose other options.)

4. Click **Create**.

Among the types of list apps you might add to your team site are these:

- **Announcements** Use an announcements list for short status reports, event news, reminders, and similar information.

- **Contacts** Track information about customers, suppliers, vendors, and other people your team works with. Information in a SharePoint contact list can be synchronized with Outlook.

- **Custom List** Start with a blank custom list and then add columns and views of your own. You'll learn more about views later in this chapter.

- **Custom List In Datasheet View** Adds a blank list that's displayed as a datasheet (like a table in Microsoft Access or an Excel worksheet), to which you add your own columns and views.

- **Import Spreadsheet** Use this list to include information from an Excel worksheet or another type of spreadsheet.

- **Issue Tracking**   An issue tracking list is handy for managing projects. You can collect information about items that need resolution or require new resources. Items in an issue tracking list can be assigned to individuals and given a priority and a status.

- **Links**   Add this list to compile a list of webpages or other resources.

- **Survey**   Use a survey to collect data and responses about issues and processes.

If you are working with a team site as you read this chapter, take a few minutes to add a task list, a discussion board, and a calendar app to your team site. (Follow the steps described earlier to add the apps.) In the next sections, you'll learn more details about how to track tasks on your team site and how you can use the calendar to schedule meetings, deadlines, and other events.

Tracking tasks

Teams can use a task list to set up a schedule for specific work items (or a group of related work items), track the status of each item, and adjust an item's priority. Task items can be assigned to team members and can also be linked to predecessor tasks to help establish a workflow.

As the task list demonstrates, each type of list in SharePoint is defined by a specific set of columns (which you can also think of as fields). When you add an item to a list, you assign a value to each column to characterize that particular item. As the number of items in a list grows, you can sort and search for items by using the values in a column.

A task is defined by fields such as the following:

- **Task Name**   The name of a task, such as Draft Due or Review Design Spec. Task Name is the only column you are required to fill in when you create a task.

- **Assigned To**   The name of the team member responsible for the task.

- **Task Status**   The five built-in status categories are Not Started, In Progress, Completed, Deferred, and Waiting On Someone Else.

- **Priority**   High, Normal (the default), or Low.

- **Start Date and Due Date**   The schedule for the task.

- **% Complete**   How much of the task is complete.

- **Description**   A field you can use to provide additional details about the work this task entails.

- **Predecessors**   Tasks that the current task depend on (for example, Review Design Spec might depend on Create Design Spec).

Teams might choose not to track all task items at the level of detail provided by this list. For example, you might use only the fields Task Name, Assigned To, and Due Date.

To add a task item to the list, open the list, and then click New Task. (You can also display the Tasks tab on the ribbon, and then click New Item.)

On the new task page, shown in Figure 2-4, fill in the fields with the information you have to date. Again, the only required field for a new task item is the task's title, but you might also know about a task's assignment, priority, due date, and predecessors when you create it. The default status for a task is set to Not Started. On the Edit tab at the top of the page, click Attach File to add a file attachment to the task item. You might attach a budget, draft specifications, or a report that's related to the task.

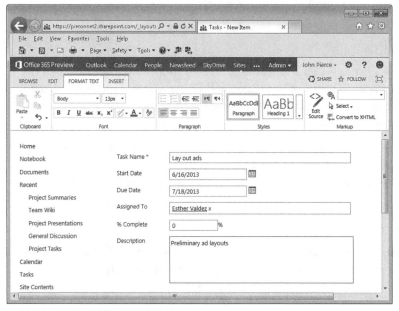

FIGURE 2-4 Define a task by adding a name and other details. You can update the task later to change its status and percent complete.

To update or view a task item, just click the item's name in the list. (You can also select the item in the list—a check box appears when you point to the item—and then click View Item in the Manage group on the Tasks tab.) Click Edit Item when you need to change an item's status or priority, specify the percent complete, add a predecessor task, or change who the task is assigned to.

On the List tab, you can use commands in the Connect & Export group to work with the task list in other Office applications. Use the Export To Excel command to create a worksheet from the task list. This step might be helpful for analysis and for creating summaries. Use the Connect To Outlook command to create a copy of this task list in Outlook.

See Also   For a detailed discussion of working with a task list in Outlook, see Chapter 5, "An integrated Outlook."

SORTING AND FILTERING A LIST OR LIBRARY

You can use column headings to sort the items in a list or library. In the task list, for example, you can use the Task Name column to sort in ascending or descending order. You can also create a filter by using a column. For example, use the Due Date column to apply a filter that shows the tasks due on a particular day. Point to the right of the column name, and then click the arrow to display the sorting and filtering options for that column. SharePoint displays an arrow (pointing up or down) to indicate the sorting column and sort order for the library. If you apply a filter, you'll see the filter icon beside the column name. You can also specify settings for how a library is sorted and filtered by creating or modifying a view. For more information, see "Creating and modifying views" later in this chapter.

Holding a team discussion

Teams have many options for gathering opinions about the issues they're working on, everything from staff meetings to hallway conversations to an exchange of instant messages. Using a discussion board on the team site is another approach.

To post an item to a discussion board, follow these steps:

1. Click the link for the discussion board on the navigation pane to open the list.

2. Click **New Discussion**.

3. On the page SharePoint displays, fill in the subject and body for the item, as shown here. Use the check box provided to pose the discussion item as a question.

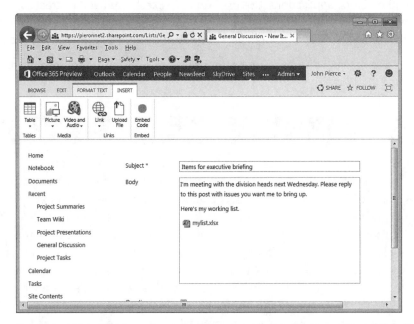

You can attach files to a discussion item, and in the Body section of the discussion item, you can use the ribbon to format the text, add hyperlinks or pictures, or insert a table.

To read a discussion thread, click the entry in the list. (To find a particular post, you can sort the thread by who posted items.) While reviewing the posts for a specific discussion, use the Create A Reply box to respond. Click Reply to post the item.

Scheduling and managing events

The team site's calendar provides a basic approach to scheduling events such as meetings, planning retreats, and other team activities. You can use the calendar to set up all-day events, meetings with defined start and end times, as well as recurring appointments.

Adding an event

You work with a calendar by using commands on two tabs, Events and Calendar. Use the Events tab to add and manage events. On the Calendar tab, you can change from Month view to Day or Week view, expand and collapse the display of items, manage views, set up alerts, and perform other tasks.

Follow these steps to add an event to the calendar:

1. On the Events tab, click **New Event**. (You can also just point to the date and then click the **Add** button.)

2. In the New Item dialog box, type a title for the event, and then specify the start time and end time.

   Title, Start Time, and End Time are the only required fields for an event, but you can provide additional information by using the following fields:

   - **Location** Type a conference room, an offsite address, or other location.

   - **Description** Provide information about the event. Use the toolbar above the Description box to format the text you type. You can, for example, create numbered and bulleted lists, align text, and highlight text to create and format a meeting agenda.

   - **Category** Use one of the values SharePoint provides (such as Meeting) or provide one of your own.

   - **All Day Event** Select this check box to schedule the event for the entire day (an event without a specific start time and end time).

   - **Recurrence** Use this option to set up a regular team meeting or another event that is scheduled at set intervals. When you select this option, the New Item dialog box refreshes, and you'll see the controls shown below:

3. Click **Save**.

Using a meeting workspace

A meeting workspace is a separate site (a subsite of your team site) that's designed for organizing and documenting meetings. You might set up a meeting workspace to manage key meetings during a project, for example, or as a tool for keeping your standing team meetings on track. When you create a meeting workspace as a subsite (the detailed steps are provided later in this section), SharePoint displays a page you use to describe and set properties for the workspace. You need to name the meeting workspace, specify the site's URL (which is added to the URL for your team site), and select a meeting workspace template. A meeting workspace inherits permissions from the team site unless you select the option Use Unique Permissions. You can also select options to include a link to the meeting workspace on the navigation pane.

See Also   For details about site permissions, see "Managing groups and permissions" earlier in this chapter.

You can choose from the following templates when you set up a meeting workspace:

- **Basic Meeting Workspace**   Creates a site with lists for tracking attendees, managing the agenda, and storing related documents.

- **Blank Meeting Workspace**   Creates a blank site you can customize.

- **Decision Meeting Workspace**   Creates a site with a task list, a document library, and a list for recording decisions.

- **Social Meeting Workspace**   Creates a site designed for social occasions.

- **Multipage Meeting Workspace**   Creates a site with lists for managing attendees and the agenda and also two blank pages that you can customize.

Figure 2-5 shows the basic layout for a decision meeting workspace when SharePoint first displays it. The workspace includes five lists (Objectives, Attendees, Agenda, Tasks, and Decisions) and a document library. Use the Add New Item and related links to populate the lists as follows:

- **Objectives**   Use the single text box provided to define a meeting objective.

- **Attendees**   Click Manage Attendees to open the list, and then use the New Item command on the Items tab to add a meeting attendee. Click the icon in the Edit column to open a page where you can type a comment about the attendee, specify whether the attendee is coming to the meeting, and specify whether the attendee is one of the meeting's organizers, a required attendee, or an optional attendee.

- **Agenda**   For agenda items, you can specify the subject, owner, time allotted, and notes.

- **Document Library**   Click Add Document to upload a document related to the meeting workspace.

- **Tasks**   The task list works the same as the standard task list described in the section "Tracking tasks" earlier in the chapter. Of course, the tasks you define in this list should pertain to the meeting or event that the workspace is set up to manage.

- **Decisions**   For decisions, you can specify the decision (for example, "Section 1 of the design spec needs input from Engineering"), a contact, and the status of the decision.

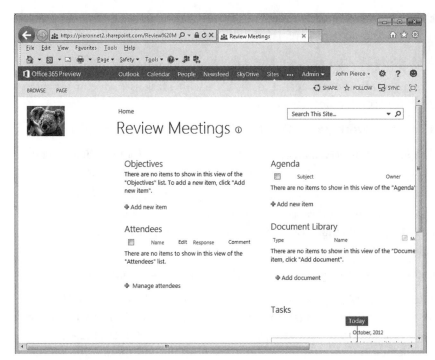

FIGURE 2-5 The decision meeting workspace is designed for tracking objectives, attendees, the agenda, and other information.

To create a meeting workspace subsite, follow these steps:

1. On the Settings menu, click **View Site Contents**.

2. At the bottom of the Site Contents page, click **New Subsite**.

3. On the New SharePoint Site page, add a name, description, and path for the subsite (for use in the URL).

4. Under Select A Template, click **Meetings**, and then select the meeting workspace template you want to use.

5. Complete the other options, and then click **Create**.

Working with documents

In this section, I'll describe some of the basic operations of a document library (such as the default Documents library that's provided with a team site). You initiate these operations by using commands on the library's Files tab.

Creating and uploading documents

Document libraries can be associated with a type of document. For example, you can associate an Excel template with a document library used for storing and editing budgets or other financial documents. The default Documents library is associated with Microsoft Word, which means that when you click New Document on the Files tab, Word starts or, if Word is already running, Word opens a new document window.

You gain more flexibility by clicking the New Document link that appears above the list of documents in a library. This link opens a menu that lets you create a new file by using the Word, Excel, PowerPoint, or OneNote web apps. It also lets you create a new folder or upload a file.

TIP Use folders to organize the files you store in a library. On the Files tab, click New Folder. In the New Folder dialog box, type a name for the folder, and then click Save.

The Upload Document command opens a dialog box you use to browse to the location where the file you want to add to the library is stored. You can specify a destination folder within the library (if folders are defined) and add a note about the version of a file you are uploading (if versioning is enabled for the library—for more information, see "Managing versions" in Chapter 3, "Managing access and preserving history.")

TIP You can also drag files from a folder on your computer to a library on your team site.

Checking documents out and in

Because the documents you store on SharePoint can be opened by anyone who has the required level of permission, you need controls in place to manage who can update a file. To address this need, you can instruct or require users of a library to check out a file before the file can be edited. When a user checks out a file, that user has exclusive access to edit the file, but other users can still view the file. When a different user opens a checked-out file for editing, a notification appears informing the user of the file's status, as shown in Figure 2-6.

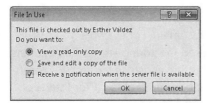

FIGURE 2-6 When a team member has a file checked out, you'll see a notification like this.

TIP   In the list of documents in a library, checked-out files are indicated with a small, downward pointing arrow.

When a checked-out file is open in Word or Excel, for example, you can click the File tab and choose Check In to save changes to the library and make the file available for others. You can also save the file and then use the Check In command on the Files tab in Share-Point. When you check in the document, type a comment about the changes you made, as shown in Figure 2-7, which helps other team members understand the status of the file.

FIGURE 2-7 Add a comment like the one shown in this image to provide information about the work you've done on a document.

The Check In dialog box provides an option for you to keep the file checked out. You might select this option when you want other users to see the changes you've made up to the point you check in the file but still retain editorial control over the document.

TIP   If you check out a file, make changes to the file, save those changes, but don't check in the file, you can restore the file to the state it was before you checked it out by choosing Discard Check Out.

USING A DOCUMENT WORKSPACE

A document workspace is similar to a meeting workspace (see "Working with a meeting workspace" earlier in the chapter) and includes a document library and an announcements list by default. You can set up a document workspace (which becomes a subsite of the team site) when you want to work with a particular document and supporting files on a separate site.

Setting up alerts

To expedite the work that's managed on a team site, team members should set up alerts for lists and libraries and for particular items (a specific document or task, for example). With alerts set, SharePoint notifies team members when documents are uploaded or modified or when items in a list change. You can be notified by e-mail or via text message (if your site is configured for text messaging).

You use the Alert Me command in the Share & Track group to set up notifications for particular items. The Alert Me command appears on the Files tab in a document library, on the Events tab for the calendar, and on the Tasks tab in the task list.

To set up an alert, follow these steps:

1. Open the list or library, and then select the document or list item you want to track.

2. In the Share & Track group on the Files tab (or the equivalent), click **Alert Me**, and then click **Set Alert On This Document**. (The text of this command will vary if you are setting an alert on a list item.)

    You'll see the New Alert dialog box, shown below.

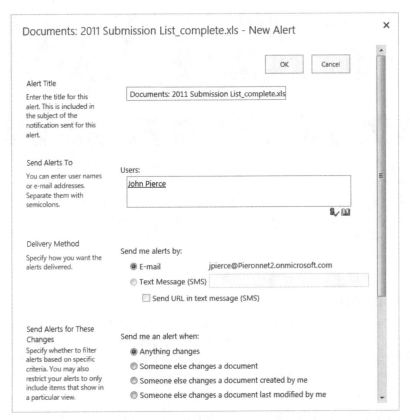

3. Type a title for the alert. (You'll see this title in the subject line of the notification.)

4. Select the delivery method. The E-Mail option is selected by default.

5. Under **Send Alerts For These Changes**, select one of the following options:

    ■ Anything Changes

    ■ Someone Else Changes A Document

    ■ Someone Else Changes A Document Created By Me

    ■ Someone Else Changes A Document Last Modified By Me

6. In the When To Send Alerts area, specify whether you want to receive notifications immediately, in a daily summary, or in a weekly summary. If you choose the daily summary option, you can specify the time you'll receive the notification. For a weekly summary, you can specify both the day and time.

The options you can select for receiving an alert are different for different types of items. For example, for an item in the task list, in addition to options such as Anything Changes, you can be notified when a task becomes complete, when a task is assigned to you, or when a high-priority task changes, among other options.

Alerts can also be set up for entire lists and libraries. Here are the steps you can follow to set up an alert for the task list, calendar, team discussion board, a document library, or other lists or libraries:

1. On the team site home page, click the **Page** tab.

2. In the Share & Track group, click **Alert Me**, and then click **Manage My Alerts**.

3. On the My Alerts On This Site page, click **Add Alert**.

4. On the New Alert page, select the list or library you want to track, and then click **Next**.

5. Use the fields on the New Alert page to specify an alert title (the name of the list or library is used by default), the delivery method, the type of changes you want to be notified about, and the schedule for receiving alerts.

TIP If you set up one or more alerts, choose Manage My Alerts from the Alert Me menu to open a page on which you can edit the settings for an alert, add other alerts, or delete an alert.

Connecting with Office and exporting items

As I mentioned at the start of this chapter, one of the main advantages of using a team site to organize and manage content is the level of integration between SharePoint and other Office programs. As one example, the Word and PowerPoint files you store on your team site can be edited by more than one team member at the same time (a feature known as coauthoring). In addition, you can compare and restore a previous version of a file that's stored on SharePoint.

See Also For details about coauthoring documents in Word and PowerPoint, see Chapter 8, "Working on shared documents in Word," and Chapter 10, "Preparing a presentation as a group."

You can set up other connections between the content you store in SharePoint and Office programs by using commands in the Connect & Export group, which appears on the Library tab for document libraries, on the List tab for the task list, and on the Calendar tab for the calendar.

For example, you can use the Connect To Outlook button to add an entry for the document library to the navigation pane in Outlook. When you display the library in Outlook, you'll see a list of the documents. If the Outlook reading pane is open, you see a preview of the document. You can open the document from Outlook to edit it. You can also link the team site's task list and calendar to Outlook. I'll cover the details of how you can connect SharePoint and Outlook in Chapter 5, "An integrated Outlook."

To set up easy access to the Documents library, open the library, click Connect To Office, and then click Add To SharePoint Sites. This command adds a shortcut to the library to your Favorites list in the Save As and Open dialog boxes in Word, Excel, and other Office applications. You can also use this menu to remove a shortcut, or click Manage Share-Point Sites to display a page on which you can modify the shortcuts you've created.

Click Export To Excel to create a list of the library's items (with column headings) in an Excel workbook. You might do this to create a tracking sheet or to cross-check an inventory of files.

The Sync Library To Computer command lets you work with a list or library offline in SharePoint Workspace.

Creating and modifying views

Lists and libraries come with built-in views. Views are defined by the columns they include and can also be set up to reflect specified sort orders and filters. In the task list, for example, the default view is All Tasks. The task list also includes the views Calendar, Completed, Gantt Chart, Late Tasks, My Tasks, and Upcoming, as shown in Figure 2-8. To change the view of a list or library, select the view you want from the menu under Current View. (You'll see this menu on the Library tab for a document library.)

You can create other views for a library or modify the views that SharePoint provides. All built-in views are public views. Users with adequate permission can create additional public views, but most all members of the site can create personal views. You might create a view to apply a specific filter or sort order to a library or to create a view that's designed for data entry (a datasheet view). When you create a view, you choose a format as the basis of the view (you'll often use the format Standard View) or select one of the library's existing views as your starting point.

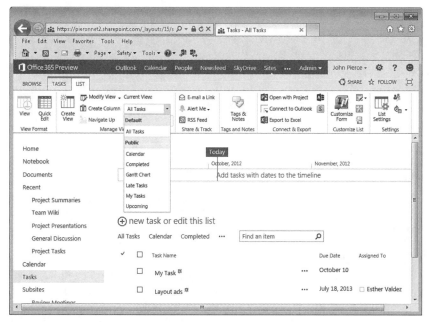

FIGURE 2-8 The task list comes with a number of built-in public views. Team members can create personal views as well.

To create a personal view, follow these steps:

1. In the Manage Views group on the Library or List tab, click **Create View**.

2. Select the format you want to use, or select an existing view for the basis of the new view.

3. On the Create View page, shown below, type a name for the view, and then select **Create A Personal View**.

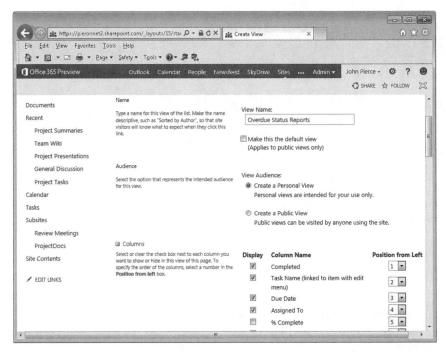

4. In the Columns area, select the columns you want to include in the view. Use the Position From Left list to specify the column order.

5. The Create View page provides a number of fields you use to define a view, and you might not need to change the default settings for many of these fields. The following list summarizes some of the fields you work with on the Create View page when you choose the Standard View template (not all these fields are available when you choose a view template such as Datasheet View):

    ■ **Sort**   You can specify two columns to sort by. Choose the columns, and then select the option to sort in ascending or descending order. In a library, users can sort library items by using column headings. If you want to maintain the sort order specified for the view, select the option Sort Only By Specified Criteria.

    ■ **Filter**   You can keep the default setting to show all items in a view or define a filter to view a selection of the items. To filter a column based on the current date or the current user of the site, type [Today] or [Me] as the column value. You can also specify a date to see only files modified after that date. Filters are especially useful in large lists because they let users work with the list more efficiently.

- **Tabular View** The Allow Individual Item Checkboxes option in this area is selected by default. These check boxes let users select multiple items to perform
  bulk operations such as deleting more than one file.

- **Group By** Specify one or two columns by which to group items. For example,
  you could group items under the Modified By field in a document library or the
  Report Status field in a report library.

- **Totals** You can use this area to calculate summary information about items in
  a library. The functions available depend on the type of column. They include
  Count, Average, Maximum, and Minimum.

- **Style** In a document library, the following styles are available: Basic Table;
  Document Details; Newsletter; Newsletter, No Lines; Shaded; Preview Pane;
  and Default. The Shaded style, for example, displays a colored background in
  alternating rows. The Preview Pane style groups items along the left side of the
  library, where you can highlight an item to view its details.

- **Folders** Specify whether to navigate through folders to view items or to view
  all items at once. If the list or library is organized by items or files within folders,
  you can provide a view in which the items or files are displayed without the
  folders.

- **Item Limit** Use an item limit to restrict the number of items shown in a view.
  You can set an absolute limit or allow users to view items in batches of the size
  you specify. By default, the number of items available for display in a document
  library is 30 per batch.

- **Mobile** Adjust mobile settings for this view by enabling it for mobile access,
  making this view the default view for mobile access, and adjusting the number
  of items to display in the List View web part for this view. You can additionally
  set the field to be displayed in a mobile list simple view.

6. Click **OK**.

If you want to make changes to a view (such as a personal view you created), select that
view in the Current View list, and then click Modify View in the Manage Views group. The
Edit View page is similar to the Create View page shown in the preceding procedure. You
work with the same fields, which are populated with values that define the view in its current state. When you modify a view, you can change the view's name, change the order
in which columns appear in the view, add or remove columns from the view, define a
filter or a sort order, or specify settings for other view fields. The Edit View page does not
let you make a public view a personal view. Base a new view on one of the built-in views
if you want to create a personal view that resembles a built-in view.

CREATING A COLUMN

Site owners or users with Full Control permissions can create a custom column and add it to one or more views. In the Create Column dialog box, you provide a name for the column and specify the column type. The options for the type of column include Single Line Of Text, Multiple Lines of Text, Number, Currency, Date And Time, Lookup (which you can tie to another field on your site), and others. You'll see an example of creating a Choice column later in this chapter in the section "Managing document approval with a workflow."

Options in the Additional Column Settings area of the dialog box change depending on the type of column. These options give you a high degree of control over the properties of a column you create. For the Number type, for example, you use the following column settings:

- Add a description
- Specify whether the column requires data
- Enforce unique values for the column
- Set a minimum and maximum value
- Set the number of decimal places
- Specify a default value
- Choose an option to show the value as a percentage
- Specify whether to add this column to all content types in the library
- Specify whether to add this column to the default view

You can also create a formula that is used to validate the data a user enters in the column. In a Date And Time column, for example, you could create a formula so that only dates later than today are valid in the column.

Custom columns are added to the library's default view if you keep that option selected in the Create Columns dialog box. They are not added automatically to other views defined for the library, but you can add them by modifying a view.

Developing the team site

The support a team gains from a team site can be extended by adding libraries and lists of other types. For example, teams that manage multiple projects that involve a variety of content (images, spreadsheets, audio files, reports, and so on) should create libraries of specific types to help manage this content. Teams can also add lists designed for managing projects or contact information.

See Also For details about the library and list apps you can add to a site, see "Working on the team site" earlier in this chapter."

In this section, I'll describe some additional features that support collaborative work as you develop your team site in SharePoint. You'll learn about workflows, how to add a page to your site, and how to work with a wiki in SharePoint.

Managing document approval with a workflow

Team members who are site owners or have full control can associate a workflow with a list or library to facilitate a business process such as approving a request for proposal (RFP), a contract, a financial report, or a similar kind of document. Two workflow templates come with a basic team site. The Disposition Approval workflow is designed to manage document expiration and retention. The Three-State workflow is designed to track items in a list—such as a document being routed for approval.

As an example, to create a Three-State workflow in a document library set up to store and track proposals, follow these steps:

1. Open the document library, and then click the **Library** tab.

2. In the Manage Views group, click **Create Column**.

3. In the Create Column dialog box, type a name (such as Status) for the custom column, and then select **Choice** as the column type.

4. In the Additional Column Settings area, type a description for the column, and then replace the generic choice options (labeled Enter Choice #1, and so on) with names such as Initiated, Under Review, and Approved.

5. Keep the options Drop-Down Menu and Add To Default View selected, and then click **OK**.

   The new column should appear in the default view of the library.

6. In the Settings group on the Library tab, click **Workflow Settings**, and then click **Add A Workflow**.

7. On the Add A Workflow page, select **Three-State** as the workflow template, and then type a name for the workflow (such as Contract Routing or Proposal Approval).

8. You associate the Three-State workflow with two lists: a task list and a workflow history list. As the workflow moves from step to step, a task is created to track its progress. Select **New Task List** to create a task list to use (or select a task list you've already defined), and keep the Workflow History (New) option selected for the history list.

9. Under Start Options, keep the default option, which is to allow an authorized user to start the workflow manually. (You can also choose an option to start the workflow when an item is added to the library.)

10. Click **Next**.

11. In the Workflow States area, select the choice column you defined at the start of this procedure. As needed, select the choices you defined for the initial state, middle state, and final state.

12. In the two Task Details sections, you define actions that occur when a workflow is initiated and when it reaches its middle state. You can set up an e-mail message to include information such as a task description and due date, who a task is assigned to, who the message goes to, and the subject line. SharePoint adds the task-related information you define to the task list you specified in step 8.

13. Click **OK**.

To initiate a workflow (if the manual start option is selected), select the item in the library, and then click Workflows on the Files tab. On the page SharePoint displays, under Start A New Workflow, click the workflow you want to apply to this item.

To move an item from one stage to the next, select the item, click Edit Properties on the Files tab, and then select the stage from the list for the choice column. To track a workflow task on the related task list, open the list, and then update the task item as you do with other tasks. The task item will include a list at the top indicating that you are working with a workflow task.

TIP   On the Workflow Settings page, you can see which workflows are in progress, add other workflows to the library, remove a workflow, and view workflow reports.

CREATING WORKFLOWS IN SHAREPOINT DESIGNER

One of the ways in which you can develop the capabilities of your team site is to design advanced workflows in Microsoft SharePoint Designer. (If SharePoint Designer is not installed on your computer, SharePoint prompts you to install it the first time you work with it on your team site.)

You can start this process by choosing Create A Workflow In SharePoint Designer from the Workflow Settings menu in the Settings group (on the Library or the List tab). After SharePoint Designer opens and sets up a connection to your team site, it displays a dialog box in which you name and describe the workflow.

You can then start defining the steps in the workflow by choosing from lists of actions and conditions. Some of the actions you can choose from are Send An Email, Log To History List, and Check Out Item. With conditions, you can define the workflow so that specific steps occur only if an item was created by a specific person, for example, or only between two dates you specify. When you finish defining the workflow, click the Publish button to make it available on your team site.

Developing workflows in SharePoint Designer involves a number of complex steps, and you can use SharePoint Designer for much more than creating workflows as well. If you are interested in learning more about SharePoint Designer, a number of books are available from Microsoft Press and other publishers.

Breaking permission inheritance

As I mentioned earlier in the chapter, lists and libraries by default inherit the permissions set up for the team site (the parent). In some cases, you might want to break this relationship and apply different permissions.

To set up permissions for a library, follow these steps. (The steps are the same for a list, except you use the List tab and the List Settings button.)

1. Open the library, and then, on the Library tab, click **Library Settings**.

2. On the Library Settings page, under Permissions And Management, click **Permissions For This Document Library**.

   On the page SharePoint displays, the notification indicates that the library inherits its permissions.

3. On the Permissions tab, click **Stop Inheriting Permissions**, and then click **OK** in the message box.

4. Select a group, and then click **Edit User Permissions** to specify the permissions for that group. To specify permissions for an individual user, click **Grant Permissions**. In the Share dialog box, type the user's name or e-mail address, click **Show Options**, and specify the permission level. (See "Managing permissions for users and groups" earlier in this chapter for more details.)

If you want to reverse your decision and inherit permissions again, click Delete Unique Permissions on the Permissions tab, and then click OK in the message warning that you will lose any custom permissions.

Keep in mind that when you break inheritance, any adjustments you make to the permissions for the team site won't affect lists or libraries with unique permissions. Similarly, changes you make to permissions for a library or a list won't affect a document or list item with unique permissions applied.

See Also   For more information about managing and granting permissions, see the "Working with groups and permissions" section earlier in the chapter.

SITE AND LIST TEMPLATES

Some teams, especially those that manage multiple projects of the same kind, can develop their team site with a particular configuration of lists and libraries and then save the site as a template they can use again. When you have developed the site as you want it, use the Settings menu to display the Site Settings page, and then click Save Site As Template in the Site Actions group. Enter a name for the template file (do not include an extension), a name and description for the template, and specify whether to include the content from the base site. You must select this option if you want to include custom workflows, but you should also include it if you have uploaded model documents to the site—for example, a budget or a presentation template.

You can apply this site template when you create a subsite (click New Subsite on the Site Contents page to start the process). Choose the template you created from the Custom category in the Template Selection area of the New SharePoint Site page. To manage custom templates, open the Site Settings page from the Site Actions menu, and click Solutions in the Galleries area.

You can also set up a list with custom views and standard items (for example, a set of tasks you perform for each product your team develops) and then save the list as a template. You can then base new lists on the template you create. Use the List Settings button on the List tab to open the List Settings page. Under Permissions And Management, click Save List As Template. Type the file name for the list template (here, too, you should not include an extension) and the name and description for the template itself. If you want to include the content of a list in the template, select that option.

If you need to edit the properties for a list template (to change its name, for example), open the Settings menu and choose Site Settings. Under Galleries, click List Templates. Select the list template, and then click Edit Properties in the Manage group.

Creating pages

In addition to libraries and lists, you can add pages to your team site. You develop a new page following steps similar to those described earlier in the chapter in the sidebar "Editing the home page." You can add text to a page and then format it, and you can also add a variety of media (pictures, for example), as well as apps and web parts. You might create a page to combine information from several lists—the calendar and task list, for example. Pages you add to your team site are stored in the Site Pages library, which you can open from the Site Contents page.

To add a page, follow these steps:

1. On the Settings menu, click **New Page**.

2. In the Add A Page dialog box, type a name for the page, and then click **Create**.

When the new page is displayed, use the Insert tab and the Format Text tab on the ribbon to add content to and design your page. When you click App Part on the Insert tab, you'll see a list of the apps (the lists and libraries) already configured for your site. Choose Calendar or Tasks, for example, to add those lists to this page, where you can examine this information and compare it in a single view. Figure 2-9 shows a new page under construction, with a calendar added to the page and the list of other available apps at the top.

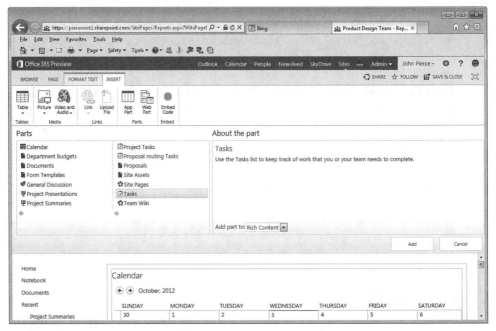

FIGURE 2-9 Use apps, tables, media types, and links to create a page. The Format Text tab provides standard tools for applying styles and formats.

Using a wiki page library

Teams that want to use SharePoint as a location for collecting notes and other research should consider adding a wiki page library to their team site. A wiki page is set up for more free-form entry than a page designed with specific web parts. On the pages in a wiki library, team members can quickly add text (and use the ribbon to format it) as well as upload files and insert tables, web parts, images, and links.

To add a wiki page library, select Add An App from the Settings menu, and select Wiki Page Library on the Your Apps page. Click the tile, type a name for the wiki, and then click Create.

A wiki page library comes with two pages by default (Home and How To Use This Library), which serve to introduce you to the purpose of a wiki and describe how to use it. Both pages appear on the navigation pane (under Updated Pages) when you display the library.

Before you can add content to a wiki page, you need to place the page in edit mode. Click the Edit button in the group of commands at the top right of the page. (You can also click the Page tab on the ribbon and click Edit.) Team members can then work with the Format Text and Insert tabs to format text, apply styles, change layouts, and insert objects. When you finish editing, click Save & Close in the Edit group (or click Save & Close at the top right).

TIP   To work on a wiki page exclusively, check out the page before you edit it.

Part of the way to make a wiki useful is to link the wiki's pages. The links create relation-ships within the wiki (for example, by linking a page named Product Ideas to a page named Market Research). To create a link to another page in a wiki library, you only need to enclose the name of the page in double brackets—for example, [[Market Research]]. After you type the first pair of brackets ([[), the library suggests pages already in the library (on the basis of the characters you type). Select a page, and then finish the link by typing]]. Links do not become active until you save and stop editing the page.

TIP   The page How To Use This Library contains examples of the types of links you can include.

You can also use the bracket syntax to create a new page. Follow these steps:

1. Click **Edit** to put the wiki page in edit mode.

2. Click on the page, and then type the opening double brackets ([[ ).

3. Type the name of the page you want to create, and then type the closing brackets ( ]]).

4. Click **Save & Close**.

5. Click the link (links to pages that do not yet exist have a dashed underline), and SharePoint displays the Add A Page dialog box, shown here:

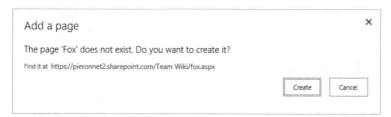

6. Click **Create**.

Figure 2-10 shows a new wiki with four pages and a link to background reading on the library's home page.

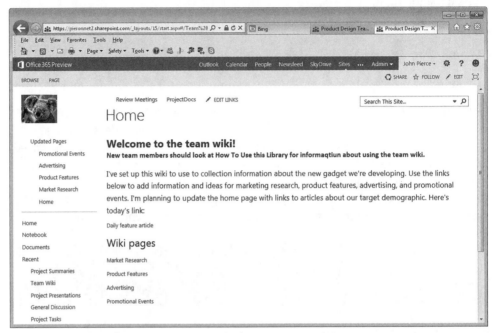

FIGURE 2-10 Set up a wiki page library to assemble information and research your team needs.

Click View All Pages in the Page Library group on the Page tab to see a list of the pages in the library. In the list of pages, you can view a number of page properties, delete pages from the library, view the version history of a page, and see who last modified the page.

Use the Page History command (in the Page tab's Manage group) to open a page that shows a list of previous versions of a page. Recent changes are highlighted in the preview of the page. Click a link for a previous version (listed with version numbers under Versions in the navigation pane) to view it, and use the links at the top of that page to delete a version, restore a version, or view more information about the page's version history.

Classifying and searching for content

Your team site will eventually contain many documents, list items, announcements, and other information that pertains to a project, your department, or another aspect of your team's activities and responsibilities. The search capabilities that are built in to SharePoint help you locate a document, for example, when you aren't sure which library the document is stored in. You can also use the search feature to find related content, such as all the files that a specific team member created.

To help annotate the content on your team site, you can use tags and notes. By adding a note or a tag to an item such as a site page or a document, a team member classifies the content, which increases the ability of other team members to find specific content. Users can add notes and tags to documents, list items, libraries, pages, and webpages outside the site.

Adding a note

The note board lets users record comments about an item in the context of a list or library. For example, a user can add a note about a webpage while they view the page. Other users can see the note and a link to the webpage. Notes can be used on items such as a page, a document, or an external site. When notes are created, they appear in the note board that's associated with the list, library, or content item. You can also edit or update a note, and you can review notes made by colleagues.

To add a note to a document, follow these steps:

1. Open the library or list to which you want to add a note.

2. Select a list item or document that you want to add a note to.

3. On the ribbon, on the Files tab, in the Tag And Notes area, click the **Tags & Notes** button to display the Tags And Notes dialog box.

4. Click the **Note Board** tab.

5. In the text box, type the note you want to make about the item, list, or library, and then click **Post**.

Adding a tag

A tag is a term that you want to assign to content. For example, you might create three tags for a document titled "Landscape Proposal for Contoso": "proposal," "landscape," and "Contoso." You might also use tags that identify who created the proposal and your contact at Contoso. Assigning a tag lets people locate documents more easily and improves searches when you use common terms. (Terms are stored in a central location so that they can be reused.) As you type a tag, SharePoint might suggest a term, and when you save tags, a list of suggested tags appears at the bottom of the Tags tab, as shown in Figure 2-11. Click one of these suggested tags to display a page showing links to the content tagged using that term.

FIGURE 2-11 Add tags to a document to classify it, which makes finding the document easier.

To add a tag, follow these steps:

1. Open the library or list where you want to add a tag.

2. Select an item that you want to tag.

3. On the ribbon, click the **Tags & Notes** button on the Files (or Items) tab.

4. Click the **Tags** tab, and then use the Tags text box to add tags you want to assign. Separate multiple terms by using a semicolon (;).

5. Click **Save**.

Searching

The team site's search box appears at the top of the home page and on list and library pages. You can search for content using keywords, a value such as a document author's name or a file name, or a particular phrase that you enclose in quotation marks.

By default, SharePoint uses context to set the search scope. As the prompt in the search box on the home page indicates, when you run a search from that page, SharePoint looks for content across the site. If you run a search from a list or library, the scope is set to that list or library, and the search results include only matching items in that list or library.

In addition to search scopes such as This Site, you can use a menu in the search box to select a different search scope: Everything, People, or Conversations.

- **Everything**   Use Everything if you want to search files in libraries as well as list items and conversations, which includes items from discussion boards and announcements.

- **People**   If you choose People, the results page includes links with which you can open a person's My Site (a personal SharePoint site that individuals can use to share information and documents), send an e-mail message, view the person on the organizational chart, and so on. Setting the search scope to People doesn't always apply. You would not use this option when you are searching for a specific word or phrase in the site's content.

- **Conversations**   Includes items from discussion boards, announcements, and similar items.

Using advanced search

When you need to define criteria for more complex searches, use the Advanced Search page. (A link to this page appears at the bottom of the search results page.) In an advanced search, you can work with fields that are set up to combine terms using operators such as AND and OR. You can also specify that the search results should include only a specific type of document. By combining advanced search criteria, you can, for example, search for Excel documents in English that contain the phrase "Overhead projections" whose author is Sam Smith and were modified later than last week. Figure 2-12 shows the Advanced Search page.

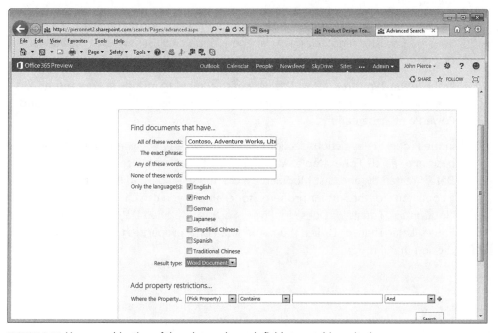

FIGURE 2-12 Use a combination of the advanced search fields to combine criteria.

Keep in mind that combining many criteria in an advanced search can affect the speed at which SharePoint returns results.

Set up an advanced search by using the following options and fields:

- **All Of These Words**   The search results will contain items that include each word you specify. For example, to find documents written by Samantha Smith about the companies Contoso and Adventures Works, type Smith Contoso Adventure Works. The logic of this search parameter assumes that you included the AND operator, so the search phrase becomes Smith AND Contoso AND Adventure Works.

- **The Exact Phrase**   The search results will contain items that include the phrase you enter.

- **Any Of These Words**   The search results will contain items that contain any of the words you enter. In other words, the terms are combined with OR—for example, Budget OR Proposal.

- **None Of These Words**   The search results will contain items that do not contain the word or words you enter.

- Use the Language area to search for items in the language you specify. The options are English, French, German, Japanese, Simplified Chinese, and Traditional Chinese.

- In the Result Type area, select the type of document to include in your results. The options are All Results, Documents, Word Documents, Excel Documents, and PowerPoint Presentations.

- In the Property Restrictions section, specify a property you want to use as the basis of a search. For example, Author, Description, Name, Size, URL, Last Modified Date, Created By, and Last Modified By. Use the second list in this area to specify a condition. For the Author property, for example, you can choose Contains, Does Not Contain, Equals, or Does Not Equal. For Last Modified Date, choose either Equals, Later Than, or Earlier Than. Add additional properties to the search by clicking the plus sign.

Working with search results

Along the left side of the search results page SharePoint displays the refinement panel. By using this panel, you can tailor the search results to see items by a particular author, for example, or to see only Excel files. SharePoint provides categories such as the following:

- Result Type
- Site
- Author
- Modified Date
- Tags

Within each category, you can click one of the links listed to apply a filter to the results. For example, under Result Type, click Word to show only Word documents. Under Modified Date, use the slider to see results related to the time period you select.

CHAPTER 3

Managing access and preserving history

COLLABORATIVE WORK IS often facilitated through approaches that don't enforce rigorous structures. Brainstorming sessions serve this purpose, of course, where some or all of a team's members gather to generate ideas about future work, exchange ideas about what processes can be improved, or outline solutions to particularly difficult problems that keep coming up. In Part 2 of this book, you'll learn how Microsoft Lync supports various types of informal (and formal) communication that let teams exchange ideas in these ways and how teams can use a Microsoft OneNote notebook as a kind of ad hoc repository for recording all types of content and ideas.

See Also For more details, see Chapter 6, "Working together in Lync," and Chapter 7, "Keeping track of discussions and ideas."

In this chapter, you'll learn more about procedures and controls that teams can put in place to manage content they produce. Procedures such as these ensure that the formal processes, decisions, and finalized content that are born from practices such as brainstorming are applied and retained. Although the idea of applying "controls" can sometimes sound exclusionary (even punitive), that isn't the intent. The types of restrictions and controls described in this chapter help protect sensitive and potentially valuable information, set up processes to ensure that team members work with content that's complete, and help teams track and classify the files they use. In addition, restricting access to files and allowing only some team members to view documents that are still in draft form helps team members with expertise in certain areas (legal, financial, sales, engineering, and others) work without concern that the information they are preparing will be mistakenly distributed or modified before final versions are reviewed and approved.

This chapter also builds on some of the concepts you learned about in Chapter 2, "Building a SharePoint team site." In the last two major sections of this chapter, I'll expand on how you can use a document library to keep track of and manage content. To start the chapter, I'll describe some of the basic ways in which you can control access to and protect Office documents. You saw in Chapter 2 how to use groups and permission levels to manage a team site in SharePoint. Those permissions go a long way toward managing which team members can work on documents and what they can do, but some of a team's work will inevitably take place on documents that don't take advantage of the structure of the team site. In these cases, you can use tools like passwords and rights management to control access to documents.

Protecting Office documents

When teams work with sensitive and confidential information, they can use rights management to manage access to files and e-mail messages and to control what users can do with a file.

Rights management restricts permissions to a file to prevent unauthorized access and distribution. For example, you can apply rights management to documents that you don't want everyone on your team to forward, copy, or print. Permissions you set up by using rights management are stored with the file, which means that the restrictions you apply are in effect whether the file is stored in a SharePoint document library, in an Outlook message store, or on a network drive, for example.

A simpler approach to protecting documents—but one without the degree of control offered by rights management—is to protect files with a password. In Microsoft Word, Excel, and PowerPoint, you can define a password that's required to open a file and a different password that's needed to modify it.

Specific applications also include capabilities for protecting the data and formatting in files. In Chapter 8, "Working on shared documents in Word," you'll learn the steps involved when you want to restrict the formatting and editing of a document. Later in this section, I'll describe similar steps you can take to protect workbooks and worksheets in Excel.

First, I'll describe the protections offered by rights management.

Using rights management

Rights management helps teams and organizations enforce policies that control the copying and distribution of confidential or proprietary information. Rights are assigned to content when it is published, and the content is distributed in an encrypted form that provides protection wherever the content resides. In other words, a document that's protected with rights management carries that protection whether it is opened from SharePoint, SkyDrive, a network share, or as an e-mail attachment.

NOTE	Rights management isn't a complete solution for protecting information. Rights management can't prevent the theft, accidental deletion, or corruption of data, and rights management is not the same as an antimalware program. People with keen intent to hand over restricted content can still type it in a new document or copy important information by hand.

Some of the restrictions you can impose by applying rights management are the following:

- Prevent an authorized recipient of restricted content from forwarding, copying, modifying, printing, faxing, or pasting the content

- Prevent restricted content from being copied by using the Print Screen key

- Define a file expiration date so that content in documents, workbooks, or presentations can no longer be viewed after the specified period of time

You can apply rights management by using a template or through user-defined rights. For the Office 2013 Preview, Microsoft provided templates such as the Company Confidential template and the Company Confidential Read Only template. With the Company Confidential template, users of the content are allowed all rights needed to work with and modify the content but are not permitted to copy and print the content. With the Company Confidential Read Only template, users can only read or view the content but are not permitted to modify the content from its original published form. If you need a higher degree of control, you can apply permissions manually by defining user-defined rights.

To apply rights management to a file you are working with in PowerPoint, Excel, or Word, you work on the Info page in Backstage view. Use the Protect Presentation, Protect Workbook, or Protect Document command, depending on which program you're working with. In a message item in Outlook, click Set Permissions on the Info page.

You can also enable rights management for a list or library on your SharePoint team site. You might take this step to protect the content in a document library that's set up to store the specifications for new products or other valuable intellectual property. When rights management is applied to a library, it applies to all the files in that library. For a list, rights management applies only to files that are attached to list items, not to the list items themselves.

When a team member downloads a file from a list or library protected with rights management, the file is encrypted so that only authorized people can view it. Additional restrictions can be applied to users who can view the file. For documents in lists and libraries (as for documents you apply rights management to directly), these restrictions include making a file read-only, disabling the copying of text, preventing people from saving a local copy, and preventing people from printing the file.

The restrictions that are applied to a file when it is downloaded are based on the individual user's permissions on the site that contains the file. For example, a site owner can generally work with a file to edit it, copy it, or modify how rights management is applied. A team member with Edit Items permission for a library can edit, save, and copy the file, but these users cannot print the file unless specifically granted that permission.

> **NOTE**   Before you apply rights management to a list or library it must be enabled by an administrator for your site. Additionally, a server administrator must install protectors on all front-end web servers for every file type that the people in your organization want to protect by using rights management.

To apply rights management to a list or library, you must have at least the Design permission level for that list or library. If you have that level of permission, follow these steps:

1. Open the list or library.

2. On the Library tab (or List tab for a list), click **Library Settings** (or **List Settings**).

3. Under Permissions and Management, click **Information Rights Management**.

> **NOTE**   If the Information Rights Management link does not appear, rights management might not be enabled for your site. Contact your server administrator to see if it is possible to enable rights management for your site.

4. On the Information Rights Management Settings page, select the **Restrict Permission To Documents In This Library On Download** option.

5. In the Create A Permission Policy Title box, type a descriptive name. For example, you might use the name Team Confidential for a policy that applies to a list or library that will contain documents that are confidential within your team.

6. In the Add A Permission Policy Description box, type a description that explains to team members who use this list or library how they should handle protected content. For example, use a description such as "Only discuss with members of the team."

7. To apply additional restrictions to the documents in this list or library, click **Show Options**. You can then select exceptions such as allowing some team members to print a document. You can also set an option that prevents team members from uploading documents that don't support rights management to the list or library.

Using a password

When you save a file in Word, Excel, or PowerPoint, you can assign a password that other users need to enter to open or modify the document. In all three programs, open the Tools menu in the Save As dialog box and then click General Options to open the dialog box where you define the passwords.

Some additional options are included for each program:

- In Excel, you can select an option to always create a backup of the workbook or an option to prompt users to open the file as read-only.

- In Word, you also have the Read-Only Recommended option. The Protect Document button opens the Restrict Formatting And Editing pane, which you'll learn about in detail in Chapter 8.

- In PowerPoint, the General Options dialog box includes the Privacy Options area. The option Remove Automatically Created Personal Information From This File On Save controls whether PowerPoint removes or retains information such as the presentation author and other properties. You'll learn more about document properties later in this chapter.

The Info page also provides an option for applying a password that encrypts the contents of the current file. To encrypt an Excel workbook with a password, follow these steps (the steps in Word and PowerPoint are similar):

1. Click **File, Info**.

2. On the Info page, click **Protect Workbook** and then click **Encrypt With Password**.

3. In the Encrypt Document dialog box, type the password you want to use and then click **OK**.

4. Reenter the password.

    Be sure to take note of the warning in the dialog box about lost passwords: you can't recover them. Be sure to record the password in a safe place so that you can provide it to other users or refer to it yourself in the event you forget the password.

5. Click **OK**, and then save the workbook.

> **TIP**   Not all file formats are compatible with passwords. For example, Excel files stored in the .csv format do not accept a password.

PREPARING TO SHARE A FILE

The Inspect Workbook area on the Info page provides three commands on the Check For Issues menu. The Check For Accessibility and Check For Compatibility commands apply in specific situations—when you want to know which elements of a document, workbook, or presentation could pose issues for people with disabilities, and when you want to know whether any features in a file aren't supported in earlier versions of a program.

You should make regular use of the third command—Inspect Document—before you distribute files to customers or partners, for example, or share a file with colleagues who aren't regular members of your team. You'll see an example of how you use the Document Inspector in PowerPoint in Chapter 10, "Preparing a presentation as a group." Figure 3-1 shows the Document Inspector for Excel.

In general, you can use the Document Inspector to detect elements in a file that you might want to remove or revise before you share the file. As you can see, one category for Excel is Hidden Rows And Columns. Imagine that you enter worksheet formulas that calculate the markup on a set of products or services or formulas related to performance bonuses or new salary ranges. If you hide these cells to focus on the results of the formulas—which users of Excel often do—it's easy to overlook the fact that you hid them later, or someone else getting ready to post the file might not realize that the formulas are contained in a hidden column or row. Inspecting a document will indicate that the workbook has hidden rows or columns. If you don't want to share the formulas with other users, you can return to the worksheet and convert the calculated values to static values, for example, or you might decide to keep the rows or columns hidden and save the workbook as a PDF file. For more details about saving a workbook as a PDF file, see "Creating a PDF/XPS document" in Chapter 9, "Collaborating in Excel."

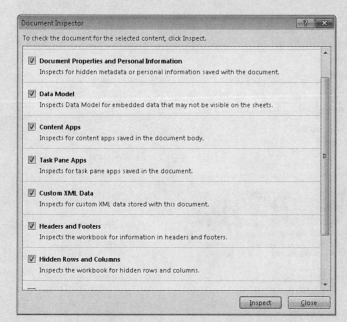

FIGURE 3-1 The Document Inspector can find content and properties you don't necessarily want to share.

Protecting workbooks and worksheets

In this section, I'll cover some specific steps you can take to protect the data and structure of Excel workbooks and worksheets. Because teams use Excel to compile and analyze financial data, these procedures are often applicable. These protections serve several purposes: they can retain the structure of a workbook, for example, or restrict which operations some users can perform. You can also specify editable cell ranges and protect the rest of a worksheet so that it is read-only. The intent of applying these restrictions has as much to do with preserving the work that team members did to construct specific financial scenarios or complex formulas as it does with limiting what other team members can do.

To apply permissions and protection to a workbook or a specific worksheet, you can use a menu of commands on the Info page in Backstage view, as shown in Figure 3-2.

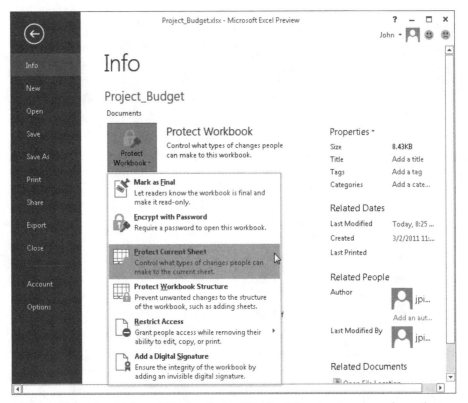

FIGURE 3-2 Select Protect Current Sheet or Protect Workbook Structure to manage how other users can interact with an Excel file.

To protect the structure of a workbook, follow these steps:

1. On the Info page, click **Protect Workbook**, and then click **Protect Workbook Structure**. (Or click Protect Workbook in the Changes group on the Review tab.)

2. In the Protect Structure And Windows dialog box, shown below, select the options you want and then enter an optional password.

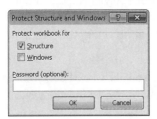

When you protect a workbook's structure, users cannot insert, delete, or rename worksheets or display worksheets that are hidden. When you protect a workbook's window, users can't change the size or position of windows.

You can also restrict the operations users can perform on specific worksheets—for example, you might restrict what users can do to worksheets that contain summary formulas that are referenced in other worksheets designed for entering data.

To protect the current worksheet, follow these steps:

1. On the Info page in Backstage view, click **Protect Workbook**, and then click **Protect Current Sheet**. Or, on the Review tab, click **Protect Sheet** in the Changes group.

    You'll see the Protect Sheet dialog box, shown here:

    You protect worksheets by selecting the specific operations users are allowed to perform. By keeping a check box clear, you prevent users from performing that task. The operations you can control include formatting cells, columns, and rows; inserting columns, rows, and hyperlinks; deleting columns and rows; sorting data; making use of automatic filters; using PivotTable reports; editing objects such as charts or illustrations; and editing scenarios, a feature related to the Excel Scenario Manager. The options Select Locked Cells and Select Unlocked Cells are selected by default.

2. Enter a password that allows you to remove sheet protection.

The next step in protecting a worksheet is to define cell ranges that specific users can edit after providing a password that you define. You can also grant specific users permission to edit ranges without a password.

Follow these steps to define editable cell ranges:

1. In the Changes group on the Review tab, click **Allow Users To Edit Ranges**.

2. In the Allow Users To Edit Ranges dialog box, click **New**.

3. In the New Range dialog box, shown in the following screen shot, enter a name for the cell range. (You can also accept the name Excel provides.) In the Refers To Cells box, enter the cell range you want to protect. You can also click in the Refers To Cells box and then drag through the range to define it.

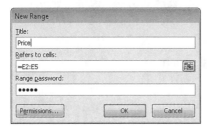

4. In the Range Password box, type a password that a user must provide to edit data in this range.

5. To grant permission to specific users to edit a range without a password, click **Permissions**.

6. In the Permission dialog box, click **Add**.

7. In the Select Users Or Groups dialog box, type the names of the persons or group you want to give permission to, and then click **OK**.

8. In the Permission dialog box, keep the Allow option selected in the Permissions area.

9. Click **OK** to close the Permission dialog box, and then click **OK** in the New Range dialog box.

10. When prompted, type the password again to confirm it, and then click **OK** in the Allow Users To Edit Ranges dialog box.

You can open the Allow Users To Edit Ranges dialog box again to modify or delete a range, add another range, set permissions for other users, and to set or change options for how the worksheet is protected. Select the option Paste Permissions Information Into A New Workbook to keep a record of the permissions you granted to the editable ranges that were defined.

Managing versions

Teams often need to be very deliberate about the information they produce and distribute. In addition to controlling access to files and placing restrictions on sensitive content, teams can use features on their team site to maintain a history of their work and to manage when content is approved and made generally available.

See Also   As you'll see in Chapter 4, "Building team templates," you can also use a template to help control the formatting and content of a document.

When you set up a document library, a slide library, or another type of library or list on your team site, you can select an option to track versions of the items the library or list will contain. Versioning settings let you manage how content is added to and edited in a list or library, and versioning also helps teams track the history of a document. For example, you can specify the number of versions you want to retain and choose to create and track both major and minor versions of a document. By maintaining this history, you can see how the team developed important documents and view previous versions if questions arise about why the final content ended up as it did.

For tight control, you can select an option that requires an authorized user (a user with at least Edit Item permission) to approve content that is submitted to a list or library and also specify a permission level at which users can view draft items. Users without the permissions you specify won't see draft items in the library until a team member with permissions publishes a draft. The set of versioning options also includes an option by which you can require that users check out a document before the document is edited.

■ **IMPORTANT**   Only team members who are site owners or have full control of the site can set up versioning. For more information about site permissions, see "Working with groups and permissions" in Chapter 2.

To set up versioning and specify versioning options for a document library, follow these steps:

1. Open the library, and click the Library tab on the ribbon.

2. In the Settings group, click **Library Settings**.

3. In the General Settings area of the Library Settings page, click **Versioning Settings**.

4. On the Versioning Settings page, set the following options:

- In the Content Approval area, select Yes if you want items to be approved before they can be submitted to this library. (Items uploaded to the library are listed with a status of Draft until they are published and a status of Pending until an authorized user approves them.) If you select this option, you can then select options in the Draft Item Security area to specify who can view items that are pending approval in the library.)

- In the Document Version History area, specify how to manage versioning. You can choose not to use versioning, to create major versions, or to create major and minor versions. You can also indicate how many major versions and drafts of major versions to retain.

- If you select Yes under Content Approval, under Draft Item Security, you indicate who can see draft items. The default option is Only Users Who Can Approve Items. You can broaden the scope for who has access to draft items by choosing Any User Who Can Read Items or Only Users Who Can Edit Items.

- In the Require Check Out section, change the setting to Yes if you want to make it mandatory that users of the library check out a document before it can be edited.

When versioning and content approval are enabled for a library and you require that users check out and check in a document, the steps required to publish and approve a major version will go something like this:

1. A team member who is part of the team site's Members group uploads a document to the library. SharePoint recognizes that users are required to check in files and flags the file as checked out. Even authorized users will not see this item in the library until the user who uploads it checks it in.

2. When the team member checks in a file, SharePoint displays the Check In dialog box. As shown in the following screen shot, you can specify whether to check in a major or a minor version, keep the file checked out, and add a comment about the file and version. Checking in a minor version creates a draft item in the library. Checking in a major version sets the item's status to Pending (assuming that content approval is enabled). An authorized user needs to approve the item before it becomes accessible to all users of the library.

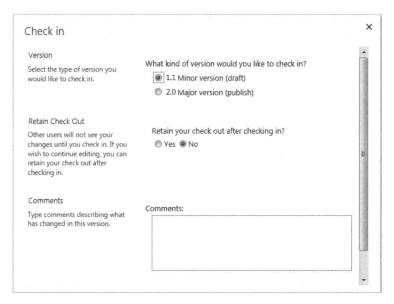

3. At this point, a draft item has been added to the library. To publish a draft item, a user with at least Edit Item permission (a site owner, a team member with full control, or a member of the Members group) selects the document and then clicks the Publish button on the Documents tab (in the Workflows group). In the Publish Major Version dialog box, shown here, add a comment about the version you are publishing before you click **OK**.

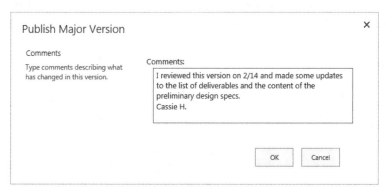

Because content approval is enabled for this library, publishing a draft document sets its status to Pending. A user with approval authority now needs to approve the document to change its status.

4. In the library, select the document that's pending approval.

5. In the Workflows group on the Documents tab, click **Approve/Reject**.

6. In the Approve/Reject dialog box, shown below, select the **Approved** option (or select Rejected, if necessary), add a comment about the action, and then click **OK**.

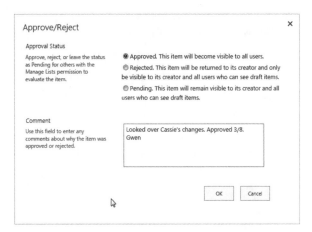

The Workflows group on the Documents tab provides the following additional commands:

■ **Unpublish**   Click this command to unpublish the current version, which returns an approved item to Draft status.

■ **Cancel Approval**   Click this command to cancel the submission of an item for approval. Cancel Approval returns a pending item to Draft status.

You can manage versions in the Version History dialog box, shown in Figure 3-3. To open the Version History dialog box, select the document you want to work with, and then click Version History in the Manage group.

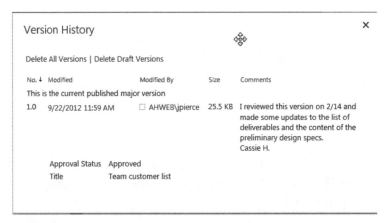

FIGURE 3-3 Select a version in the Version History dialog box to view it. You can also unpublish major versions if you have permission.

The Version History dialog box shows major versions of a document (and minor versions if you have permission to view draft items and you are tracking minor versions) and a version's status. In the Version History dialog box, point to a version you want to examine, and then click the arrow to open a menu you can use to view, restore, or unpublish the current version or to view, restore, or delete a previous version. If you retained draft versions of the document, use the link at the top of the dialog box to delete these versions. (They are moved to the site's Recycle Bin.) Use the Delete All Versions link to send previous versions of the document to the site's Recycle Bin.

Working with document properties

In the final section of this chapter, I'll describe how to work with document properties. Properties provide facts about a document. For example, when you create, fill in, and later edit a workbook in Excel, Excel sets and tracks properties such as the file's size, the dates on which the workbook was created and last modified, and the name of the workbook's author. Properties such as these are read-only. Other properties, including many advanced properties and custom properties you define, can be set in the program and updated by team members as needed.

Document properties aren't in themselves an aspect of collaboration. People who work all on their own might find properties a helpful device for categorizing and identifying content, and while teams gain the same organizational benefits from using properties, they can also use properties to require specific information—the due date for a proposal, for example, or the prospective revenue associated with a contract or service agreement, or who the lead attorney is on a pending case.

You can set some document properties when you work in Word or Excel, for example, and these programs (as well as PowerPoint) let you define custom properties. You can also set up a list or library on your team site to track properties in addition to those that the list or library contains by default. You do this by adding columns to a view or by defining a custom column, which you'll learn how to do in this section.

See Also   For details about list and library views, see "Creating and modifying views" in Chapter 2.

Setting properties in an Office program

Many of the basic document properties are listed on the Info page in Backstage view. In PowerPoint, for example, the list shows the number of slides, the title, the date the presentation was created, and the date it was last modified. You'll see similar information for workbooks in Excel and for Word documents.

You can fill in or update some properties on the Info page. In PowerPoint, click Add A Category and then type a term you want to use—a project or customer name, for example. You can also specify properties such as an additional author. To see the full list of properties available on the Info page, click Show All Properties at the bottom of the list. In Excel, the list expands to display the properties shown in Figure 3-4. Several of the properties that are not filled in automatically, such as Title, Tags, Status, and Categories, have been filled in here.

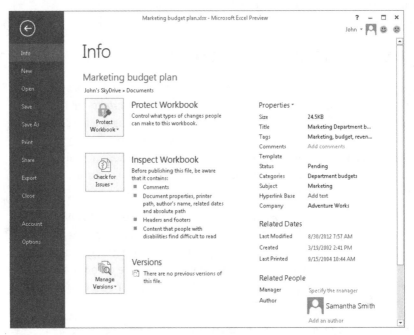

FIGURE 3-4 This screen shot shows the expanded list of properties on the Info page in Excel. You can add information for properties such as Tags and Title on this page.

To work with additional properties, click Properties at the top of the list, and then click Advanced Properties. You'll see the Properties dialog box. Figure 3-5 shows the Summary tab and the Custom tab.

The General and Statistics tabs display information about the file, including the creation and modification dates and when the file was printed. The Contents tab shows information such as the name of a document template, named ranges in a worksheet, or slide titles and themes. On the Summary tab, you can type values for properties such as Title and Subject. (Many of the properties listed on the Summary tab also appear in the list on the Info page.)

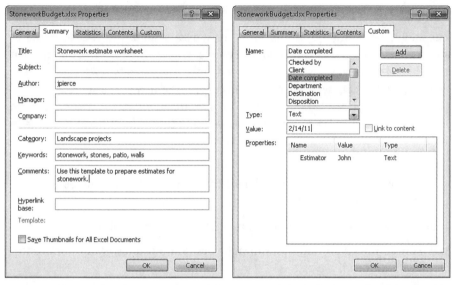

FIGURE 3-5 You can also view properties and document statistics in the Properties dialog box. Use the Custom tab to define properties of your own.

The Custom tab shows a list of properties designed for more specific purposes—Checked By, Client, Project, and Typist among them. These properties let you identify additional attributes about a workbook, document, or presentation. You can use the properties listed as a starting point for a custom property or define a custom property that reflects specific information your team wants to collect—a property that records who approved an estimate for a new project, for example.

To set the value for a property listed on the Custom tab, select the property in the list, type the value for the property, and then click Add. To define a custom property, follow these steps:

1. On the Custom tab, type the name of the property in the Name box.

2. From the Type list, select the data type for this property. You can choose from Text, Date, Number, and Yes/No.

3. In the Value box, type the value for the property.

4. Click **Add**.

The name, value, or type of an advanced or custom property can be modified by selecting the property in the Properties list at the bottom of the Custom tab, and then updating the property by using the Name, Type, and Value boxes. Click Modify, and then click OK to complete the steps.

Defining properties for a list or library

To provide additional information about the items in a list or library on your team site, you can create your own column and add it to one or more views. Custom columns then serve as additional properties for the items stored in the list or library. By specifying that a column is required to contain a value, you can collect information about a document or a list item when it is added to your team site. For example, you might create a column named Due Date to use in a library where you store sales proposals. When a team member uploads a document, he or she has to fill in the due date, which helps you track when each proposal must be complete.

To create a column, a team member must be a team site owner or have Full Control permission. Follow these steps to define a column:

1. In the Manage Views group on the Library tab, click **Create Column**.

2. In the Create Column dialog box, shown below, type a name for the column and then select the column type.

The options for the type of column include Single Line Of Text, Multiple Lines of Text, Number, Currency, Date And Time, Lookup (which you can tie to another field on your site), and others.

3. In the Additional Column Settings area, type a description for the column and then specify other settings as required for the column.

Options in the Additional Column Settings area of the dialog box change depending on the type of column. These options give you a high degree of control over the properties of a column you create. In the preceding screen shot, you can see some of the options for a Choice column. For the Number type, you use this area to specify the following:

- Whether the column is required (so that it must contain data)

- Whether the column must contain unique values

- A minimum and maximum value

- The number of decimal places

- A default value

- Whether to show the value as a percentage

- Whether to add this column to all content types in the library

- Whether to add this column to the default view

4. Set up a validation formula if necessary.

   In a Date And Time column, for example, you could create a formula so that only dates later than today are valid in the column.

5. Click **OK**.

> **TIP** Custom columns are added to the library's default view if you keep that option selected in the Create Column dialog box. They are not added automatically to other views defined for the library, but you can add them by modifying a view.

When a document is uploaded to a list or library with required columns, SharePoint displays a dialog box such as the one shown in Figure 3-6. Notice that, even though check-out and check-in are not required for this library, SharePoint uploads the document and checks it out to the person uploading the file. That person needs to fill in the required fields and then check in the document to make it accessible to other members using the team site.

FIGURE 3-6 In a list or library with required columns, you can't add an item or check in a document until you fill in those properties. This screen shot also shows notifications you see for a library in which content approval is required.

For documents stored in the library—or for documents you create by using the New Document command in the library (or the New Item command for a list)—mandatory properties you define for a list or library are also accessible on the Document Panel in the related Office program. For a new document, the team member creating the document can fill in values for required properties before saving the file to the team site.

To view the Document Panel, first display the Info page in Backstage view. Click Properties at the top of the list of properties, and then click Show Document Panel. (If the Developer tab is displayed on the ribbon, you can also click Document Panel in the Templates group.) Figure 3-7 shows a blank Document Panel in a new Word document created from a document library. Filling in required properties at this point saves a step when the file is saved to the team site.

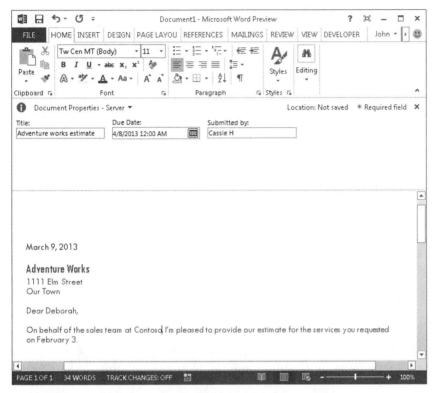

FIGURE 3-7 An asterisk indicates required fields in the document panel.

Another advantage of using properties is that SharePoint includes some properties in its search results. For example, SharePoint searches the text included in the Comments property in Word, Excel, or PowerPoint, and also searches the Title property. As you can with other columns in a list or library, you can sort and filter by a custom column to locate specific items of interest.

CHAPTER 4

Building team templates

ONE OF THE goals of effective team work is to ensure that processes used to successfully manage ongoing work are repeatable. The detailed circumstances of each project or event will often require some flexibility, but in general you want to avoid reinventing the wheel. As teams gain experience working together, they need to determine what's worked and solidify those actions, improve on the steps that weren't successful, and then organize their evaluations and decisions into processes they can rely on to move work forward.

But it's not just the processes themselves that you want to streamline, it's also the results—the records, budgets, presentations, and other content that teams create to document the work that took place. For example, if your team manages a group of similar projects, you want to collect and report the same information about those projects so that you have an accurate basis for comparison.

In cases like these, you want to set up Microsoft Excel workbooks that you can use to track standard financial information and maybe schedules and resource assignments. In Microsoft Word, you want documents such as proposals or status reports to not only look the same but have the same organization and a set of common elements—such as tables, lists, and descriptions—so that those reviewing the documents and making decisions based on them can find the information they need. For presentations in Microsoft PowerPoint, a common look and feel can accentuate the professionalism your team wants to convey and can also ensure that you provide a regular baseline of information when you need to compare one product with another, for example, or want to communicate the qualities you hope will make next month's marketing launch a winning one.

In this chapter, you'll learn how you can use and build templates to help facilitate these goals. Templates are only starting points, of course. Teams still need to collect raw data, write proposals, and develop and rehearse presentations. But as starting points, templates provide an array of tools, placeholders, prompts, and styles that lessen the work that team members need to do to identify what information is required, as well as the effort involved in finalizing the appearance of a work product they will share.

You can begin to understand the usefulness of templates simply by recognizing how much time Microsoft has spent defining and producing Office templates of all sorts. For the three applications covered in this chapter—Excel, PowerPoint, and Word—you can find hundreds of templates by searching on the New page. Figure 4-1, for example, shows just a couple of the templates that show up in Word when I searched for "status reports." As the list on the right suggests, 32 templates related to status reports are available.

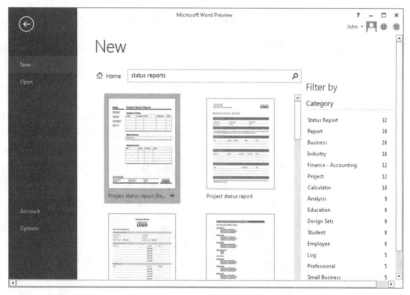

FIGURE 4-1 Search for templates on the New page in an Office program, such as this one in Word. Click an item in the Category list to display templates of a particular type.

After you find a template that looks promising, click the template preview on the New page. In the window the Office program displays, you'll see a description of the template, a rating, and who provided the template (Microsoft or one of its partners, usually). Click Create to open a document based on the template.

> **NOTE**   The templates shown and illustrated in this chapter were available in the Office 2013 Preview available during the summer of 2012.

Use the built-in templates in Office to become familiar with the elements a template can contain. You can also start with a built-in template and modify it. I'll illustrate a couple of the built-in templates in this chapter as a way to introduce template elements. I'll also provide some details about how you can create your own templates. Many of those details also apply if you want to start with a built-in template and modify it.

Using Excel templates

There are clear advantages to using templates for documents such as invoices, expense reports, and budgets. The information that's needed for approval, compliance, and analysis remains consistent. It can be easily compared and can also be summarized and totaled when teams or departments need to look at data over months, quarters, and years.

Excel templates often include a mix of data, formatting, and formulas. They can include graphical elements such as charts and PivotTables and also implement features such as conditional formatting to highlight information and data validation to ensure that the information provided meets specific requirements (that the dates of invoices fall within a specific time period, for example).

In this section, I'll cover two Excel templates. The first is a template for an inventory list, and the second is a simple event-tracking template. Through these illustrations, you'll see some of the components of an Excel template and learn how to add similar features to the templates you design.

Looking at the inventory list template

The inventory list template described in this section (see Figure 4-2) is defined as a table in Excel. (In Excel, tables are also referred to as lists). The template is set up with the following columns (not all of these appear in the figure):

- ID
- Name

- Description

- Unit Price

- Quantity in Stock

- Inventory Value

- Reorder Level

- Reorder Time

- Quantity Reordered

- Discontinued

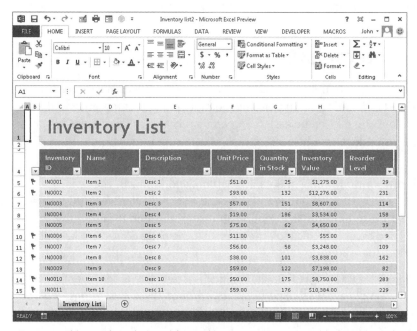

FIGURE 4-2 This template, designed for tracking inventory, uses a table for its basic format. It also implements conditional formatting to highlight important information.

I selected this template because it illustrates why setting up data in a table can be beneficial in any template that's designed for tracking lists of items. A team might use a table to track events, projects, media purchases, office space, resource assignments, and so on. As you read about the details of this template, keep in mind how you might implement them in a template that's relevant to the work your team does—whether that involves managing inventory or something else.

Creating a table to manage data provides at least a couple of advantages. First, in a table, Excel configures each column so that you can filter and sort based on the values in the column. Figure 4-3 shows the menu that appears when you click the down arrow beside a column name. In the figure, the menu for the Unit Price column is open and displays the options for number filters. To see only unit prices greater than a certain amount, select Greater Than and then specify the value you want to use. Filtering options such as these also appear in columns that use text, where you can filter by using options such as Begins With (to view all product names that begin with *S*, for example) or Contains (to see only products that include the word "pasta" or descriptions that contain the words "on sale"). Date columns have filtering options such as Before, After, Between, Next Week, Next Month, and so on.

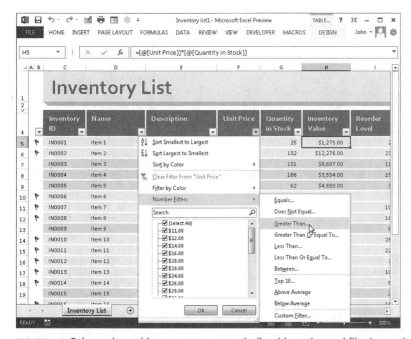

FIGURE 4-3 Columns in a table are set up automatically with sorting and filtering options.

You don't need to take any additional steps to set up columns in this fashion. The act of defining a table in Excel configures the columns in this way. To create a table, select the cell range (including column headings) that will contain the data, and then click Table on the Insert tab. (You can also simply press Ctrl+T or Ctrl+L.) Excel displays the Create Table dialog box, in which you can adjust the cell range (if needed) and select the option that tells Excel that the table has headings.

Another aspect of tables demonstrated in this template is the use of what Excel refers to as *structured references*. A structured reference is a formula that uses the names of column headings instead of cell references. In the formula bar in Figure 4-3, you can see the formula *=[@[Unit Price]]*[@[Quantity in Stock]]*, which multiplies the value in the Unit Price column by the value in Quantity in Stock. The advantage of using a structured reference such as this (which Excel defines when you create a formula in a table) is that the names adjust whenever you add or remove data from the table. A formula like this can also be easier to understand. A formula such as *=C3*D3* doesn't tell you immediately what value the formula is designed to calculate—you need to look back at the worksheet to see what data is contained in columns C and D. Structured references are also used when you create a formula in a cell that's outside an Excel table but makes reference to the table's data. The column heading names in the formula let you find relevant data more easily.

If you want to see a simple example of how Excel creates a structured reference, follow these steps:

1. Open a blank worksheet from the New page on the File tab. (If you have the inventory list template open, you can add a blank worksheet to that file.)

2. In row 1, in columns A through D, enter the headings January, February, March, and Total.

3. In rows 2 and 3, enter numeric values for each of the months. Don't enter values in the Total column.

4. Select the cell range A1:D3, and then press **Ctrl+T**. In the Create Table dialog box, click **OK**.

5. Click in the Total column in row 2, type an equal sign (=), and then click in row 2 for January. Notice that Excel enters the column name instead of the cell reference in the formula.

6. Type a plus sign (**+**), click in the February column, and then repeat this step for March.

7. Press **Enter** to finish the formula and perform the calculation. Notice that Excel copies the formula to row 3—you don't need to copy the formula to the other rows in the table yourself.

8. Click in the column heading for March. In the formula bar, change March to April. Now check the formula in the Total column, and you'll see that Excel updated the column name in the formula.

The inventory list template also uses conditional formatting to highlight the status of information. With conditional formatting, you define rules for conditions that Excel evaluates.

When those conditions are true—for example, when a value in a cell is less than an amount you specify or greater than the amount in another cell—Excel applies formatting you define to highlight information. In the inventory list template, conditional formatting is used to emphasize rows for items that need to be reordered and also to strike through the data in rows for items that have been discontinued.

To see the conditional formatting rules applied to a workbook, click Conditional Formatting in the Styles group on the Home tab, and then click Manage Rules, which opens the Conditional Formatting Rules Manager, shown in Figure 4-4. Here, the Show Formatting Rules For list at the top of the dialog box is set to This Table. The list will show Current Selection if you have a cell range selected. Choose a setting from the Show Formatting Rules For list to see the conditional formatting rules that affect different areas of a worksheet.

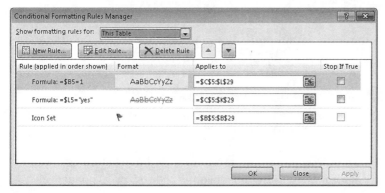

FIGURE 4-4 You can create and edit conditional formatting rules using the Conditional Formatting Rules Manager dialog box.

The inventory list template includes three rules. Using the first rule (Formula: = $B5=1), Excel adds a background color to rows when the value in column B equals 1. The background color indicates that the quantity in stock for items in the highlighted rows has reached the reorder point. The rule depends on a formula in column B that essentially compares the value in the Quantity in Stock column with the value in the Reorder Level column. If Quantity in Stock is less than Reorder Level and an item isn't discontinued, the background color is applied. Whether the formatting is applied is also managed by a check box control that appears in the template above columns K and L. Selecting the check box turns on the formatting, clearing the check box removes it.

The second rule (Formula: $L5="yes") applies to the Discontinued column. If the value in that column equals "yes," the strikethrough formatting is applied. In the third rule, a flag icon is added to column B when the formula in that column equals 1. This rule also demonstrates some of the flexibility of conditional formatting. In addition to formatting such as background colors and strikethrough, you can use icon sets such as these flags to mark cells that meet the conditions you define.

To set up your own conditional formatting rules, you can take a number of approaches. Figure 4-5 shows options available on the Conditional Formatting menu.

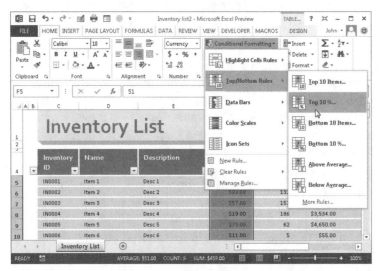

FIGURE 4-5 You can create conditional formatting rules by using built-in options that show the top 10 percent of items, those above or below average, and many others.

For example, let's say you are designing a budget template. In the Actual column, you could define a conditional formatting rule that highlights the top 5 or 10 budget categories so that you know where most of your expenses occur. You could use data bars (another option on the Conditional Formatting menu) to display colored bars that appear in various lengths to show the relative values among a group of cells.

You can also use a formula to define a conditional formatting rule. Click New Rule on the Conditional Formatting menu to display the New Formatting Rule dialog box. In this dialog box, select the option Use A Formula To Determine Which Cells To Format. You then need to define the formula that Excel applies to the selected cell range to determine whether the formatting you define is shown. In a template in which you track a series of dates, you could write a formula that compares two dates (whether an expiration date is within 30 days of today, for example) to highlight rows that need your closer attention.

Creating a simple tracking template with data validation

In this section, I'll walk through how to create a simple template for tracking information about a series of events your team has planned. You wouldn't want to use this template in real life—it's only an illustration—but it reinforces some of the benefits of using tables and conditional formatting and also introduces you to data validation, a feature that lets you specify what values can be entered in specific cells.

Setting up the template

To start, open a blank workbook from the New page, and then follow these steps:

1. In cell A1, type the heading **Event Tracker**.

2. Select cell A1. In the Styles group on the Home tab, click **Cell Styles** and then choose **Heading 1**.

3. In row 2, in columns A through E, enter the column headings **Location**, **Coordinator**, **Invitations Due By**, **Start Date**, and **Budget**.

4. Select the column headings, and then choose a Themed Cell Styles option from the Cell Styles menu to format the column headings.

5. Select the cell range A2:E7, and then press **Ctrl+T**.

6. In the Create Table dialog box, select the option **My Table Has Headers**, and then click **OK**.

   That's it, but of course you could add much more to enhance this template. At this point, the template should look something like the following screen shot:

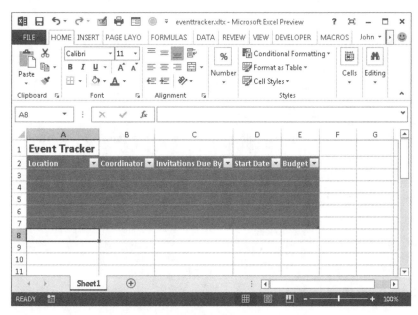

7. Click the **File** tab, click **Save As**, and then click **Computer**.

8. Click **Browse**, and then choose Excel Template (*.xltx) from the Save As Type drop-down list. Choose a location, and then click **Save**.

Adding data validation

Some cells or cell ranges require a specific type of data or specific values to be valid. You can set up data validation rules in Excel templates to restrict the type of data—to allow only dates or whole numbers, for example—or to define a range of valid values—for example, dates between July 1 and September 30 or the locations Brussels, London, Paris, and Rome. Setting up data validation rules helps maintain the integrity of the data that a template is designed to capture, and it can also make the process of entering data in the template more accurate and convenient.

You define validation rules in the Data Validation dialog box, shown in Figure 4-6, which you open by clicking Data Validation in the Data Tools group on the Data tab. In the dialog box, you can also define notifications that appear on the screen to tell users of the template what data is valid and to alert users when they enter data that's not.

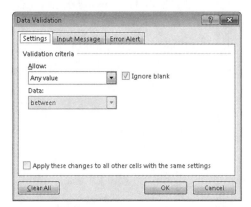

FIGURE 4-6 Define rules for valid data input, along with messages to assist users, in the Data Validation dialog box.

In the Data Validation dialog box, the Allow list gives you several choices for the type of data that will be defined as valid:

- Any Value
- Whole Number
- Decimal
- List
- Date
- Time
- Text Length
- Custom

Based on the data type you select, the dialog box displays text boxes in which you specify other details. For example, if you select Text Length, you need to specify the minimum and maximum length (which might be the same). You could use the Text Length option in a template in which you record product IDs that all have a specific number of characters. If you select List, you need to identify the valid items. You can do this by entering the items in the Source text box in the Data Validation dialog box, separating each item with a comma, or you can add the list to a worksheet and refer to the cell range where the list items appear. (You'll see how to do this in detail shortly.) If you keep the In-Cell Dropdown check box selected when you create a list of valid values, Excel displays the items in a drop-down menu in the cell.

The Custom option in the Data Validation dialog box lets you define a formula that Excel calculates to determine whether data is valid. For example, you might prevent someone from entering an expense item in the Travel category unless the travel budget (defined in a different cell) still has available funds.

You use the Input Message tab of the Data Validation dialog box to define the text for a ScreenTip that indicates what kind of data should be entered. You could, for example, define a message that tells users of a template that a valid date must be later than today. On the Error Message tab, you can create a custom message box that Excel displays when invalid data is entered.

Keep in mind that validation rules let you control the data that is entered directly in a cell. If a user enters invalid data, Excel displays a generic message or the message you define, and the user must cancel the entry or try again. Excel does not display these messages when data is copied to a cell, when a value is entered by filling a cell range, when a formula calculates an invalid value, or when the data is entered by the operations of a macro. You can check whether a worksheet contains any invalid data by clicking Circle Invalid Data (in the Data Tools group on the Data tab). Excel marks the cells and ranges in which faulty data resides. With this information at hand, you can correct the data or (as necessary) relax the validation rules.

TIP ✓ In addition to the messages you create to tell users about the data validation rules active in a template, users can check whether a worksheet contains data validation rules by pressing Alt+E+G to open the Go To dialog box, and then clicking Special. In the Go To Special dialog box, select Data Validation and use the All option. Click OK, and Excel highlights the cell ranges subject to validation rules. A user can then open the Data Validation dialog box to examine the rules that apply. You can also identify cells with data validation rules applied by clicking Find & Select on the Home tab, and then clicking Data Validation.

To set up some validation rules for the event tracker template, follow these steps:

1. In the template, select cells B3:B7 (the blank rows under Coordinator).

2. On the Data tab, click **Data Validation**.

3. In the Data Validation dialog box, in the Allow list, select **List**.

4. In the Source box, type the names of several of your team members, separating each name with a comma.

5. Click **OK**.

In the Coordinator column, you should now see an arrow next to the border with cell B3. Click the arrow to display the list you just created. A user of this template can choose an entry from this list—which presumably contains only the team members who act as coordinators. You can type a name not in the list in one of the cells under Coordinator. When you press Enter, Excel display its generic error message indicating that the data you entered is invalid.

You could also set up a rule for valid dates in the Invitations Due By column. Let's say that for logistical reasons, invitations can't be sent later than 30 days before the start date. Select the cells in the Invitations Due By column, open the Data Validation dialog box, and then choose Custom in the Allow list. In the Formula box, you could use a formula such as <=[Start Date]+30 to define the valid data.

To finish a template like this, you could define additional data validation rules (a list of valid locations, for example, or a maximum amount for a budget). You could also apply conditional formatting rules, as you saw in the inventory list example earlier. For example, you could create a rule for the Start Date column as follows:

1. Select the cells in the Start Date column.

2. On the Home tab, click **Conditional Formatting** and then click **A Date Occurring**.

3. In the Date Occurring dialog box, select **Next Week** (or Next Month), and then define the formatting you want to apply.

   With this rule in place, Excel displays upcoming events using the formatting you specified.

With data validation and conditional formatting in place, you can manage the information collected in the template and see important data when it needs your attention. And with custom error messages in place, users of the template receive instructive warnings if they inadvertently enter data that's not correct, as you can see in Figure 4-7.

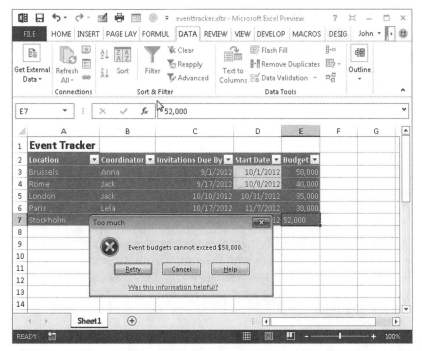

FIGURE 4-7 With data validation rules in place in this template, data that doesn't meet defined criteria can't be entered directly by users.

Developing a PowerPoint template

PowerPoint templates generally include examples of slides designed for specific purposes. Some slides feature bulleted lists or other short text descriptions that outline goals, milestones, resources, and processes. Other slides in a template are built to emphasize visual elements using SmartArt shapes, charts, tables, or images.

In this section, to introduce PowerPoint templates, I'll walk through a template designed for project overviews and highlight some of the elements it contains. After that introduction, I'll go through the steps you can follow to develop a template of your own, where you'll work with a template's slide master, learn how to customize design elements and placeholders, and create a custom layout.

A slide master defines settings for presentation elements such as a background, colors, fonts, text effects, and the size and position of placeholders. When you apply or change these settings on the slide master, the settings are applied to every slide in the presentation. For example, you might place an image or a logo on a slide master so that it appears in the same location on each slide. You can overwrite the settings defined in a template when you develop and format a presentation in Normal view.

■ **IMPORTANT** Don't mistake a template's theme for the template itself. Themes contain a set of coordinated colors, fonts, and text effects. Templates can have a theme, but templates also contain a set of slide layouts with content placeholders that are customized for each presentation based on the template. Placeholders can be used for text prompts as well as SmartArt, images, and other graphical elements.

Elements of a PowerPoint template

Because the focus of many teams is to plan and manage projects, I picked a template designed for presentations that describe the goals and details of a project to illustrate some of a PowerPoint template's basic elements. The sample template (named Project Overview) contains 11 slides, which each contain prompts and placeholder objects that are customized by teams when they report to others about the current details of the projects they manage. Figure 4-8 shows the title slide with several placeholders that you replace with information specific to your project. The template shown here uses the Trek theme.

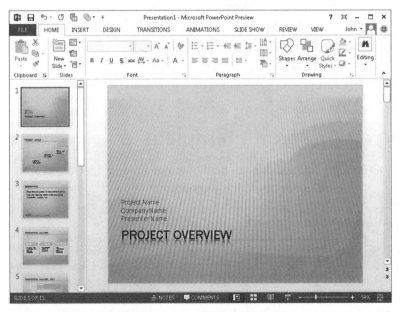

FIGURE 4-8 PowerPoint templates rely on placeholders that prompt you to enter information for a specific presentation.

Other slides in this template are designed to present information about project goals, a project description and schedule, analysis of competitive information, technologies that might be involved, resources, procedures and processes required, current status, and a slide that points to additional resources. One step teams can take when they start developing PowerPoint templates is to create a list of the slides the template should contain and define what information should be presented on each slide. Tie the list of slides to the standard slide layouts in PowerPoint. Does your template need a simple blank slide? If the template is designed for presentations that compare information, which of the two-column layouts will you need? To see a gallery of standard layouts, click Layout in the Slides group on the Home tab.

In addition to prompts and placeholders for information related to the purpose of the slide, this template uses various SmartArt elements—a bold arrow that arcs upward toward the project's ultimate goal and a series of circles designed to present information about team resources. As you can see in Figure 4-9, to change the text displayed in the SmartArt graphic, you can click the small handle at the left side of the selection box to display a pane where you can update the text.

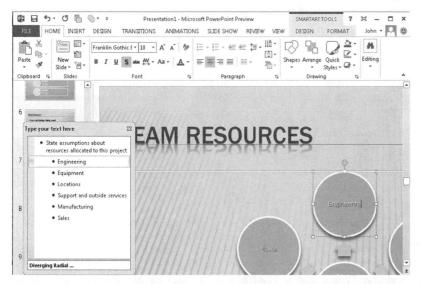

FIGURE 4-9 To update the text in a SmartArt graphic, select the object, click the arrow on the left border, and then use the pane that PowerPoint displays to change and edit the text.

The project overview template doesn't include slide transitions or animations, but you could add them for a particular presentation by selecting a slide or an object and then using the options on the Transitions and Animations tabs. For the purposes of a specific presentation, you could also apply a different theme or otherwise modify the appearance of slides by changing the formatting of fonts, text effects such as shadows, the fill colors for the SmartArt elements, and so on. You could make these changes without altering the basic template, which would remain intact for when you need it again for similar presentations.

Creating your own PowerPoint template

Your team might find that one or more of the PowerPoint templates that come with Office serve most of your needs. You could modify a built-in template to better capture the work and personality of your team and organization, but you might find that the effort required is better spent designing and saving your own template. I'll outline the steps you follow to do that in this section.

To start, open a blank presentation by clicking the File tab, clicking New, and then clicking Blank Presentation. On the View tab, click Slide Master to open the presentation in Slide Master view. As shown in Figure 4-10, in the pane at the left you'll see the slide master (the larger thumbnail at the top of the pane) and various side layouts.

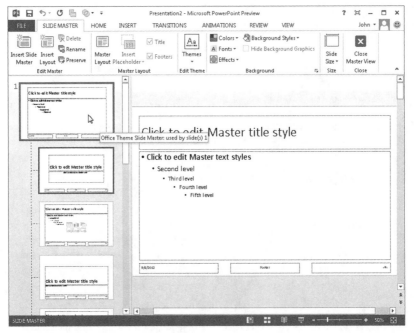

FIGURE 4-10 To start building your own template, open a blank presentation and switch to Slide Master view.

You can point to a thumbnail to see the name of the layout—for example, the Title Slide layout, the Title And Content layout, the Title And Two Content layout, and others. Changes you make to the slide master (to font formatting, for example) apply to all the individual layouts. Changes you make to a specific layout affect only slides that use that layout.

Customizing template design elements

Because you're working with a blank presentation, the generic Office theme is currently applied. To apply a different theme to the template, be sure the slide master is selected and then open the Themes gallery in the Edit Theme group on the Slide Master tab. Select a theme or click Browse For Themes to see other choices. The theme you choose— with its collection of fonts, backgrounds, and colors—is applied to the slide master and the available layouts.

You can use the theme as is at this point or start adjusting elements such as the color scheme, fonts, and text effects. Use the command groups on the Slide Master tab to make the following changes:

- In the Background group, click Colors and then select a color scheme for the template. Rest your pointer on an option to see a preview. To fine-tune the color scheme for your template, click Customize Colors at the bottom of the Colors gallery to open the Create New Theme Colors dialog box, shown here.

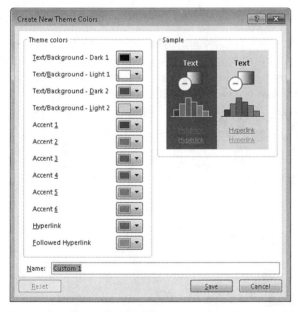

Open the palette for each color element (Text/Background - Dark 1 and so on) you want to change, and then select the color you want. The image in the Sample area is updated to reflect your choice. You can select More Colors at the bottom of the palette you're working with to mix colors of your own. When you finish making changes, type a name for the custom color scheme and click Save. Your new scheme is now available in the gallery.

- Open the Fonts gallery to select a different base font for the template. (This changes the font scheme that's built into the theme you selected.) The choices in the gallery show the heading font and the body font. If you want to use a combination not available in the gallery, click Customize Fonts to display the Create New Theme Fonts dialog box, shown here.

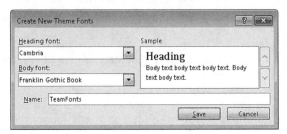

Select a heading font and a body font, type a name for the new scheme, and then click Save. This font scheme is now added to the gallery, and you can use it for other templates you develop (or apply it to a presentation that you're creating).

- Use the Effects gallery to choose a set of shadows, edges, and other text effects.

- To modify the background, click Background Styles, select one of the options available, or choose Format Background to display the Format Background pane, shown in the following screen shot. In the Format Background pane, you can make detailed changes to fill formatting, effects, and the background image.

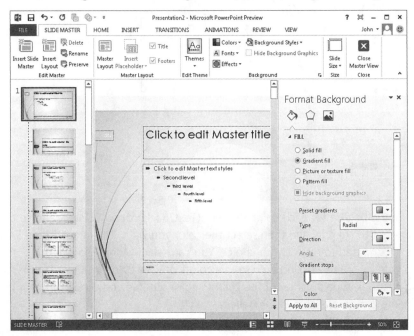

- To change the size of slides, click Slide Size, and then select Standard, Widescreen, or Custom Slide Size. To set up a custom slide size, you need to fill in the Slide Size dialog box with information about what the slides are being sized for (a paper size, a screen display, and so on), slide dimensions, and orientation (portrait or landscape).

Working with placeholders

Updating the design of your template with color and font schemes addresses how slides look. You also should consider the content you want to include on the slides in your template. To do this, you work with placeholders.

Figure 4-11 shows the Insert Placeholder menu, which lists the types of placeholders you can add to a slide. In the figure, the slide layout named Picture With Caption is selected. Initially, this layout included a single placeholder for an image, together with a text placeholder for the caption. I resized the default placeholder and then inserted a second one to provide a layout that's designed for a side-by-side comparison of pictures. Notice that the default placeholder contains the helpful prompt "Click icon to add picture." The placeholder I added doesn't yet include a prompt. It's simply labeled "Picture" in the top-left corner.

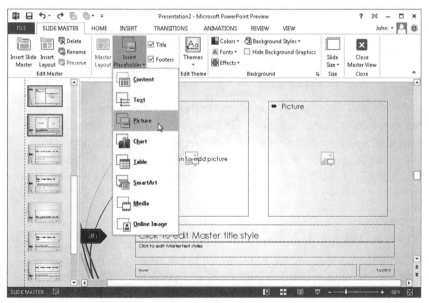

FIGURE 4-11 You develop a PowerPoint template in two stages—refining the design with colors, fonts, and text effects, and then adding content placeholders to build the slide layouts you need.

Because you're designing this template for use in a collaborative environment, adding prompts such as the one shown in Figure 4-11 can be very helpful. These prompts can describe actions a user needs to take or can point to the type of information you want the users of your template to enter. (For example, look back at Figure 4-8, which shows placeholders for company name, project name, and presenter name.)

Here are the steps you follow to add a text placeholder in Slide Master view:

1. Select the layout.

2. In the Master Layout group, click **Insert Placeholder**, and then click **Text**.

3. Click a location on the layout, and then drag to draw the placeholder.

4. To resize a placeholder, drag the corner of one of its borders.

5. Type descriptive text that prompts the users of your template to enter specific information.

USING MORE THAN ONE SLIDE MASTER IN A TEMPLATE

In some PowerPoint templates, using a single slide master provides the consistency in appearance that you need. However, you aren't restricted to using only one slide master when you build a template. You might consider adding a slide master to a template you know will be used for presentations that cover multiple topics. You can distinguish topics by using the variations in look and feel provided by more than one slide master.

In Slide Master view, click Insert Slide Master in the Edit Master group. A new slide master is added to the thumbnail pane along with the standard slide layouts. You can then apply or define a different theme to this slide master. When you are building a specific presentation in PowerPoint's Normal view, you'll see the additional layouts available under New Slide and Layout on the Home tab.

Creating a custom layout

As you saw earlier in this section, a template—even a blank presentation—comes with a set of slide layouts. The layouts are designed for slides in which you want to present graphical elements, those in which you want to compare information side by side, and so on. You can make adjustments to built-in layouts, but you can also create your own. Custom layouts will include placeholders (and possibly distinctive design elements) in an arrangement that fits the purpose of the slide.

To create a slide layout, display your template (or the current presentation) in Slide Master view, and then click Insert Layout. You'll see a basic layout with a title placeholder. To build the layout, add placeholders following the steps described earlier in this section. Select the kind of placeholder you want, and then drag to place it where you want it to appear. Then use the options in the Background group on the Slide Master tab to update the look and feel of the new layout.

PowerPoint names custom layouts as Custom Layout or Custom Layout_1 by default. To provide a more descriptive name, select the layout's thumbnail and then click Rename in the Edit Master group on the Slide Master tab. (The Rename command is also available on a shortcut menu if you right-click a thumbnail.)

Working with notes and handout masters

When you develop a PowerPoint template, most of your attention will be focused on altering the slide master or updating specific slide layouts. As part of your template, you can also work with handout masters and notes masters. Notes and handouts apply mainly to presentations you plan to print, but a few customizations to bring notes and handouts up to date with the appearance of the template's slides is a good finishing touch. For example, apply the same theme or color scheme to handouts and notes. For handouts, you can also specify the slide size and how many slides will be printed on a single page. In addition, you can include or remove header and footer information in handouts, and add the date and page number. You have the options for a header, footer, the date, and page numbers in notes as well. In notes, you also have the options to include a slide image and to change the page orientation, among other things.

To work with notes or handout masters, switch to the View tab, and then click the command you want in the Master Views group.

Saving the PowerPoint template file

PowerPoint templates use the .potx file name extension. To save your template, click Save As on the File tab. Select a location (such as Computer), and then click Browse. Type a file name, and then select PowerPoint Template (.potx) in the Save As Type list.

To create a presentation based on the template, open the template and then save the presentation using the .pptx file name extension. Unfortunately, custom templates you create in PowerPoint don't show up on the New page—at least not in the Office 2013 Preview.

Designing a Word template

If you want to design your own template in Word, you have a few choices as your start-ing point. You can use a document you've created as the basis of the template, you can use another template file as your foundation, or you can create a template from the ground up.

Some of the elements you should consider using in a Word template include the following:

- **Styles**   What styles do you need? Can you work with only the built-in styles, or do you need to define each style from scratch? Depending on the purpose of the template, you need to consider styles for headings, normal paragraphs (indented or unindented), lists, tables, illustrations and images, and other elements. For more information, see "Working with paragraph styles" and "Defining character styles" later in this section.

- **Headers and footers**   Add page numbering, the date, a document title (for ex-ample, "Request for Proposal"), and other information (the label "Confidential" or your department name) that you want each document based on this template to contain in these areas. To define a header and a footer, click Header or Footer on the Insert tab and then select the format you want to use. For more information, see "Creating headers and footers" later in this section.

- **Images**   Add a company logo or other graphic that should be part of each docu-ment. Click Picture on the Insert tab to add a picture to a document.

- **Page layout**   Use the commands and tools on the Page Layout tab to set mar-gins, the page orientation, page size, the number of columns, and other layout-related settings.

- **Document references**   Add a placeholder table of contents, if applicable. If the template is for documents that include a number of illustrations, indicate whether captions are required and define a default style for captions.

- **Placeholder text**   Add placeholder text for elements such as an address block, product references, agenda items, meeting notes, and other content that should be included in documents based on the template.

- **Tables**   What type of table formats do you need? Can you use one of the built-in table styles provided by Word, or do you want to define your own?

- **Building blocks**   Building blocks are content elements (such as cover pages, headers and footers, and watermarks) that are stored in galleries. You can save your own building blocks and distribute them with templates. When you send or make the template available to others, the building blocks saved with the template are available in the galleries. For more information on creating building blocks, see "Creating building blocks and Quick Parts " later in this section.

- **Content controls**   You can add certain types of content controls to a template to help you and other users manage information. For example, you can add a drop-down list control to a template, define the items in that list, and then select the items you need as you build a document. By setting properties for a content control, you can restrict the content the control allows (only certain items in a list) or provide more flexibility. You can find more information about specific content controls later in this section.

To start building a Word template, click the File tab, display the New page, and then click Blank Document. Click File, and then click Save As. For now, save the template on your local drive by clicking Computer and then clicking Browse.

In the Save As dialog box, in the Save As Type list, choose Word Template (*.dotx). Notice that the dialog box opens the folder Custom Word Templates, which is a subfolder in the Templates folder in your user profile. Type a name for the template, and then click Save. Click OK if you see a message about file formats. You're now ready to start making the customizations and additions that will define the template.

> **NOTE**   If you are creating a template in which you want to create and save macros, select Word Macro-Enabled Template (*.dotm) in the Save As dialog box.

Working with paragraph styles

Start by considering the various elements that documents based on this template will contain. It's likely that you'll want styles for at least two or three levels of headings, for regular (normal) paragraphs, for lists of various types (numbered and bulleted), and perhaps tables, image captions, and so on.

Remember that every paragraph in a Word document is assigned a particular style, and although you can create an entire document that uses only the default Normal style and then format the text by adding bold or italic, increasing or decreasing font size, applying different fonts, and adding text effects, even in a document that contains only one or two levels of headings and regular paragraphs of text, you need to do a lot of work to make elements of the same type consistent. Styles provide much more control and consistency, and after you apply styles, you can change style properties once and apply them throughout the current document and every document based on the template.

The Styles gallery on the Home tab displays several of Word's default styles, including the paragraph styles Normal, Heading 1, and Title and character styles such as Emphasis, Strong, and Subtle Reference. (You'll learn more details about character styles later in this section.)

Let's say you want to modify the default Heading 1 style. To modify a built-in style, right-click the style in the Style gallery and then choose Modify. This opens the Modify Style dialog box. In the dialog box, shown in Figure 4-12, the style's properties are described below the preview box. Here you can see font properties such as size, color, and space before.

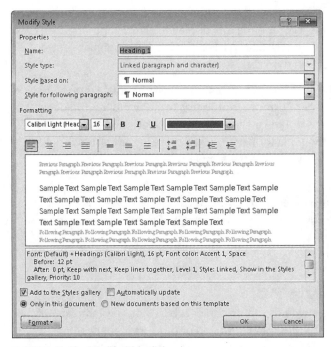

FIGURE 4-12 The Modify Style dialog box.

In the Modify Style dialog box, make changes to the style's properties by choosing a different typeface or font size, for example, or by setting a heading to a different font color, adjusting line spacing, setting indentation, and so on. To specify more detailed settings for a style, click Format at the bottom of the dialog box, and then choose Font, Paragraph, Numbering, Text Effects, or another item to open a dialog box with options you can set for that element of the style.

Be sure to review the settings in the check boxes and option buttons at the bottom of the Modify Style dialog box. Keep the Add To Styles Gallery option selected if you want to add this style to the gallery on the Home tab. Select New Documents Based On This Template so that the changes you make carry over to all documents that are based on the template you're creating. When you finish defining the style, click OK.

To create a style, first click the Styles dialog box launcher on the Home tab. In the Styles pane, select the style you want to use as the basis of the new style. For example, select Heading 1 or Heading 2 to create a new heading style, or select Normal to create a new style for running text. The style you select in the Styles pane provides the basic formatting attributes for the new style.

At the bottom of the Styles pane, click New Style (the icon at the far left in the row of icons at the bottom of the pane) to open the Create New Style From Formatting dialog box, which provides the same set of options as the Modify Style dialog box shown earlier in Figure 4-12. Type a name for your style, and then select the type of style. In many cases, just leave Paragraph selected in the Style Type list, but you might also choose Character, Table, or List if you're creating a style specifically for character emphasis (italics or bold, for example) or a style you'll use in tables and lists. The style you selected as the base style should be displayed in the Style Based On list. If you want to change your selection, choose a different style here. If you want to apply a specific style to paragraphs that follow the style you're defining, select that style in the Style For Following Paragraph list. For example, you might choose Normal in this list to follow a heading style you're defining.

You can also create a style based on text you format in the body of a document. Type a heading, for example, apply the font formatting and text effects you want, and then select the text. Click the More button in the bottom-right corner of the Style gallery and then click Create A Style. You'll see an abbreviated version of the Create New Style From Formatting dialog box, shown in Figure 4-13. Type a name for the style, click Modify if you want to change any of the style's attributes, and then save the new style.

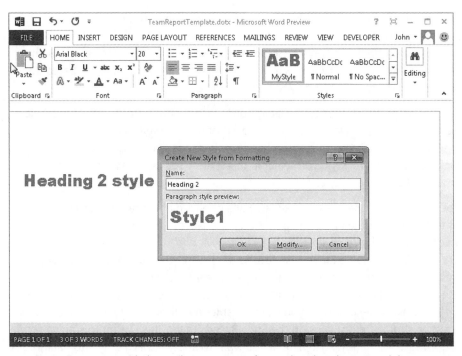

FIGURE 4-13 Format text with the attributes you want for a style, select the text, and then name a style based on it.

TIP You can import (and export) styles to get a headstart on defining the styles you want to use in a template. To manage styles in this way, you use the Organizer. At the bottom of the Styles panes, click Manage Styles, and then click Import/Export in the Manage Styles dialog box to open the Organizer. You should see the currently active document or template in the Styles Available In list on the left. Use the Styles Available In list on the right to open the document or template that includes the styles you want to import. Select the styles in the list on the right, and then click Copy to include them in the document or template listed on the left—the template you are building. (You can copy styles in either direction.) You can also delete styles or rename styles—for example, you might use names such as RFP_Heading 1 for your Request For Proposal template and Fax_Heading 1 for the style for your fax cover sheet.

Defining character styles

In many cases, you can capture all the formatting details you need in a paragraph style—indentation, font size, line spacing, and other such details. Within a paragraph, you can apply local formatting to characters by using the controls in the Font group on the Home tab or by choosing options in the Font dialog box. But you can also create styles specifically for groups of characters and then apply those styles as you format the document. Here again, the advantage of applying a character style (for example, to hyperlinks or to company names) is that you can update the style and have those updates reflected everywhere the style is applied. If you use only local formatting, you have to reformat each and every instance to remain consistent.

To define a character style, click the Styles dialog box launcher to display the Styles pane. At the bottom of the pane, click New Style. In the Create New Style From Formatting dialog box, name the style (for example, Product Name) and then select Character from the Style Type list. When you make this selection, the options in the dialog box change so that they apply only to character styles.

In the Style Based On list, you'll see Default Paragraph Font listed. Open the Style Based On list, and choose from among the built-in character styles if you want to use one of them as a starting point. Use the buttons and lists in the Formatting area of the Create New Style From Formatting dialog box to specify the properties you want to include in this style's definition, or click the Format button at the bottom of the dialog box to gain access to more options for formatting the font, border, and text effects.

Creating headers and footers

The information you define for a header or a footer is repeated on each page (or alternating pages) of a document or a document section. Page numbers are the simplest example of the type of information that a header or a footer presents (and whether you place page numbers in a header or a footer depends on factors such as page margins and page size, organizational preferences, or style conventions). Headers and footers can contain other information as well, including a document's title, an author's name, a project or department name, the time and date, or labels such as "Draft" or "Confidential."

Word comes with a gallery of headers and footers that you can add as is to a template you're designing or customize to provide more or less information. You can also define your own headers and footers as part of a template.

Headers and footers have their own group on the Insert tab. This group also includes the Page Number command, which lets you insert a page number in one of several locations and in a choice of formats. More options for formatting page numbers are provided in the dialog box that appears when you click Format Page Numbers. Use the Page Number

Format dialog box to change from the default format, which uses Arabic numerals (1, 2, 3...), to one that uses uppercase or lowercase roman numerals, letters (A, B, C...), or negative numbers (–1, –2, –3...).

Another option in the Page Number Format dialog box gives you control over whether a chapter number appears with a page number (a convention such as 3-1 or 3:1, meaning "page 1 of Chapter 3"). To use a chapter and page numbering scheme, select the Include Chapter Number check box and then select the style that marks the start of each chapter. (Only the built-in heading styles appear in this list.) In the Use Separator list, select the character that should separate the chapter number from the page number.

If you expect to define sections in documents based on this template, indicate whether you want pagination to continue from the previous section or whether the next section of a document should start at a particular page number. Use this option if you set up a template for documents that will use roman numerals for page numbers in elements such as the table of contents, foreword, preface, and other front matter and Arabic numerals for page numbers in the body of the document.

Headers and footers appear in galleries that Word displays when you click Header or Footer on the Insert tab. Choose one of the built-in headers or footers, click the option to find other styles on Office.com, or click Edit Header (or Edit Footer) to create your own header or footer. If you select one of the preset headers or footers, Word opens the header or footer area and displays placeholder text that you replace.

To work with custom headers and footers (and to modify those that come with Word) you use the Header & Footer Tools Design tab, which makes an array of possibilities available. This tab includes the Header, Footer, and Page Number commands again, as well as various controls that let you define the header or footer you need:

- **Insert**   Use the Insert group's commands to add the date and time (you can choose from a variety of formats), a Quick Part, a picture such as a company or department logo, or a piece of clip art. For Quick Parts, you might insert a custom AutoText entry you saved, such as "Confidential, For Internal Review Only," a document property (for example, the document's author or keywords that describe the document), or a field. The Quick Parts menu also gives you access to the Building Blocks Organizer, where you can select AutoText entries again or a building block from another category.

See Also   For more information about saving AutoText entries and working with Quick Parts and building blocks, see "Creating building blocks and Quick Parts" later in this chapter.

- **Navigation**   Use the controls in this group to switch between the header and the footer or to move between the header or footer on the next or previous page. Click Link To Previous to tie the current page's header or footer to the previous one.

- **Options**   In some types of documents (generally long documents such as books), tradition calls for excluding a header or footer on the first page of a document section (or having only the page number) and varying the information that appears on odd and even pages. For example, you might display the document title on even-numbered pages and section titles on odd-numbered pages. Options for both circumstances are included in the Options group. Also, clear the check box for the Show Document Text option if you want Word to hide the document's content so that you see only the information in the header or footer for the time being.

- **Position**   Use the Header From Top and Footer From Bottom controls to set the position of a header or a footer. The Insert Alignment Tab command helps you gracefully arrange the elements of a header or a footer.

Creating building blocks and Quick Parts

Very often, documents of the same type should use the same language in the same situation—for example, disclaimers and boilerplate language in a contract. Even in documents of different types, certain elements need to remain consistent in the information they present. An address block is one example. Being able to insert a ready-made piece of content when you are building a document from a template saves time and works as an effective control to ensure that the document's elements are up to date and valid.

Using building blocks

The galleries you work with in Word are filled with what are known as *building blocks*. Building blocks are available for document elements ranging from headers and footers to cover pages and tables. To add a building block to a document, you often use commands on the Insert tab—for headers and footers, for example—although the Watermarks gallery appears on the Design tab.

You can see the assortment of building blocks that come with Word by viewing the Building Blocks Organizer, a dialog box you open by clicking Quick Parts on the Insert tab and then clicking Building Blocks Organizer. Sort the list of building blocks by clicking a column heading. (The list is initially sorted by gallery.) Select a building block in the list to see a preview and a description. If you want to insert a building block in your template or document—for example, the Stacks footer—select that building block and click Insert.

To make changes to a built-in building block—to modify a cover page, for example—add the building block to your template, revise it (by changing the font styles, background image, and other properties), and then click Save Selection To Gallery (in this example, the Cover Page gallery, which you open under Pages on the Insert tab). Word displays the Create New Building Block dialog box, shown in Figure 4-14. (You can also click Quick Parts, Save Selection To Gallery on the Insert tab or press F3 to open this dialog box.)

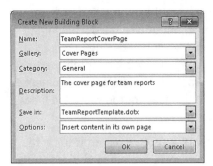

FIGURE 4-14 In creating a building block, you define properties such as what gallery the building block belongs in.

Type a name for the building block, and then fill in the following fields:

- **Gallery** The Gallery list provides a long set of options for adding the entry to a built-in gallery (Headers, for example) if you don't want to stick with the default. Use these galleries to maintain building blocks in an orderly fashion.

- **Category** Each building block is assigned to a category. Many are assigned to the Built-In category, and others to categories that describe the building block. You can find built-in watermark building blocks assigned to the Confidential category, for example. In defining your own building blocks, you can use a category Word provides or create one or more categories of your own. You might categorize building blocks by department or by team role, for example. In the Building Block Organizer, you can group building blocks by category, which might let you find the building block you need more easily.

- **Description** Use this field to enter a description that appears in a ScreenTip when you point the mouse to the item in a gallery and when you select the item in the Building Blocks Organizer.

- **Save In** Select the template in which you want to save the building block. Choose Normal.dotm to save it in Word's general template so that you can insert it in any document. Select the name of the template you are creating to store the building block there. This choice makes the building block available to new documents based on this template. Select Building Blocks.dotx to save it in the Building Blocks template. This choice also makes the building block available for all the documents you create.

- **Options**   Specify how you want to insert the building block. The choices are Insert Content Only, Insert Content In Its Own Paragraph, and Insert Content In Its Own Page. The first of these choices places the building block at the cursor without adding a paragraph or page break.

> **NOTE**   The Edit Properties button in the Building Blocks Organizer opens the Modify Building Block dialog box, which provides the same fields as the Create New Building Block dialog box. Although you won't often need to change the properties of built-in building blocks, you might do so for a building block you create.

Saving and inserting Quick Parts

Quick Parts come in several varieties—AutoText entries (a type of building block), document properties, and fields. You gain access to Quick Parts by clicking the Quick Parts command in the Text group on the Insert tab.

AutoText entries can play a particularly effective role in templates. For example, you could define a standard disclaimer or other boilerplate language as an AutoText entry. To define an AutoText entry, type the text you want it to include, and then select the text. Open the Quick Parts menu, click AutoText, and then click Save Selection To AutoText Gallery. You'll see the Create New Building Block dialog box (shown earlier in Figure 4-14), with the gallery you selected shown by default. In the dialog box, set the Save In list to the template you are building if you want this AutoText entry available only in this template.

To insert an AutoText entry, click Quick Parts, AutoText on the Insert tab, and then select the entry you want to insert. A faster way to insert an AutoText entry is to type its name (or just the first few characters). Word can recognize the AutoText and display a preview. Press Enter at this point to add the AutoText entry to your document.

Document properties and fields are useful but might not be applicable in many templates. However, as you learned in the section "Working with document properties" in Chapter 3, "Managing access and preserving history," you can tie document properties to column names in a SharePoint list or library. If you are creating a template for documents in which you want to capture information such as Author, Manager, Subject, and so on, add document properties to the cover page of your template, for example.

On the Quick Parts menu, point to Document Properties, and then choose from the list that includes Abstract, Company, Keywords, Manager, Title, and others. Values for some properties (Author, for example) are filled in automatically by Word. You can specify values for other properties on the Info page in Backstage view, in the document's Properties dialog box, or in the Document Panel that you can open from the Info tab. If a value hasn't been set for the property you choose, you can enter the value when you insert the property as a Quick Part.

See Also   For more information, see "Working with document properties" in Chapter 3.

Fields, the third Quick Part type, are placeholders for specific types of content and data. The information a field contains can be updated automatically. Word uses fields for many different features that you might use regularly, including tables of contents, index entries, and the date and time. Use the Field dialog box to insert a field and specify formatting or other related information. You can view all fields or select a category from the list box at the top.

For example, to insert a field that shows who last saved a document, select LastSavedBy in the list of fields, specify the format you want to use (uppercase, lowercase, and so on), and then click OK. This bit of information might be helpfully placed on the first page of a document that a group is collaborating on or in the header or footer for that document.

To see the inner workings of a field, right-click the field and then click Toggle Field Codes. You'll see that the field's name appears along with a formatting reference and other information, depending on the field you are using. Fields are enclosed by curly braces—{author}, for example. You can enter field codes on your own by pressing Ctrl+F9, but using the Field dialog box is much easier. There, you see the required information as well as a description of the field.

Adding content controls

Like some types of Quick Parts, content controls aren't a key element in many Word templates, but in some situations (in forms, for example), content controls help teams collect and manage information in specific ways. This section provides an overview of the types of content controls you can add to a template (or to a document).

Content controls let you define elements such as a list, a date picker, or a rich-text control for a template. You add a content control by using the Controls group on the Developer tab.

TIP

If the Developer tab isn't displayed on the ribbon, click the File tab, click Options, and then click Customize Ribbon. Under Customize The Ribbon, click Main Tabs, select the Developer check box, and then click OK.

Here's a brief description of the content controls you might use. In the Controls group, point to an icon to see a ScreenTip that identifies each control:

- **Rich text**   Used to hold text. You can format text as bold or italic, include multiple paragraphs, and add other formatting.

- **Plain text**   Used to hold text. Use the plain text control if you want to limit what users can do with respect to formatting the text.

- **Combo box**   Users can select from a list of defined choices or type their own information. If you select the Contents Cannot Be Edited check box in the properties for this control, users won't be able to add their own items to the list.

- **Drop-down list**   In this control, users can select only from the list of defined options.

- **Building block**   Use a building block control when you want people to choose a specific block of text. In a proposal, for example, you might include a building block control that indicates the length of time for which the proposal is valid or other types of boilerplate text. For more information about building blocks, see "Creating building blocks and Quick Parts" earlier in this chapter.

- **Picture**   Use this control to embed an image file.

- **Date picker**   This control inserts a calendar control that lets you select a date.

- **Check box**   Use the check box control to provide a set of options in the template.

TIP

To group content controls, select the controls and then click Group in the Controls group. For example, if you want to keep three check boxes together as a unit so that they cannot be edited or deleted individually, select those controls and then click Group.

Working with content control properties

Protecting the content controls you add to a template can prevent users from deleting or editing a content control or a group of controls. For example, you can set an option that lets a user edit the content in a control but not delete the control from the template or from a document that uses that template. Word also gives you an option with which users can delete the control but not edit its content. You might use the second option (delete but not edit) in documents that require specific wording but not in every instance.

Changing the text in a content control

Content controls often include a simple text statement that tells users what the control is for. Changing this text so that it provides precise instructions helps users work with a template efficiently.

Changing the text is a simple operation. Open the template that contains the content control, and then click Design Mode in the Controls group on the Developer tab. Select the control whose text you want to change, select the text it contains, and then type the new text.

Protecting a template

You can use the Restrict Editing command (on the Review tab or under Protect Document on the Info page in Backstage view) to assign a password to a template and also to control formatting. If you don't use a password, the work you've done designing the template is subject to anyone's changes, and if you don't control formatting to some degree, a document based on the template might come back looking nothing like what the template was intended to provide.

As you'll see in more detail in Chapter 8, "Working on shared documents in Word," the Restrict Formatting And Editing pane provides an option named Limit Formatting To A Selection of Styles. Select this option, and then click the Settings link to open the Formatting Restrictions dialog box. You can then select the set of styles you want users to work with when they base a document on this template. The options in the Formatting area of the dialog box let you control whether autoformatting settings can override formatting restrictions, whether users can switch themes and schemes such as for fonts and colors, and whether users can modify styles listed on the Styles gallery.

In the Restrict Formatting And Editing pane, click Yes, Start Enforcing Restrictions to define a password. (You don't need to set any restrictions unless you need them.) In the dialog box that appears, define the password you want to use to protect the template.

Adding custom templates to your team site

Having spent time creating templates your team will use—or modifying some of the templates that come with Office—how do you put these templates into use? You might assign one or more team members to be in charge of each template. This team member or group could help other team members apply the template when questions come up and would update the template when changes are needed. The "master" template file could be stored in a Templates library in SharePoint, and then you could manage permissions on this library so that only team members with responsibilities for maintaining templates could access files with permission to change them. Through notifications in SharePoint and communication through e-mail, the team members responsible could let the whole team know when a new version of the template became available. And, with centralized storage of your team's templates in SharePoint, each team member should know where to go when they need one.

A document library on your team site can also be associated with a template you create. When you set up a document library, the default setting is that new documents created from the library are based on a generic Word template named template.dotx. As part of defining the document library, you can specify a different Office program that new documents will be based on. This gives you the ability to associate a library named Budgets with Excel, for example, but you still get only a generic template.

Through a few steps, you can replace the generic template with a custom template you've created.

1. On your team site, open the library.

2. On the Library tab, in the Connect And Export group, click **Open With Explorer**.

   You'll now see the library as you would other folders in Explorer.

3. Open the library's Forms folder, and then copy your custom template into the folder.

4. Switch back to the document library (you can close the Explorer window at this point).

5. On the Library tab, in the Settings group, click **Library Settings**.

6. On the Settings page, click **Advanced Settings**.

7. In the Template URL box, update the path so that the library's document template points to your custom template (instead of to template.dotx), as shown here.

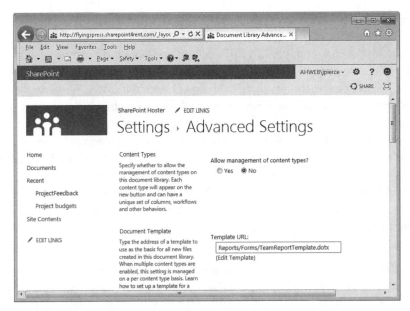

When you choose the New Document command on the Files tab, the document is based on the custom template you defined.

2

Working day to day as a team

CHAPTER 5

An integrated Outlook

THIS CHAPTER demonstrates practical examples of two time-management concepts—finding shortcuts and taking time to plan. First, you'll see how to connect libraries and lists on your team site to Microsoft Outlook. This connection creates a folder in Outlook (accessible from the navigation pane) where you can, for example, open and edit documents, add discussion items to a discussion board, and create and update tasks on your team site's task list. Those are the specific examples you'll see in this chapter. The process I describe works with other types of lists and libraries as well, including a team site calendar or contact list.

As you'll see, this shortcut to your team site cuts down on the need to open and sign-in to your team site, navigate to the library or list you need, and then open a document or update a list. Many users of Microsoft Office spend a lot of time working in Outlook anyway—especially writing and answering e-mail—and the ability to access and update items on your team site from Outlook saves time for certain tasks. Another shortcut you'll learn about is linking Outlook items to notebooks in Microsoft OneNote. This relationship isn't as dynamic as the one between Outlook and SharePoint, but it does provide team members a way to associate notebook sections and pages with specific meetings, contacts, and tasks that are defined in Outlook.

The third major section of this chapter is about sharing calendars, a tool teams can use to help schedule time for individual projects, keep team members advised of each other's free and busy times, and make scheduling information available to people outside the team.

TWO OUTLOOK BASICS

Here are two basic steps you can take to organize your work (as an individual and as a member of a team) in Outlook:

- Be sure to create folders to store messages. Use a different folder for each of your major projects or for each person you correspond with regularly. To create a folder at the same level as Inbox and other default folders, right-click your account name in the navigation bar and select New Folder. To create a subfolder, right-click the parent folder, choose New Folder, and then type the name.

- Archive messages when projects are complete. This step helps keep your inbox and mail folders from overflowing and also collects the messages related to a project in a single file. Ask each team member involved in the project to archive his or her messages as part of wrapping up a project.

Outlook is a program with many organizational tools. Others to consider are custom views and conversation settings. In addition, be sure to create a contact group that includes all the members of your team. Use the contact group to address e-mail messages and meeting requests to the team at large.

Working with the team site from Outlook

At least some team members might resist the idea of using a SharePoint team site. They could say that the benefits a team gains from managing access to files or by exchanging ideas in a discussion board don't offset the time that's required to upload a document and then check out the document to edit it, or the time it takes to initiate discussion items, read through them, and reply.

These team members have a point—there are numerous ways to store files that more than one person needs to use (a network share, for example) and to collect opinions and engage team members (a team can just use e-mail, for example). Alternatives like these might not require as much administration and don't require team members to sign in to the team site and open a list when they have an idea or a file they want to share.

The perspective of these team members probably overstates the ease with which teams can implement less structured approaches and then manage and use them day to day. It also understates the benefits teams get from making the effort to set up a team site from the start. Once the team site is in place, the need to add content and update list items will be rewarded by access to previous versions, for example, or to workflows that help automate approval processes, or to a record of the status of specific tasks.

See Also   For detailed information about setting up a team site, see Chapter 2, "Building a SharePoint team site."

Still, it's always nice to find a shorter path to the work you need to do, and by connecting Outlook with lists and libraries, you can accomplish a lot of work that's centered on the team site while you manage your day in Outlook. I'll show three examples in this section: how to work with a document library, how to add to a discussion list, and how to manage tasks.

Connecting to a document library

To set up a connection between Outlook and a document library in SharePoint, sign in to the team site, open the library you want to work with, and then follow these steps:

1. In the library, click the **Library** tab

2. In the Connect & Export group, click **Connect To Outlook**.

   You will probably see one or more dialog boxes prompting you to allow a website (the team site) to open a program (in this case, Outlook). Click **Allow** in these dialog boxes to proceed. (The prompts vary with different web browsers. The information described here relates to Internet Explorer.)

3. After Outlook starts, it displays a dialog box you use to confirm that you want to connect the library to Outlook. Before you click Yes, click **Advanced** to open the SharePoint List Options dialog box, which is shown in the following screen shot.

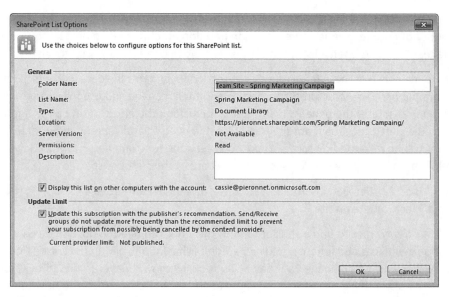

When you connect the library to Outlook, Outlook creates a folder in which you can access items in the library. You can change the name of the folder (as you'll see it in Outlook; this doesn't rename the library in SharePoint). You can also add a description. By default, the folder for the library (referred to generally as a *list*) is included on other computers where you use your account. Clear this option if you want the list only on the computer you're working on. The Update Limit option is related to how often Outlook and SharePoint synchronize the items in the list. Keep this option selected.

4. Click **OK** in the SharePoint List Options dialog box, and then click **Yes** to confirm you want to connect the list.

Outlook adds an entry for the library to the navigation pane under the group heading SharePoint Lists. Outlook also downloads the items into the list (the time required will vary depending on the number and size of the documents in the library). When you select an item in the list, Outlook displays a preview of the file in the reading pane (when the reading pane is displayed). Figure 5-1 shows how the list of files in a SharePoint library appears in Outlook.

To move beyond the preview and open a file to read or edit it, double-click the item in the list in Outlook. When the file opens (in Excel or Word, for example), you'll probably see a notification that you are working with an Offline Server Workbook or Offline Server Document (even if you are online at the time). Also, notice that the title bar in the program's application window indicates that the document is read-only. You can review the document in this state by using the arrows on each side to move from page to page. To make changes to the document, click Edit Offline in the notification bar.

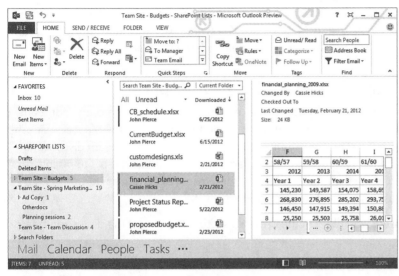

FIGURE 5-1 You can work with items in libraries and lists on your team site by connecting them to Outlook. The reading pane previews a file. Folders for the lists and libraries appear on the navigation pane.

At this point, Outlook displays the Edit Offline dialog box. The text in the dialog box informs you that to edit the file, an offline copy will be stored in a folder named SharePoint Drafts. (You can change this location by clicking Offline Editing Options, which takes you to the Office program's Options dialog box.) Click OK in the Edit Offline dialog box to make the file editable.

If you are online when you save your changes and close the file, Outlook displays a notification in the reading pane that indicates that the updated file is available only on your computer. If you are offline when you save and close the file, you'll see information in the reading pane about the most recent version on SharePoint. When you connect to your network again and open Outlook, the notification in the reading pane points to the copy you edited locally.

The reading pane notification prompts you to open the file again to check in your changes. Follow that step, and you see the Edit Offline dialog box, shown in Figure 5-2. Click Update to add the updated copy to the team site.

FIGURE 5-2 Click Update in the Edit Offline dialog box to add the file you edited locally to the team site.

After the updated file is uploaded to the library, a read-only copy of the file is opened in the program you're working with. Close the file if you are finished editing it, or click Edit Document in the notification bar to work with the updated file that's now on the team site.

Managing team discussions from Outlook

One way to encourage team members to make use of a discussion board on your team site is to have team members connect the discussion board to Outlook. Most people who use Office spend a lot of time working in Outlook, so managing your team discussions from there is usually convenient. Team members can post, read, and reply to discussion items while they manage their daily e-mail, and the team gains the benefit of having a record of the discussion on the team site.

Follow the same steps described in the previous section to connect the discussion board to Outlook:

1. Open the list on the team site.

2. Click the **List** tab, and then click **Connect To Outlook** in the Connect & Export group.

3. Work through the dialog boxes to allow the connection to occur.

4. After the list is connected, open it from the navigation pane in Outlook. The folder appears on the navigation pane (under SharePoint Lists) when you are working in Mail view in Outlook.

To add a discussion item to the list, use the New Post command in the New group. The window Outlook displays shows that the post will be added to the team discussion list (or to a discussion board with a different name if you connected to one). Type a subject and then the body of the post in the window. You can insert attachments or Outlook items, format the text of the post, add a signature, categorize the item, and so on. Use the Insert tab to add various types of illustrations. A variety of other commands—including commands that open the Research pane or the thesaurus—are available on the window's ribbon.

If you want to respond to a discussion thread, select the item in the list in Outlook and then click Post Reply in the Respond group. You can also reply to the item via e-mail or by forwarding the post.

If you are working offline when you create a discussion post or reply to a current thread, the discussion board on the team site is updated when you go online again and Outlook completes its Send/Receive operation.

Using Outlook to add and update the team site task list

The task lists you set up on the team site are also good candidates for lists you work with in Outlook. Follow the steps outlined in the previous sections to connect to the list. When the list is connected, it appears on the navigation pane (in a group named Other Tasks) when you display the Tasks view in Outlook.

To add a task, open the list from the navigation pane, and then click New Task on the Home tab (or simply click and type the subject for a new task in the text box below the Subject column heading in the list in Outlook). To add details to a task or update its status, priority, or other fields, double-click the task's entry in the list.

To create a task or update a task that's already defined, you work in an Outlook task item. You can use the task form to change or make assignments and to update fields such as subject, start date, due date, status, priority, and percentage complete. Figure 5-3 shows an example. In the Show group on the item's Task tab, click Details to see additional fields, such as Date Completed, Total Work, Actual Work, and others.

FIGURE 5-3 You work in a regular Outlook task item when you use Outlook to add or update a task that's defined in SharePoint.

In the Actions group, click Open In Browser to display the task item in the browser-based form you work with in SharePoint. You can click Edit Item in this view to make additional changes, or click Version History to see earlier instances of this task. (You can also click the Team Site - Tasks link at the bottom of the task item in Outlook to open the task list in SharePoint.)

> **NOTE**   You can link Outlook tasks to a OneNote notebook, but you cannot link tasks that are stored in a task list on your team site. You'll learn about working with tasks in Outlook and OneNote in the next section.

As with items in a discussion board or another type of list, you can add and update tasks when you work offline in Outlook, and Outlook synchronizes changes to the team site task list during its Send/Receive operation the next time you connect to the network.

Linking Outlook items to OneNote

As you'll learn in Chapter 7, "Keeping track of discussions and ideas," teams can use OneNote as a way to collect information of all kinds (images, files, links, and so on) and to keep track of ideas that the team wants to develop and refine over time. To support that work, you can add Outlook items to a notebook and also link related tasks, contacts, and calendar items. By adding items such as an e-mail message to a notebook, you create context and establish relationships between projects and activities and routine (or more consequential) communications. For example, the team member managing a product development project might send an e-mail message to colleagues outlining the goals of the project, the status of prototypes, and other related information. If this team is using OneNote to document the product's development—background research, notes from review meetings, and so on—the project manager can add this e-mail message to a page in the project notebook. No one has to retype the goals, and the message serves as a reference and touch point as development proceeds.

E-mail messages you send to OneNote are more or less static entries in a notebook. The note displays the subject line, the To and From fields, the date the message was sent, and the message's body. If the message body contains links, the links remain active. If a message contains attachments, the attachments are included and can be opened from OneNote.

Contact items you send to OneNote from Outlook are linked, meaning you can open a contact in Outlook from OneNote. But don't mistake "linked" for "synchronized." For example, when you add a contact item to a page in a notebook, the entry lists the contact's name, business phone, e-mail address, and other information stored in the contact item in Outlook. It also includes a link that lets you view the contact item in Outlook. You can't, however, update details in OneNote (for example, change a business address) and have those changes travel back to Outlook. If you want to make changes to a contact's information, you need to use the original item in Outlook.

Working with Outlook tasks and meetings in OneNote offers more of a relationship. For example, you can mark a task complete in OneNote, and that action also marks the task complete in Outlook. For meetings, you can set up a meeting so that the notes you take in OneNote are shared with people invited to the meeting. Attendees can click a link in the meeting request to review the notes you take.

Adding e-mail to OneNote

Adding an e-mail message (or messages) to OneNote is simple. In Outlook, select the item or items (in the inbox or another mail folder), and then click OneNote in the Move group on the Home tab. You'll then see the Select Location In OneNote dialog box (a dialog box you'll become very familiar with as you spend more time working in One-Note), which is shown in Figure 5-4. Specify the notebook, section, or page you want to add the message to, and then click OK.

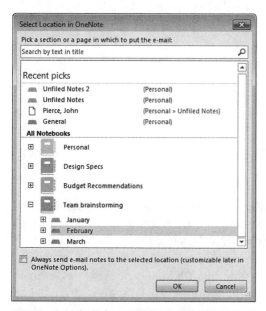

FIGURE 5-4 In the Select Location In OneNote dialog box, select the section or page where you want to place the Outlook item.

Using meeting notes

The links you can set up between meeting items in Outlook and OneNote notebooks can help establish and maintain a record of important and routine team gatherings. The team member taking the notes can share them at the start or keep notes locally and then share them with the team later after editing the notes and adding related content.

To link a meeting set up on an Outlook calendar, select the meeting (or open the meeting item), and then follow these steps:

1. On the Appointment tab, click **Meeting Notes**.

    Outlook opens the item (if it isn't open already) and displays the Meeting Notes dialog box, shown below:

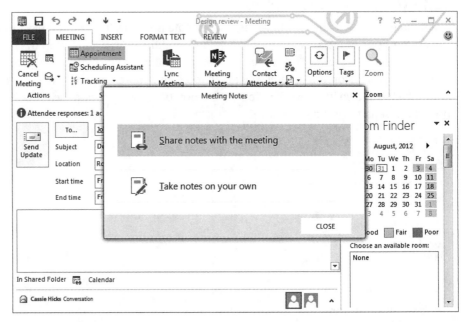

2. If you click **Share Notes With The Meeting**, you'll see the Choose Notes To Share With Meeting dialog box. Select the section or page in OneNote where you want to include the notes. You can also use the New Notebook button at the bottom of the dialog box to create a notebook for this meeting (which you can, of course, use for related purposes as well). When you click **OK** in the Choose Notes To Share With Meeting dialog box, OneNote sets up the notebook for sharing, and a link to the meeting notes is added to the meeting request. Attendees can follow this link to view the notebook being used to document the meeting.

3. If you click **Take Notes On Your Own**, you'll see the Select Location In OneNote dialog box, where you specify the notebook, section, and page where you want to record the notes. A summary of meeting details is added to the notebook (meeting date and time, location, and participants, for example). The note container also provides a heading (Notes) where you can start recording your notes.

Working with Outlook tasks in OneNote

To add an Outlook task to OneNote, select the task in Outlook and then click OneNote in the Actions group. (This group appears on the Task tab in the task form and on the Home tab in Tasks view.)

When you link a task item you create in Outlook to a new page in a notebook, the page is named using the task's subject. (You can also add a task to a page that's already defined.) You don't see many details about a task (as you do for contact items and calendar items, for example). The task's title is provided, and any attachments added to the task item are included as well. Point to the flag icon beside the task's title to see details such as the start date and due date. Right-click the flag icon to open a menu that lets you work with the task. You can assign a follow-up flag, mark the task complete, and delete the Outlook task. These actions update the task item in Outlook.

Sharing and publishing calendars

Too often, the effort required to coordinate team members' time and schedules takes away from more important work. To make this process more manageable, Office provides a number of tools. You can, for example, add a calendar to your team site and use it to record meetings, events, and project milestones. (For details, see Chapter 2.) Microsoft Lync, as you'll learn in the next chapter, provides status and presence information so that you know when another team member is available or busy. In Lync, being able to see someone's status has more to do with the near term—knowing that someone's status is Available means the chances are good that the person will answer a Lync call or an instant message.

Sharing calendars in Outlook is another way to make the scheduling information a team needs available. The Share group on the Calendar view Home tab provides three commands for sharing a calendar: E-Mail Calendar, Share Calendar, and Publish Online. You'll learn more about each command in the following sections.

First, it's important to keep in mind that many people use their calendars not only for work-related appointments and meetings but for personal appointments—visits to the doctor, family activities, and so on. Team members who use their calendars in this way might not want every detail of an appointment (subject, location, and so on) available in a calendar they share. Similarly, details about some work-related appointments might be best known only by a small group.

When you share or otherwise make an Outlook calendar public, you can choose one of three options for the level of detail you want to provide:

- **Availability Only**   People viewing the calendar see only time indicators—when you are free, busy, out of the office, and so on.

- **Limited Details**   This option allows people to see the subjects of calendar items in addition to your availability.

- **Full Details**   This option shows your availability and all the details of each calendar item.

These options are clearly identified and described in the Outlook user interface, and you can select additional options to keep specific appointments and meetings private.

Sending a calendar by e-mail

Imagine circumstances in which you want other people to know what your schedule is over a set period of time. For example, you might be one of the team members about to depart on a series of sales calls, but you're also one of the team members responsible for approving a set of new advertisements being prepared by your outside design firm and scheduled for release in the next few weeks. You don't need to share your whole calendar (see the next section) with the design firm, but you can select the upcoming week's appointments, choose the Availability Only option, and send that information via e-mail. That way, the design firm knows when you're free and when you're busy so that they can schedule your time when they need you.

When you click E-Mail Calendar, Outlook opens a blank message and displays the Send A Calendar Via E-Mail dialog box, shown in Figure 5-5.

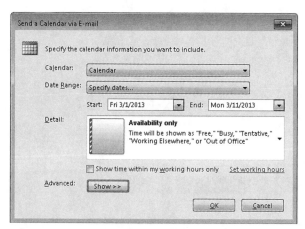

FIGURE 5-5 In the Send A Calendar Via E-Mail dialog box, review the options under Detail so that you know what information the recipient of your calendar will see.

Choose a calendar (if you have more than one set up) or keep the default calendar (named Calendar) selected. Under Date Range, make a selection from the group of preset choices (Today, Tomorrow, or Whole Calendar are a few of the options), or click Specify Dates, which adds Start and End date lists to the dialog box. Type the date range you want to provide or choose from the calendar that appears when you click the arrow to the right of each list box.

In the Detail section, the default choice is Availability Only. As the description indicates, the message's recipients will see only time indicators—when you are free, busy, and so on. The other options available are Limited Details and Full Details.

If you choose Limited Details or Full Details, click Show to work with two other options. For Limited Details, you can select the option Include Details Of Items Marked Private. In this case, recipients will see the subjects for appointments you've marked as private. For Full Details, you can select Include Details Of Items Marked Private and also Include Attachments Within Calendar Items. (You can also use the Advanced area to choose an e-mail layout—Daily Schedule or List Of Events.)

When you click OK, Outlook adds the calendar information to the message, including the date range that you've shared, time zone information, thumbnail calendars and sum-maries of free and busy times, and other details if you selected one of those options. An example is shown in Figure 5-6, where the Availability Only option was selected.

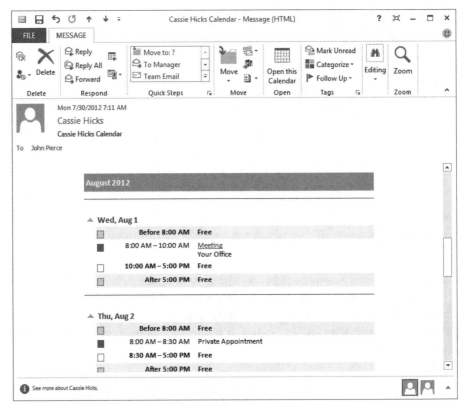

FIGURE 5-6 This calendar shows only availability (free and busy times).

MANAGING CALENDARS AND CALENDAR PERMISSIONS

By default, Outlook provides a single calendar (called Calendar). You aren't limited to using a single calendar, however, and creating calendars for specific uses can aid the work of a team. For example, you might create a calendar for a specific project or other extended activities, share the calendar with team members working on the project, and use that calendar when you schedule project meetings.

You can use the Create New Blank Calendar command (under Open Calendar in the Manage Calendars group) to create a calendar. Then follow the steps described in the next section to share the calendar. You can also use the Open Calendar menu to open shared calendars or open calendars published to the Internet (which you'll learn about later in the chapter.)

When you share a calendar you create, you send an invitation to other users via e-mail. In the invitation Outlook sends, you can select an option (under the subject line) that grants the recipients permission to add, edit, and delete items in the shared calendar. This option is not selected by default, so if you don't select it, recipients have only read access to the shared calendar.

You can also manage permissions for a shared calendar by clicking the Calendar Permissions command in the Share group, which opens the Calendar Properties dialog box with the Permissions tab displayed. You can add other people and grant them permission to view the calendar or refine the level of permission granted. Figure 5-7 shows the Permissions tab with the options available. Use the Permission Level list to select a permission level such as Owner, Editor, Publishing Editor, Author, and others. The selection you make in this list determines which options are selected under the Read, Write, Delete Items, and Other areas. You can also configure these options on your own to create a custom level. Select Default in the list at the top of the dialog box and change the permission level if you want to grant people a specific level of permission by default.

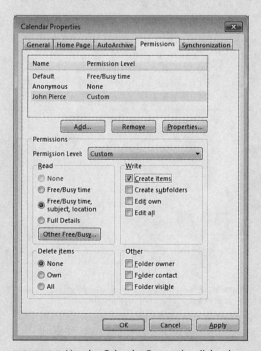

FIGURE 5-7 Use the Calendar Properties dialog box to control permissions for a shared calendar.

Sharing a calendar

Sharing a slice of your calendar to inform people about your free and busy times is helpful when you're just beginning a business trip or need to coordinate your time with people who can't otherwise see when you're free or busy. You can also make your full calendar available to team members, and with the same degree of control over the level of detail you show.

To share a calendar, first select the calendar in the navigation pane. (If more than one calendar is displayed, the calendar that appears first in the list is the one you'll share. For best results, select only the calendar you want to share.) To complete the process, follow these steps (which document how to share your default calendar with others):

1. In the Share group, click **Share Calendar**.

    Outlook creates an e-mail message item with a preset subject line ("Sharing Invitation: Cassie Hicks - Project Calendar," for example) and embeds sharing options in the message, as shown in the following screen shot. When you share your own calendar with other people, you can request permission to view their calendars as well.

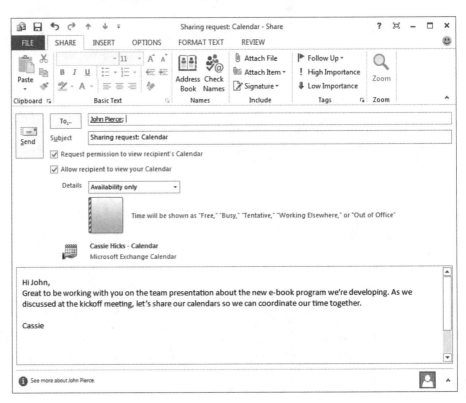

2. Address the message, select the option for the level of detail you want to provide, and then click **Send**.

3. When the recipient receives the shared calendar invitation—and assuming you selected the option to ask the recipient to share his or her calendar, the recipient needs to allow or deny this request, as shown below:

Assuming the recipient allows the request to share his or her calendar, Outlook creates a similar message that goes back to the sender. Each person sharing a calendar then needs to click the Open This Calendar button in the message that confirms the calendar is shared. This step adds a Shared Calendar group to the Outlook navigation bar (or adds the new shared calendar to this group if more than one shared calendar is available) and displays the shared calendar side by side with your own. Clear the check box for the calendar in the navigation bar to show or hide the calendar.

Publishing a calendar online

The third way that information about a schedule can be shared is over the Internet. You might take this step if you are a member of a virtual team, for example. In this approach, too, you can control the degree to which the details of appointments and meetings are accessible.

Under Publish Online in the Share group, click Publish This Calendar to open a page in your browser. The title of the page, shown in Figure 5-8, is Calendar Publishing. If you aren't already signed in to a Microsoft account, you are prompted to sign in before the page is displayed.

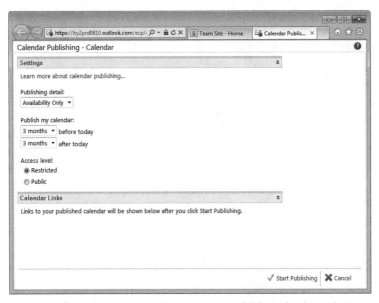

FIGURE 5-8 Use the Calendar Publishing page to publish a calendar to the Internet.

Use the Publishing Detail list to specify the level of detail to provide—Availability Only, Limited Details, or Full Details. (When you open the list, a ScreenTip is displayed that describes each of these options.) Under Publish My Calendar, select the time period you want to publish, starting from the current day. Three months is selected by default. Other choices include 1 day, 30 days, and 1 year. You cannot select a specific range of dates (as you can when you send calendar information in an e-mail), and you can't type in a custom value (say, 60 days).

The options under Access Level control who can see the calendar online. Restricted, the default choice, lets you manage access by sending a link to the calendar to the people you want to grant access to. If you choose the Public option, anyone who finds the calendar on the Internet—through a search engine, for example—can view it.

When you click Start Publishing at the bottom of the page, links to the calendar are created. The first link is for subscribers, who are people who will automatically see updates to the calendar. The second link is for people viewing the calendar. Click Copy Links To Clipboard and then paste them into an e-mail message that you send to others to alert them about the calendar's availability.

For a calendar published on the Internet, you can return to the Calendar Publishing page by selecting the calendar in the navigation pane and then clicking Publish Online,

Configure This Published Calendar. You can modify the level of detail shown, the time period, and other fields.

Avoiding scheduling conflicts

Keeping track of appointments and meetings on more than one calendar—your default calendar, calendars that your team uses to track projects and events, and any personal calendar you add in Outlook—is simplified by seeing the calendars in an integrated view. By using the Overlay command in the Arrangement group on the View tab, you can see your time commitments from each calendar together. If you are juggling a lot of meetings and other events, keeping the Overlay view selected can save time because you don't need to check all your calendars individually before you add an entry to one. Click the tab for a particular calendar to make it active so that you can add and modify appointments and meetings.

Calendars that other team members have shared with you aren't included in Overlay view, but you can see a composite arrangement of your schedule by clicking Schedule View on the View tab, as shown in Figure 5-9.

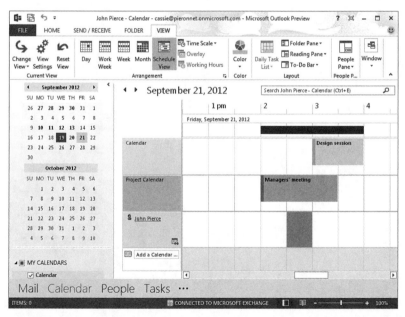

FIGURE 5-9 Use options in the View tab's Arrangement group to check for scheduling conflicts across a group of calendars.

In this view, the entries on each calendar, including shared calendars, are displayed in rows. Anywhere you see entries overlap across the rows is likely to be a time when you're overbooked.

CHAPTER 6

Working together in Lync

AS I MENTIONED IN THE EARLY CHAPTERS OF THIS BOOK, teams need both formal and informal communication tools, capabilities to access shared content when team members are working together and when they're working on their own, and record-keeping tools to document their deliberations and decisions. In their everyday conversations, in meetings, and in sharing content of all kinds, teams can find support for these needs in Microsoft Lync.

> **NOTE** Keep in mind that Lync isn't a program that you can run on its own. The Lync client must be associated with an instance of Lync Server. Your organization might have this configuration in place, or you might be using a hosted version of Lync from Microsoft.

You'll see in this chapter that the capabilities in Lync make it especially well suited for teams that don't share the same physical location and for circumstances when colleagues who are usually housed together aren't—when one or more members are traveling or working offsite, for example. For ease of communication, you start from a contact list in Lync. From there, you can send instant messages or call one or more of your contacts. Through a status indicator, Lync tells you when a colleague is available, busy, away, or doesn't want to be disturbed. Lync is also well integrated with

Microsoft Outlook for scheduling meetings and with Microsoft OneNote, which a team member can use to take notes during a conference call or a meeting. In programs such as Microsoft Word, Microsoft Excel, and Microsoft PowerPoint, you can share content in Lync from the ribbon.

Lync also offers a range of content sharing options that simplify collaboration at almost any stage of content development—from brainstorming sessions to meetings in which members agree on the final wording of a document, the analysis behind a sales forecast, or the images and text in a presentation.

If you aren't familiar with Lync, look at Figure 6-1, which shows the windows you work in most often and identifies elements of the Lync user interface.

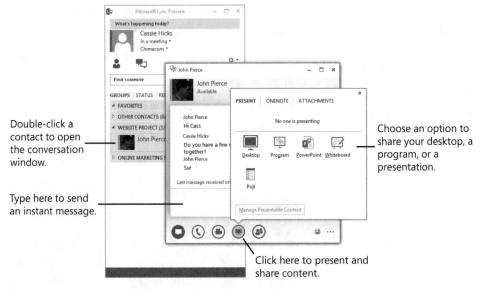

Double-click a contact to open the conversation window.

Type here to send an instant message.

Choose an option to share your desktop, a program, or a presentation.

Click here to present and share content.

FIGURE 6-1 The contact list appears in the main Lync window. Double-click a contact to open the conversation window. Use the conversation window to send an instant message or access other options for team communication. Click the monitor icon in the conversation window to collaborate on files, brainstorm on a whiteboard, or conduct a poll.

TIP

To keep the main Lync window visible when you are working in other programs, click Always On Top on the Tools menu. The Lync window is small enough that you can position it in a corner of the screen and continue working in other programs.

Contacts and presence

The first step you take to make effective use of Lync is to create a contact group that includes the members of your team. Organizing contacts into groups helps you find a contact and, more importantly, lets you communicate with the members of the group in a single step.

To create a contact group, do the following:

1. Above the contacts list, click **Groups**.

2. In the list, right-click a group name (for example, Other Contacts), and then click **Create New Group**.

3. Type a name for the group, and then press Enter.

Now use the Search box above the contact list to locate a contact you want to add to the group. You can search by name, e-mail address, or phone number. In the list Lync displays, right-click the contact you want to add, click Add To Contacts List, and then choose the contact group from the menu that's displayed. (Other options on the shortcut menu let you add a contact to the Favorites group, tag a contact so that you see status change alerts, communicate with a contact, and more.)

As an alternative, click the small contact icon below the Search box (at the right side of the window) and then click Add A Contact That's In My Organization or Add A Contact That's Not In My Organization. Fill in the information required, and specify the group you want to add the contact to.

Sharing status information with your team

When you add a contact to your list, that person is notified of the action and can choose to add you to a specific contact group as well. The new contact can also select a privacy relationship to apply. Privacy relationships determine the level of detail a contact can see about your contact information, status, and activities. For the most part, making more information available rather than less aids team communication.

For contacts in your organization, Lync sets the privacy relationship to Colleagues by default. Colleagues can see basic information such as your display name and e-mail address and can also see your work phone number, your free and busy times, and your designated working hours. Some teams may decide that the level of information for the Colleagues relationship is enough for their purposes. An alternative is to set the privacy relationship for team members to Workgroup, a relationship that allows those contacts to also see your mobile phone number, meeting locations, and meeting subjects and to interrupt you when your status in Lync indicates that you don't want to be disturbed.

(You'll read more about status later in this chapter.) That might be more information than your team members want to share, but it does enable teams that work on fast-paced projects—teams facing daily deadlines, for example—to find each other when the need is critical.

To view the list of privacy relationships or to change the relationship for a contact, right-click the contact entry and point to Change Privacy Relationship. On the menu Lync displays, you can read a brief description of each privacy relationship. For a full list of the information that's available for each category, look for the Lync Help article "Control Access to Your Presence Information."

TIP   Another category you might use in the set of privacy relationships is External Contacts. Contacts in this category can't see phone numbers or meeting details, for example. Contacts outside your organization—contacts who don't share your company's domain name—don't have to be designated as External Contacts. You can set their relationship to Colleagues or to Workgroup if they are integrated into your team and you want to share more information with them.

Getting in touch

After you add contacts to the team contact group, group communication is easily facilitated. To start a conference call with the group's members—or at least those members who are currently available—right-click the group's name in the contact list, and then click Start A Conference Call. This shortcut menu, shown in Figure 6-2, has options for managing contacts and additional options for communicating with your team, such as the following:

- Send an instant message to the group

- Start a video call

- Send an e-mail message to group members

- Schedule a meeting with group members (if your account is set up to use Outlook)

You'll learn more details about several of these options later in this chapter in the section "Instant messages, video calls, and online meetings."

FIGURE 6-2 Use this menu to contact team members who are available or to rename, delete, or change the order of contact groups.

Viewing and managing your status

Using the options on the shortcut menu that appears when you right-click a contact group is great for informal communication. But as Figure 6-2 illustrates, not every member of your team will be around when you call (Chris Green, for example, is offline) or send an instant message. Scheduled meetings, of course, are when team members are expected to be present. At other times, you can rely on the status indicator in Lync to know when a colleague is available, offline, or away momentarily. Your current status appears under your name in the Lync window. The status of your contacts appears just to the right of their names.

By default, Lync uses entries in your Outlook calendar to set your status. For example, during a time period you have blocked off for an appointment, Lync sets your status to show that you are busy. When you are engaged in a call, Lync changes your status to In A Call. Likewise, Lync uses the status settings In A Meeting and In A Conference Call when you are involved in those activities.

You can change your status on your own to alert colleagues that you are away or don't want to be disturbed. To see the choice of status indicators, click the arrow beside the indicator. The choices include the following:

- **Available** Your status is set to Available when Lync detects you're using your computer. You can manually set your status to Available as well.

- **Busy** Lync sets your status to Busy when you have an appointment on your calendar in Outlook. You can also set your status to Busy manually.

- **Do Not Disturb** When you set your status to Do Not Disturb, you'll see conversation notifications only from contacts you assigned the Workgroup privacy relationship. When one of your Workgroup contacts chooses the Do Not Disturb status, you see Urgent Interruptions Only next to that contact in your instance of Lync.

- **Be Right Back** This is another status setting that you can set yourself.

- **Off Work** You select this status when you are away from your office and from work.

- **Appear Away** Set your status to Appear Away when you don't want other contacts to know you're online but still want the ability to get in touch with other team members.

TIP   To revert from the status you set and have Lync resume automatically updating your status, click Reset Status.

You will also see status settings such as Offline or Unknown for your contacts. Lync sets your status to Offline when you log off your computer. The Unknown status setting is shown when Lync can't detect the status of a contact.

Lync sets your status to Inactive and then to Away after your computer is idle for the period of time that's specified in the Lync Options dialog box. The default interval is five minutes for each change in status. If you want to change this setting, click the Options button at the top-right of the Lync window, and then display the Status page in the Lync Options dialog box. The settings you need to change are at the top of the page.

The presence states defined in Lync can't be customized, and you can't create presence states of your own. If you want to give team members more details about what you're doing or where you are, add a note in the text box above your name (which displays the prompt "What's happening today?") The note you add appears with your contact information. You can also add a place to the Set Your Location box to associate a location with the network you are connected to.

Instant messages, video calls, and online meetings

As I mentioned at the start of this chapter, Lync supports both formal (scheduled meetings) and informal (instant messaging) modes of communication. Coupled with the information Lync shows about a contact's availability, absence, or current activity, the various options for communicating let team members find each other whenever an issue needs consideration.

Communicating through an instant messaging program is familiar to many people. Lync's basic implementation of instant messaging is similar to other programs, and Lync lets you build on the messages you type by providing Voice over Internet Protocol (VoIP) calls, video feeds, and collaboration tools. We'll explore some of the regular instant messaging features in this section, look at the video capabilities in Lync, and then finish with information about how the integration of Lync and Outlook lets teams schedule and conduct meetings online rather than in a conference room.

See Also   The tools you use to share content and collaborate in Lync are covered in detail later in the chapter.

Exchanging instant messages

To send an instant message, double-click a contact's entry in the Lync window to open the conversation window. Type your message in the window's bottom pane, and then press Enter. The contact then receives a notification of the message from Lync and can accept to read the message and reply, ignore the message, or indicate that he or she doesn't want to be disturbed.

You can add multiple contacts to a single instant message session by selecting the first contact, pressing the Ctrl key, and then selecting the other contacts you want to include. To send an instant message to a group of contacts, right-click the group name in the contact list, and then click Send An Instant Message. (You can also drag a contact's entry into the conversation window to add that contact to the conversation.)

In the conversation window, shown in Figure 6-3, you can move beyond a simple exchange of typed messages to do the following:

- Click the phone icon to reach the contact via a Lync call or at a phone number. (Not all configurations of Lync will support calls of both types.)
- Click the camera icon to initiate a video conference with participants.

- Click the monitor icon to share your desktop, a program, or a presentation, for example, or to set up a poll or a whiteboard. These commands are useful even when just two members of a team are talking or exchanging instant messages. For example, a team member responsible for updating a presentation who wants feedback from the team's PowerPoint expert can send an instant message to the expert and then, once she's engaged, share the presentation. (For details, see "Sharing a PowerPoint presentation" later in this chapter.)

The monitor icon also lets you start OneNote to take notes during a conversation and to add attachments that participants in a conversation can review. When an attachment is added, the participants can then choose to accept the file, save it, or decline its delivery. The recipient can open the file once the attachment is accepted. (By default, files that are accepted, saved, or transferred are stored in the My Received Files folder in the user's Documents library. You can change this setting on the File Saving page of the Lync Options dialog box.) The sender of the instant message sees a message indicating the action taken by the recipient.

TIP You can copy and paste text and links to websites or documents into the instant message window.

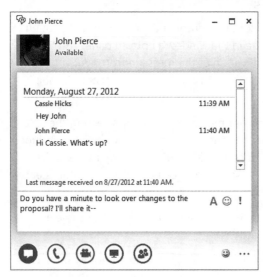

FIGURE 6-3 Click the icons at the bottom of the conversation window to start a call, a video conference, or an online presentation.

RESPONDING TO A CALL WITH AN INSTANT MESSAGE

When a contact calls you in Lync, you can respond with an instant message. Click Options on the notification Lync displays when you receive the call, and then click Reply By IM. When you click this command, the instant message window opens, and the person who called is informed that you chose to reply with an instant message. Type your reply in the instant message window, and then click Enter to continue.

Holding a video conference

With a webcam connected to your computer, you can include a video feed in a conversation in Lync. Right-click a contact or your team contact group, and then click Start A Video Call. If you are already engaged in a group conversation or instant message session, click the camera icon in the conversation window and then click Turn My Camera On.

TIP Open the Video Device page in the Lync Options dialog box to check the settings for focus, brightness, and other properties of the webcam.

The video feed from your computer appears in a preview window inset at the bottom-right corner of the conversation window. Point to the window and then click the down arrow in the top-right corner of the preview to hide it. Click the up arrow to show the preview again.

To change views, click Pick A Layout, and then choose Speaker View, Compact View, or Presentation View. Choosing Compact View hides the video feed, but you still have audio communication. Click the camera icon to temporarily turn off the video feed. Click the icon again to resume. You can also pause the video by pointing to the camera icon and clicking Turn My Camera Off.

As in other conversations and meetings, point to the monitor icon at the bottom of the conversation window to share your desktop, a specific program, a whiteboard, or an online poll with the participants in the video call. To end the video feed, point to the camera icon and click End Video. Note that the conversation itself is not ended. Participants can carry on via voice or instant messaging.

Using your conversation history

Lync maintains a history of the calls and conversations you have with contacts. A typical list is shown in Figure 6-4. You can review this information to see calls you missed or to pick up a conversation you want to continue. You can also view recent conversations you had with particular contacts.

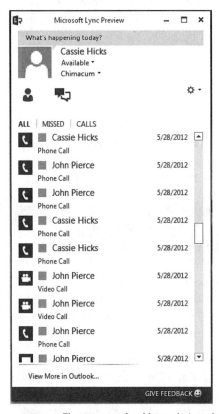

FIGURE 6-4 The conversation history in Lync includes calls you missed. Double-click an entry to resume the conversation.

Above the Search box in the main Lync window, click the conversations icon (at the right of the contacts icon). Lync displays a list of phone calls, missed calls (if any), meetings, instant message sessions, and group conversations. Use the filters at the top of the list to see all conversations, missed calls only, or all calls (including group conversations, missed calls, and online meetings). Here is an explanation of the options you see:

- *All* shows your 100 most-recent conversations.

- *Missed* shows any missed conversation during a certain timeframe (up to the 100 most recent).

- *Calls* shows any calls during a certain timeframe (up to the 100 most recent).

To continue a call or an instant message session from the conversation history list, right-click an entry in the list and then click Continue Conversation. You can also simply double-click the entry to open the conversation window.

If you are using Outlook with Lync, you can also work with a list of your previous conversations in Outlook. To find these entries, look in the Outlook folder Conversation History. (You can also click View More In Outlook at the bottom of the conversation history in Lync.) In Outlook, point to a contact's name in the message item to reveal a small contact card that you can use to send that contact an instant message, call the contact, start a video call, or send the contact an e-mail message.

Holding meetings online

One quick way to get a group together is to click the arrow next to the Options button, click Meet Now, and then click Invite More People to ask people to join the discussion. On the Add People page, search for contacts you want to include.

By default, each person who accepts your invitation to this impromptu meeting joins the meeting as a presenter, which is an important point to keep in mind if you plan to share content in the meeting. Presenters can share content and perform other operations during a conversation that participants designated as attendees cannot. For informal meetings among peers, having everyone enjoy the same status is often fine. On occasions when you need or want more control, you might want to be the only participant designated as a presenter. To address situations like these, when you invite people to the meeting, point to the people icon in the conversation window and then choose Everyone An Attendee, as shown in Figure 6-5. As you can see, you can also choose options to mute the audience, hide names, or invite others by e-mail.

TIP   For additional control over the meeting, click the More Options ellipsis at the bottom right of the conversation window and choose Online Meeting Options. You'll learn more about online meeting options later in this section.

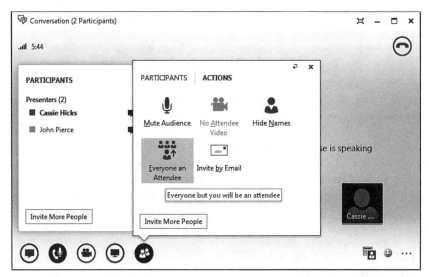

FIGURE 6-5 Use the Actions window to manage meeting options.

Using the Meet Now command or sending an instant message to teammates to get a quick opinion, to prompt them for information you need, or to invite them to coffee or lunch is part of the way Lync lets you communicate informally. For example, if a colleague's status is Available and you need to talk to him, there's probably no need to schedule an appointment. But teams can also make use of Lync for occasions that are formally on their calendars. These online meetings can be scheduled from Lync and can be managed from the desktop version of Outlook.

To start, display the calendar in Outlook, and then click New Lync Meeting on the Calendar view's Home tab. Outlook opens a new meeting request form and adds a link to the meeting (which reads "Join Lync Meeting"). The meeting organizer can then use the standard scheduling tools in Outlook to specify the time and the attendees. At the scheduled time, meeting attendees use this link to join the meeting, which is held online in Lync.

Before you send the meeting request, it's a good idea to click Meeting Options in the Lync Meeting group, which appears on the Meeting tab at the top of the meeting request. Use the Lync Meeting Options dialog box (see Figure 6-6) to change access and presenter options. By default, everyone you invite to an online meeting, including external contacts, can join the meeting without having to be admitted. Instead of admitting everyone automatically, you can set up a meeting so that only the organizer is admitted immediately, only people from your organization, or only those people in your organization whom you invite directly. If an online meeting includes people from outside your company, for example, you might want to select an option that lets you manage when to admit these participants. That way, team members from your company can talk briefly among themselves at the start of the meeting to be sure you agree about the goals and organization of the meeting.

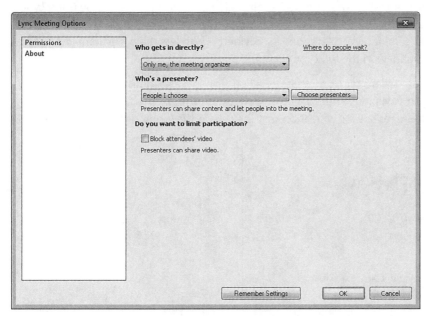

FIGURE 6-6 Review meeting access and presenter options in the Link Meeting Options dialog box. Presenters have more control of meetings, which might be what you need.

TIP By clicking Online Meeting Options from the More Options button in the conversation window, you can open the Link Meeting Options dialog box to manage presenter and access options for a meeting you initiate with the Meet Now command.

For presenters, the default setting is that everyone from your organization who attends the meeting is a presenter. You can instead choose Only Me, The Meeting Organizer, select the option that imposes no restrictions, or designate presenters. If you select People I Choose, click Choose Presenters to identify the individuals who can serve in that role. (You must have already added recipients to the meeting request to designate presenters. If you haven't done this, the list you see when you click Choose Presenters is blank.)

TIP If you want to use these settings for other online meetings, select Remember Settings in the Lync Meeting Options dialog box.

To join an online meeting, recipients open the meeting request in Outlook and click Join Meeting on the Meeting tab or click the link in the meeting request. That action opens the conversation window in Lync, with the meeting's subject line in the title bar. (A meeting participant who doesn't have Lync installed can join the meeting by using Lync Attendee, which runs in the browser. When the participant clicks the Join Meeting link, the option to download Lync Attendee is provided, which lets the participant join the meeting without having the full Lync client.)

If meeting options were set up so that not all participants are admitted to the meeting automatically, the organizer needs to admit attendees who are waiting, and while they wait, these attendees see a notification that they are in the lobby, as shown in Figure 6-7.

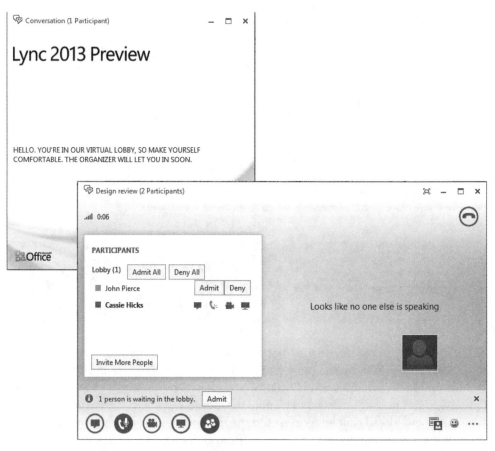

FIGURE 6-7 If meeting participants aren't admitted to a meeting automatically, they wait in the lobby for the organizer to admit them.

Collaboration tools

One practical issue when teams develop content together is how to get the content in front of everyone's eyes. This issue is magnified when members of a team can't sit down together in the same room. Teams can, of course, make use of features like coauthoring, tracking changes, or inserting comments, but these features, as useful as they are, might not be available to everyone whose input is required.

See Also Coauthoring, revision marks, and comments are important features for capturing the collective efforts of a team when its members put together a substantial document. You'll learn the details of how you can use coauthoring, track changes, and compare documents in Word, Excel, and PowerPoint in Chapters 8, 9, and 10.

Lync offers an alternative. During an online meeting, a conference call, or an instant message session, teams can supplement and focus the conversation by using Lync to share content and collaborate in developing it. You can, for example, open a PowerPoint presentation and discuss and annotate the presentation's slides, share your entire desktop or a document in a specific program, use an online whiteboard to brainstorm, or conduct a poll to collect opinions. The next few sections describe the mechanics of these options. As your team adopts Lync to help coordinate its efforts, you'll likely find numerous opportunities to make use of these capabilities.

Sharing your desktop

To work as a group on a document, to view a website your team is designing, or to review other content, you can share your desktop as part of a meeting or a group conversation. During the conversation or meeting, you can turn over control of your desktop to another participant (either a presenter or an attendee) and let that participant work with the programs or files on your computer. Participants can also request control, which you can approve or reject.

In the conversation window, point to the monitor icon, and then click Desktop to start this process. If you're the one who initiates this action, you see a notification that indicates you are currently presenting. Lync notifies participants that you have shared content, and they can then accept (or decline) to view the shared content. Lync loads and displays your desktop to participants in a portion of the Lync window referred to as the stage.

TIP Click the monitor icon to temporarily hide the stage. Click the icon again to display the stage.

Participants see activity on your desktop in real time. The numerical data or text you type in an Excel worksheet, for example, appears on their screens as you type it. To let another participant work on your desktop, click Give Control at the top of your screen, and then select the participant from the list. If a participant clicks Request Control at the top of his or her screen, you see a notification that lets you accept or decline the request. Switching control like this might apply in a meeting that you, as a project's manager, have set up with a group from your team plus managers or outside vendors. At the meeting, you want to look over a proposal from one of your partners—maybe a design firm that's providing advice on specific components. The senior partner of the design firm is part of the meeting, and having her handle the discussion while she points out aspects of the proposal makes great sense. Turn over your desktop to her at that point—or she can share her desktop directly—and let her carry on.

You regain control by clicking Give Control and choosing Take Back Control or by pressing Ctrl+Alt+Spacebar. Click Stop Presenting when you no longer need to share your desktop.

> **TIP** To avoid having to accept control requests from people you know, you can click Give Control Automatically, an option on the menu that appears when you click Give Control.

Sharing a PowerPoint presentation

Lync offers a specific option for sharing and reviewing PowerPoint presentations. Click the monitor icon, click PowerPoint, and then Lync displays the Share PowerPoint dialog box, where you select the presentation you want to describe or talk through with the team. You can't add slides to a presentation you are sharing, but the presentation isn't just static content. Team members can add annotations, images, and other objects while the presentation is open in Lync to emphasize elements on a slide or to provide directions for modifications. Click the Annotations icon in the top-right corner of the stage to reveal a set of tools that let you do the following (described as the tools appear from top to bottom):

- **Telepointer** Use the pointer if you are leading the conversation and want to point to a specific area or item on the current slide. A small ScreenTip appears in Lync to identify the participant who is pointing.

- **Select and type** Use this tool to type an annotation on the current slide. Click where you want the annotation to appear and then type. The text appears in a container you can drag to a different position if necessary. (This container resembles the note container that appears in OneNote.) You can change the font, font color, and font size by clicking the arrow to the right of this tool and then making selections from the lists Lync displays.

- **Pen** Use the pen to write or draw freehand on the slide. Use the down arrow beside the icon to select a different color or line weight. Participants can choose specific colors to identify their additions to the slide.

- **Highlighter** Select a highlighter from the options presented, and then highlight content that needs changes, further review, or different formatting, for example. You can choose from 10 colors for highlighters (or pens) and can also change the line thickness.

- **Eraser** Use the eraser to remove an annotation made with the pen or highlighter.

- **Stamp** Another way to annotate a slide is by using one of the stamp shapes available. You can add an arrow, an X, or a check mark. Use the arrow at the right of this tool to choose the stamp you want to add.

- **More shape tools** Click this button to add a line, an arrow, a rectangle, or a circle to the slide. Use these shapes to draw attention to specific elements that need more attention. You can choose from 10 colors here as well.

- **Insert picture** Choose an image file to add to the slide. Use the handles to resize and position the image.

- **Delete selected annotations** Select annotations and then click this button to remove them.

The More Options ellipsis at the bottom of the annotation tools opens a menu with commands that let you manage annotations (select all of them, undo an annotation, copy, cut, paste, and so on). You can also use this menu to save the annotated presentation as an XPS file or to send the annotated file to OneNote.

TIP   You can view an XPS file in most web browsers or in a viewer application available from Microsoft.

Attendees as well as presenters can annotate slides, but only presenters can save an annotated presentation. As the group reviews the presentation, a presenter can use the navigation arrows at the lower right of the stage to navigate between slides. Presenters can also click the Thumbnails button to display thumbnail images of the slides along the bottom of the stage. To see the notes related to a slide in PowerPoint, click Notes. To turn off either of these features, click the feature's button again.

MANAGING PRESENTABLE CONTENT

During a presentation session in Lync, when you have a PowerPoint file open and have also set up a whiteboard, for example, you have several options for how you and other participants can work with the content. Point to the monitor icon and then click Manage Presentable Content. You'll see a window like the one shown in Figure 6-8. Click Present Now to switch back to a file you shared earlier. Click Stop Presenting to remove the file, program, poll, or whiteboard from the stage. Use the Permissions list to specify who can download a shared file. Click More to see details about the shared content and to gain access to commands such as Save As, Send To OneNote, Save With Annotations, and others. Click Remove to stop sharing that content during the current conversation.

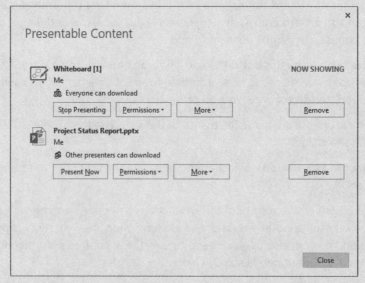

FIGURE 6-8 Use the Manage Presentable Content button to open this window, where you can adjust permissions, save shared content, and remove content from the stage.

You can also add attachments to the conversation window during a meeting. Point to the monitor icon, click Attachments, and then click Add Attachment. Select the file or files you want to provide to participants. Participants then click in the notification area of their conversation window to view or save the attachments.

TIP   You can also drag a file into the conversation window to attach it to a conversation. If you want to cancel the transfer of an attachment, press Alt+Q.

Sharing a program

Sharing a computer's desktop lets participants in a group conversation see everything that's currently running on that computer. If instead of sharing the desktop, you want to share a document in a particular program or two, start the program or programs, click the monitor icon in the conversation window, and then click Program. In the Present Programs dialog box, shown in Figure 6-9, select which programs you want to share and then click the Present button.

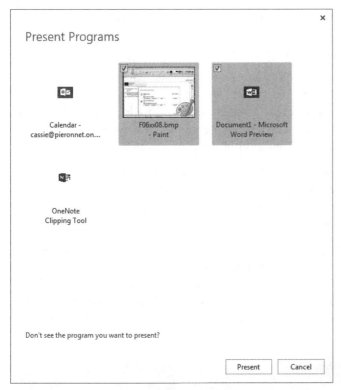

FIGURE 6-9 Lync doesn't give you the option to start a program when you choose the Program option. The program you want to share must be running on your computer before you share it.

A shared program comes to the foreground on the computer from which it's shared and is displayed in the stage on participants' computers. Whoever shares the program can give control of the program to a different participant, who can then interact with the program. Use the Give Control button to select a participant, to choose the option to automatically accept control requests, and to take back control. A participant can also request control.

If a presenter switches to a program that's running but that hasn't been shared, other participants see a message in the stage indicating that the presenter's programs are currently minimized or participants will simply not see the program (if its window overlaps a shared program's window, for example).

■ **IMPORTANT** You can't share some programs. Use the link at the bottom of the Present Program dialog box to open a Help topic that lists the reasons why. For example, you cannot share Lync, File Explorer (in Windows 8), Sticky Notes, Windows Sidebar, and so on. You can share these programs when you share your full desktop, however.

Conducting an online poll

Your team is together and talking about development plans for your new product. The team needs to make a decision about some issue or another—maybe which cities you should travel to in Europe to conduct focus groups. You could ask for a show of hands as each city's name is announced, but the team is online, so that won't work especially well. Instead, use Lync to conduct a simple opinion poll.

The Poll option opens the Create A Poll dialog box. Provide a name for the poll, type a question, and then enter the set of choices. You can provide up to seven options for users to choose from. When you click OK in this dialog box, the poll question appears in the stage area, as shown in Figure 6-10.

When you first post a poll, the poll is open but responses are hidden from attendees. Presenters can use the menu at the bottom of the stage to close the poll, show results to all participants, edit the poll question and choices, and clear votes. When you edit the poll question and answers, the current answers are cleared. Once the results are in, you can save the poll as a PNG file or as a comma-separated value file (.csv) that you can open in Excel.

TIP To conduct a poll with multiple questions, define the first question, collect answers, and then save that poll. Then edit the current poll and define a new question and set of answers.

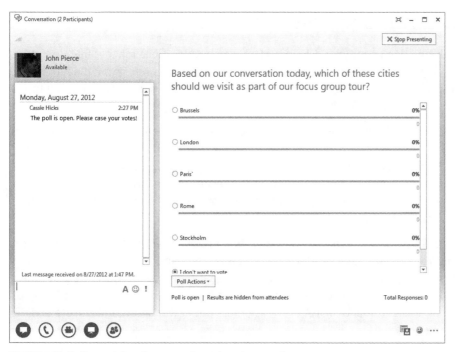

FIGURE 6-10 Gather opinions from your team by using a poll.

Working together on a whiteboard

For a group brainstorming session, share a new whiteboard. Lync displays a blank page in the stage area and provides a set of tools along the right side of the window that let you sketch and outline your ideas. The tools available are essentially the same as those you can use to annotate a shared PowerPoint presentation. For a description of these tools, see "Sharing a PowerPoint presentation" earlier in this chapter.

Everyone in the group conversation can contribute to the whiteboard. With a whiteboard displayed, you won't see the Give Control or Request Control buttons. To preserve the working session you conduct with a whiteboard, make sure someone saves it. You can save a whiteboard as an XPS file or a PNG file. You can also send a whiteboard to One-Note to preserve it in a related notebook.

Recordings and meeting notes

Almost always, document your activities as a team, but do so in a manner that doesn't simply create clutter. You can follow this golden rule in Lync as well as in other applications, and for group conversations and online meetings, Lync is often the best tool to start with.

As you learned in the previous sections, during meetings and calls that teams hold using Lync, presenters can share content. They can also record conversations, capturing audio and video presentations and the discussions of content that was shared. You won't always need to make a recording, but when you want a record of what was said and decided or if you need to share a meeting's proceedings with an absent team member, a manager, or anyone else, it's simple to do.

An alternative to making a recording is to use the option in Lync to take meeting notes in OneNote. You can start OneNote from Lync; compile text, images, and other files related to the discussion; and then revise and organize the OneNote pages as a more permanent record. I'll touch on how you get to OneNote from Lync in this section. Chapter 7, "Keeping track of discussions and ideas," provides details about working with OneNote and sharing notebooks.

Making and managing recordings

It's good business practice (and in some locations might be legally required) to advise people who are gathered for a meeting if you are going to record the meeting. It's fair to say that some people might be less willing to contribute or agree with controversial or dissenting opinions if a meeting is being recorded. This doesn't apply in all cases—you may just want to record the rehearsal of a presentation—but you need to balance the importance of creating an environment that's conducive to gathering a range of perspectives with your need to create a full recording. Also, recordings can consume a lot of disk space, so if space is limited, you probably need to develop a process for retaining and archiving the recording files.

To begin recording a meeting, click the More Options ellipsis at the right side of the conversation window, and then click Start Recording. You can use the same menu to pause or stop recording. When you stop a recording, Lync Recording Manager displays a notification. You can click this notification to see the progress in processing the recording. When the recording is available, you'll see a second notification. If you open the Lync Recording Manager (click the icon in the system tray on the Windows taskbar), you'll see a list of recordings, as shown in Figure 6-11.

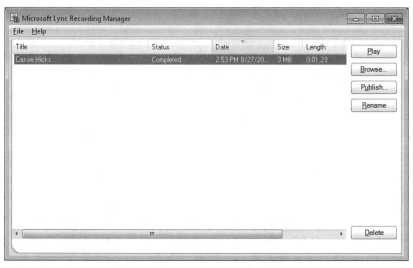

FIGURE 6-11 Use the Lync Recording Manager to play back recordings or publish them so that other team members can view them.

When you want to replay a recording, click Play, and the recording is shown in Windows Media Player. By default, recordings are stored in the Lync Recordings folder within an individual's My Videos library. The team member making the recording can use the Browse button to open this folder and move or copy the file or use the Publish button to open the Save And Publish dialog box and save the file to a location with greater access—including the team's SharePoint site. In the Save And Publish dialog box, use the Browse button to navigate to the location where you want to publish the recording. The Options button opens a dialog box in which you can specify which types of content to include in the published version. For example, if you want to reduce the size of the file you are publishing, clear the Participant Video option in the Save And Publish Options dialog box (see Figure 6-12).

> **NOTE** On the File Saving page in the Lync Options dialog box, you can change the default location Lync uses to store recordings made on a particular computer. Lync prompts you to confirm the change with a warning that using a public location can make the recordings more accessible. This points out again that recordings should be made with some sensitivity, and they should be stored and managed with that consideration in mind.

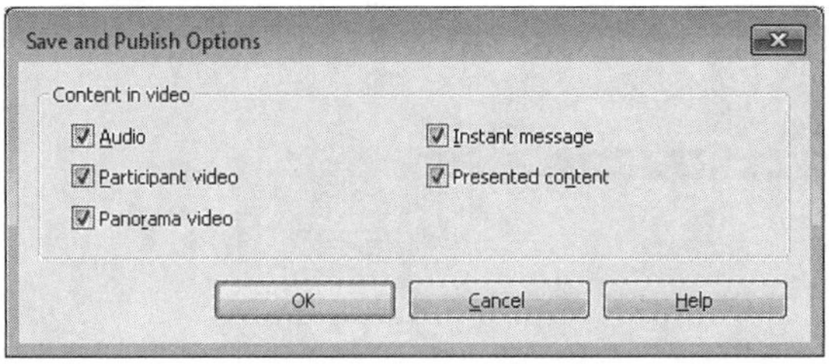

Save and Publish Options

Content in video

☑ Audio   ☑ Instant message

☑ Participant video   ☑ Presented content

☑ Panorama video

OK   Cancel   Help

FIGURE 6-12 Use the options in the Save And Publish Options dialog box to remove some content from a recording.

Taking notes in OneNote

Remember that notes that document a meeting's agenda—a formal one or just the topics that come up as a conversation evolves—can be culled for insights. A record of opinions, considerations, and decision-making criteria provides valuable information that teams can apply in the future or pass on to new members when members of the current team go on to other pursuits.

Instead of making a recording, someone can take notes on behalf of the team in One-Note during the conversation and then compile and distribute notes to participants later. In fact, it's wise to apply this practice to almost any group conversation or meeting—even ones you record—because the written notes augment what was said and can point to moments in the meeting that you want to review in detail by replaying a recording.

At the start of a conversation or an online meeting in Lync, click the monitor icon, and then click OneNote at the top of the window. This option displays a small window where you can select MyNotes. In the Select Location In OneNote dialog box, select a notebook or notebook section where you want to keep the notes. If you select a section, a new page is created, tentatively titled "My Meeting Notes." The page includes the date and a time stamp of when the conversation began, and also lists the participants. To take notes, just start typing or writing on the page. You can add notes to a different area of the page by clicking there and then typing the text.

TIP Taking notes in OneNote is not the same as sharing a program through Lync. If you start OneNote, you are the only conversation participant working in that instance of the program.

Ending the conversation in Lync doesn't close OneNote. You can keep OneNote open to edit and organize the raw notes, insert images or files to complement the notes you've taken, and so on. Also, you don't need to save your work in OneNote—the program saves new content automatically. You might also move the page to a different notebook (a notebook for the project you're meeting about, for example). As you will learn in the next chapter, which describes the collaboration features in OneNote in detail, you can distribute the notes by circulating a notebook via e-mail or by sharing the notebook on your team's SharePoint site.

Keeping track of discussions and ideas

TEAMS CAN SPEND a lot of time planning—evaluating the current state of their work and identifying the steps they need to take to ensure that they're prepared for what's ahead. All or part of the team plans together in meetings, and team members also work on their own in advance of group sessions and again afterward to follow up on decisions, tasks, and issues the team defines.

As part of planning, teams record their ideas and processes and often gather information from other sources—market research, economic trends, customer feedback, product reviews, media opinions, past projects, and so on. Much of the information that's compiled needs to be documented, designed, formatted, and edited before it's in final shape. In Chapters 8, 9, and 10, you'll learn more about how teams can review and update shared documents. This chapter describes how teams can use Microsoft OneNote to help plan their work and gather data they need. By using OneNote, teams can do the following:

- Share and synchronize notebooks.

- Store and access information in a variety of formats, including notes, files, printouts, images, drawings, video and audio, and tables.

- Build links between pages, notebooks, and other applications to facilitate navigation between related information.

- Track and manage changes made by multiple users.

- Search the current notebook or specify a different search scope to broaden or narrow the search.

- Identify and tag content to help group and locate related notes.

See Also In Chapter 5, "An integrated Outlook," you'll find information about how to add Microsoft Outlook items to a OneNote notebook. Chapter 6, "Working together in Lync," touches on how to take notes in OneNote during an online meeting or a conference call. In Chapter 11, "Working with Office Web Apps on SkyDrive," you'll learn more about using the OneNote Web App.

Before exploring these and other features in OneNote, familiarize yourself with the main OneNote window (if you aren't already a regular user of the application), as shown in Figure 7-1.

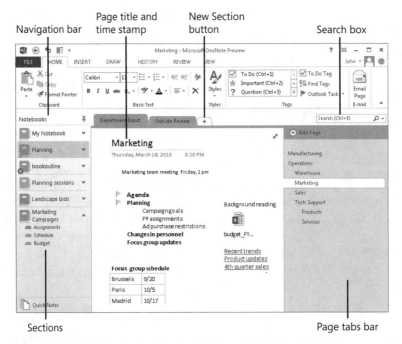

FIGURE 7-1 Use the Navigation bar to switch between notebooks and to open sections. Use the page tabs bar to create and display pages.

Here's a quick description about how notebooks are organized and how to navigate in the OneNote window.

- A notebook contains at least one section, which OneNote includes by default when you create a notebook. You can create additional sections as you need them and organize them into section groups in a notebook with many sections.

- Sections contain pages where you add notes, pictures, and other types of content. You can also create subpages to define a more detailed level of organization.

- Open notebooks are listed on the Navigation bar, which appears along the left side of the OneNote window by default. The sections in a notebook are listed under the entry for a notebook in the Navigation bar. Click a section name to display that section. You can also display a section by clicking the section tab that appears across the top of the current page.

- The pages in a section are listed in the page tabs bar, which is displayed along the right side of the window. Click a page name to display its content. Click Add Page at the top of the page tabs bar to insert another page in the section.

> **NOTE**   OneNote automatically saves changes you make to a notebook. You don't need to click a Save button or a Save command before you close a notebook.

Sharing OneNote notebooks

When you share a notebook in OneNote, you can add it to a SharePoint site, to SkyDrive, or to a folder on your network. Locations associated with your Office 365/Microsoft account will be listed on the New page and on the Share page. You can select a SkyDrive folder or a SharePoint library on the New page when you create a notebook, or you can share a notebook you're already working with—a notebook that's stored on your local computer, for example—to make the notebook available to other team members.

For a notebook already in use, first display the Share page on the File tab. The current notebook is shown at the top of the page. Select a location in the Places list, and then select the folder or a library. (Use the Browse button to select a location that's not in the list of recent locations.) When you share a notebook that's currently stored on your computer, you move the notebook to the shared location.

> **TIP**   Yet another way to share a notebook is via the Info page. In the list of notebooks, click Settings for the notebook you want to work with as a team, and then click Share Or Move. Click the Invite People To This Notebook link to let other people know about a notebook you've saved to a shared location.

SHARING A NOTEBOOK ON YOUR TEAM SITE

Many teams will favor the option to post a OneNote notebook to a team site. This step helps consolidate where information is stored and lets teams manage notebooks like they manage other files stored on the site—by applying permissions, for example, or by creating an alert to signal when a notebook has been changed.

See Also For more information about managing a team site, see Chapter 2, "Building a SharePoint team site."

When you create a new notebook on SkyDrive, for example, OneNote prompts you to invite people after it saves the file. Click Invite People in the message box to display the Share Notebook page, shown in Figure 7-2, which you use to set up an e-mail message that you send to team members and other people you are sharing the notebook with.

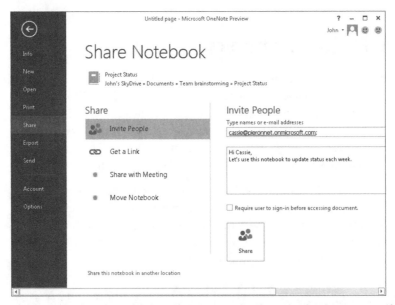

FIGURE 7-2 To share a notebook on SkyDrive, use the Share Notebook page to notify team members.

Sharing a notebook on the web by using SkyDrive makes the notebook accessible from any computer that can connect to the Internet—you don't need access to your organization's network to access the notebook. (You can restrict who has access to the notebook, however.) This option is useful for virtual teams of independent contractors, for example, who don't work on a shared domain.

As mentioned in Chapter 6, Lync and OneNote are integrated so that you can share a One-Note notebook during a Lync meeting. Click Share With Meeting on the Share Notebook page to select or set up a meeting in which you want to share a specific notebook.

Synchronizing notebooks

In OneNote, more than one person can work in a shared notebook at the same time. When a notebook is updated, OneNote synchronizes the changes so that the notebook is current for each person using it. OneNote keeps a local copy of a shared notebook on each person's computer. This lets team members work with the notebook when they are offline. When they connect to the network again, OneNote synchronizes changes automatically.

Shared notebooks are identified in the OneNote Navigation bar by a Sync Status icon, which displays a symbol to indicate the status of synchronization. Figure 7-3 shows some examples. You'll see a warning exclamation mark when OneNote has encountered problems with the synchronization process (for example, if some sections are unavailable or in an inaccessible location). Spinning arrows indicate that the notebook is being synchronized, and an X indicates a synchronization error. OneNote also notifies you when a password is required to sync the notebook.

FIGURE 7-3 Check the Sync Status icon beside a shared notebook to know whether a notebook is up to date or being synchronized.

You can let OneNote take care of synchronizing notebooks, but you can take this step yourself when you want to be sure a shared notebook is up to date. For example, you might manually synchronize notebooks just before you leave the office for a trip if you plan to work on them while you're away. OneNote provides several ways to manually synchronize notebooks:

- Right-click a notebook in the Navigation bar and click Sync This Notebook Now. You can also press Shift+F9 to synchronize the current notebook.

- Display the Info page in Backstage view, click Settings for the notebook you want to synchronize, and then click Sync.

- Right-click a notebook, click Notebook Sync Status, select the notebook in the Shared Notebook Synchronization dialog box, and then click Sync Now, as shown in Figure 7-4.

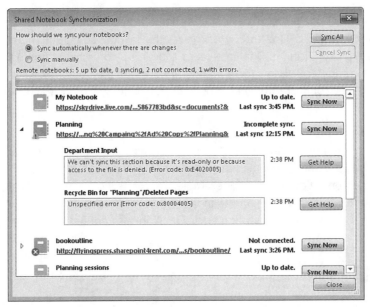

FIGURE 7-4 Select a notebook in the Shared Notebook Synchronization dialog box, and then click Sync Now.

Adding content to a notebook

As you can see, making a notebook accessible to a team of people and keeping the notebook up to date are pretty straightforward tasks. When team members need to add notes or other content to a notebook shared on a SharePoint site, they just open the notebook in OneNote. You don't need to open the team site first. OneNote synchronizes changes with any copy of the notebook that's stored locally.

In the remaining sections in this chapter, you'll see how teams can add depth of content and relationships to the information stored in a notebook. In addition, you'll learn how to see who's contributing to the notebook and how to search in OneNote to bring informa-tion to the surface when you need it.

To start, I'll cover the second capability mentioned at the beginning of the chapter—us-ing OneNote to store and access information in a variety of formats, including files, print-outs, images, drawings, audio and video, and tables. A quick glance at the commands on the OneNote ribbon's Insert and Draw tabs reveals this range of operations, which are, of course, in addition to typing or writing your own notes. To add a note, just click the page and start typing (or writing, if your computer has a pen). OneNote encloses the note in a container with handles you can then use to move or resize the note.

The fact that a notebook can contain a variety of information isn't a collaborative feature in itself, but it does support the work of a team, especially one whose members are in charge of different phases or aspects of a project. For example, marketers can compile useful statistics in a table, designers can sketch ideas and insert illustrations, and team members doing research on competitors' products can add related files, links, and printouts.

Inserting files and printouts

Teams can extend the information that's collected in and accessible through a One-Note notebook by linking to an external file or a website or by embedding a file in a notebook. You can also add a printout of a file to OneNote (by using the built-in Send To OneNote printer driver) or even insert an image from a scanner or a digital camera. When you link to a file, you can open the file to update it—the content you add to the notebook is live.

Linking to files

The Link command on the Insert tab opens a dialog box in which you can specify a website, file, or location in OneNote that you want to link to from the current page. The dialog box includes a text box where you can type display text to identify the link. For example, you could type the display text "Home page demo" to identify a link that points to a URL such as http://www.homepageprototype.net.

Here are some more details:

- To link to a website, type the site's URL in the Address box or click Browse The Web to open your default web browser and then navigate to the site. Copy the URL in the browser's address box, close the browser (or switch to OneNote), and then paste the URL into the Address box in the Link dialog box. Add the display text you want to provide for the link (for websites, OneNote does not provide any display text by default), and click OK to add the link to the current page.

- To link to a file (which could be on your local computer, on a network share, or on SkyDrive or SharePoint), type the path to the file in the Address box or click Browse For File to open the Link To File dialog box. Navigate to the file, select it, and then click OK. For files, OneNote inserts the file's name (without the file name extension) in the Text To Display box. Modify the display text if necessary.

- The Link dialog box also lets you insert a link to another OneNote notebook, section, or page. In the dialog box, select the notebook, section, or page from the list under All Notebooks. (The list shows open notebooks, not all notebooks on your computer.) Use the plus and minus signs to expand and collapse the items that are displayed. You can also search for a location in OneNote by typing the title of a notebook, section, or page in the search box. By default, OneNote uses the display name of the notebook or the title of the section or page for the link's display text. Change or add to the text if necessary.

TIP Below the All Notebooks list is the Create New Page area. Select New Page In Current Section (and type display text) if you want to link to a new page from the current page. OneNote creates an untitled page in the current section.

Attaching files

In the Insert tab's Files group, click File Attachment to attach a file to a notebook. Select the file from the Choose A File Or A Set Of Files To Insert dialog box. You can select a single file or press and hold Ctrl or Shift to select a group of files. (Press Ctrl to select a set of noncontiguous files; press Shift to select more than one file listed contiguously.) When you click Insert in this dialog box, you'll see another dialog box (named Insert File) with a list of options that depend on the type of file you selected. These options let you attach the file and display it as an icon, attach the file as a file object (such as a spreadsheet), attach the file as a printout, and others.

When you double-click an icon for a file you've attached, OneNote warns that opening the attachment could harm your computer. Select the option Don't Show This Again before you click OK in the warning box to forego this step in the future. With the file open, you can make changes to it, but you are updating an embedded copy and not the original file. Embedded files can increase the size of a notebook, so to keep the size of notebooks smaller and the content they contain live, link to files instead of embedding them. Keep in mind, however, that a link breaks if a linked file is moved.

Printing files to OneNote

When OneNote is installed, a virtual printer is set up along with the program. This printer lets you add a printout of a file—fully formatted—to a notebook. You can make use of this feature when you are working in OneNote or when you are working in another application. For example, let's say that the team member responsible for updating the budget does so just before a scheduled meeting. To make a copy of the budget available for discussion at the meeting, the team member can print the budget spreadsheet so that an image of the file appears in the team's planning notebook.

To use this feature in OneNote, click File Printout on the Insert tab, and then select the file to print. OneNote opens the file's original application and then prints and inserts the file. You don't need to make any additional settings. In addition to displaying the file's content, OneNote attaches a copy of the file. Double-click the icon to open the original file and edit it. (Be sure, of course, to save the file in the original application if you want to preserve any changes you make.) Modifications to the file are not reflected in the printout, which is a static representation of the file in the state it was when it was inserted.

When you are working in another application—another Office application or an application such as Adobe Acrobat or your web browser, for example—you can choose the Send To OneNote printer driver in the Print dialog box (or on the Print page in Backstage view) to insert a printout in a notebook. Choose the Print command in the application, choose Send To OneNote from the list of printers, and then make any other print settings you want to apply—specify a page range, for example. When you print the file, OneNote displays the Select Location In OneNote dialog box. Use this dialog box to specify the section or page where you want to add the printout. In this case, only a representation of the file is included on the page you select. OneNote does not also embed the file or provide a link to it.

SETTING SEND TO OPTIONS

When you print to OneNote from another application, by default the Select Location In OneNote dialog box is displayed, prompting you to specify where you want the printout to appear. You can change this setting (and settings for related operations, such as sending a screen clipping to OneNote) on the Send To OneNote page in the OneNote Options dialog box. You can choose from three or four options (depending on the operation) for how content is sent to OneNote:

- **Always Ask Where To Send** (default)   With this setting selected, OneNote displays the Select Location In OneNote dialog box, where you can designate a specific section or page (depending on the type of content).

- **To Current Page**   This option is available for e-mail messages and task notes from Outlook and for web content and printing to OneNote. (For information about sending Outlook items to OneNote, see Chapter 5.)

- **To New Page In Current Section**   This option is available for all types of content.

- **Set Default Location**   When you choose this setting, OneNote displays the Select Location In OneNote dialog box. Select the section or page to which you want to send this type of content by default. For example, you might create a notebook named Printouts and send all printouts to a section in that notebook.

Inserting a spreadsheet

Use the Spreadsheet command in the Insert tab's Files group to add a new or an existing spreadsheet to a notebook. When the spreadsheet is inserted, click the Edit icon that appears in the top-left corner to open Excel so that you can make changes to the file.

Adding images and drawings

To amplify and complement the text and files you add to a notebook, you can insert pictures and images and create drawings with a pen and shapes. You can compare the drawing tools in OneNote to the tools you can use on a shared whiteboard in Lync. (For more information about sharing a whiteboard in Lync, see "Working together on a whiteboard" in Chapter 6.) Neither OneNote nor Lync have the scope of capabilities of a program such as Microsoft PowerPoint or Microsoft Visio, but the drawing tools in OneNote are a step beyond the whiteboard tools in Lync and can be used to sketch flowcharts and other business diagrams with some precision.

Pictures

The Pictures command on the Insert tab opens the Insert Picture dialog box. Use this dialog box to add an image file (or multiple files) to a notebook. You can choose from many types of formats, including .png, .bmp, .jpg, and .gif.

After you insert a picture, right-click the image to open a menu with commands that let you rotate the image, move it behind or in front of other content on the page, reposition or resize it, or restore it to its original size. If the picture you insert contains text (an image of a Microsoft Visio drawing, for example), point to Make Text In Image Searchable and then choose a language, or choose Disable to turn off this feature.

See Also For more information about searching in OneNote, see "Searching notebooks" later in this chapter.

The Online Pictures command opens a different version of the Insert Pictures dialog box. Use this command and dialog box to insert clip art from Office.com, an image from the Internet (using the Bing search engine to locate the image), or from SkyDrive. You can also link your Office account to a photo hosting service such as Flickr and insert pictures from that site.

Screen clippings

Any team member who wants to add a screen capture to a notebook should become familiar with the Screen Clipping command. The command appears on the Insert tab in OneNote, but you can also add a screen clipping to a notebook when OneNote is not running. (There's a simple step you take to ensure this. If you don't see the icon for the OneNote clipping tool in the notification area of the Windows taskbar—it appears there by default—open the OneNote Options dialog box from the File tab and select the first option on the Display page—Place OneNote Icon In The Notification Area Of The Taskbar.)

Imagine you're browsing the web, looking for sites with interesting designs, or imagine you want to quickly snag a few sentences from an insightful posting on a blog that you follow. You don't need to start OneNote. Instead, press the Windows logo key+S. This key combination triggers the screen clipping feature. You'll see the current window dim and the pointer change to a cross. Drag to select the portion of the window you want to capture. When you release the mouse button, the Select Location In OneNote dialog box opens, and there you can choose the section or page where you want to add the screen clipping. (Alternatively, click Copy To Clipboard to preserve the clipping for use in a separate application).

TIP Screen clippings are tagged with the date and time they are taken. Clippings from webpages are also tagged with the page name and the site's URL.

If you're working in OneNote, be sure the program, document, or page from which you want to capture a screen clipping is open. Click Screen Clipping, and you'll see that the OneNote window is minimized and the window behind OneNote appears, with the content in that window dimmed. Drag across the window to select the portion of the screen you want to add to the current page. When you release the mouse button, OneNote becomes the active window, and the screen clipping is added to the page.

ADDING A QUICK NOTE

Typing what OneNote calls a *quick note* (or a side note) is something else you can do when OneNote isn't running (and when it is). Quick notes enable you to record an idea—even make a quick sketch—in a OneNote window that provides a subset of commands from the regular ribbon and no Navigation bar or page tabs.

When you set up OneNote, the icon for the OneNote clipping tool is displayed by default in the notification area of the Windows taskbar. When you click the icon, you'll see a small window where you can choose to create a screen clipping, send content to OneNote, or create a quick note. Type or write your note (or use the Draw tab to sketch), and then close the note window. When the window closes, OneNote sends your note to the Quick Notes section, which appears at the bottom of the Navigation bar. You can display notes and then drag them to the page in the notebook they relate to or create a notebook to house them. (If you want to keep the quick note window open and display it on top of other windows, click Keep On Top on the View tab of the note window.) When you are working in OneNote, you can display the clipping tool by clicking Clipping Panel on the View tab.

Working with drawing tools

To add a sketch, a rough floor plan, or a simple business diagram to a notebook, work with tools and commands on the Draw tab. The following list describes the details of working with the commands in each group on the tab.

- In the Tools group, the Select & Type tool is selected by default. Use the Eraser tool (you can select an eraser of various sizes) to delete pen strokes and portions of lines and shapes you've added to a page. Use the Lasso Select tool to select irregularly shaped areas of a drawing. Use the Panning Hand tool to scroll a page by using the mouse, a pen, or a finger (for touch-enabled computers).

TIP   When you want to type a note again, you don't need to click the Select & Type tool. Just click the page where you want the note to appear and type; OneNote automatically enables the Select & Type tool again.

The Tools group also includes a variety of pens and highlighters you can choose from. See the following section for more detail.

- The Shapes group provides several line styles (with arrows and without), five basic shapes, and three basic graph patterns. Select a shape (click More to reveal the full set of shapes), and then click the page where you want the shape to appear. The shape is selected when you add it, and you can use the handles on the shape's border to change the shape's dimensions. Drag the shape to reposition it.

TIP When you select and point to a shape, you'll see a mini toolbar that includes a number of commands. Use the mini toolbar to add a fill color, to flag a shape, and so on.

If you want to use a different color or a different line thickness for a shape's borders, click Color & Thickness in the Insert Shapes group, and then make the selections you want to use in the Color & Thickness dialog box. The color of the line thickness options changes when you select a line color, which gives you a preview of how the shape borders will appear.

- The commands in the Edit group let you do the following:

  - Insert Space adds or removes space between note containers and other elements on a page. Click the button, and then position the pointer between the two elements whose spacing you want to adjust. Drag up to decrease the space between the elements; drag down to increase the space.

  - Delete removes the selected note container or other element.

  - Arrange provides a menu of options for positioning an element behind or in front of other elements.

  - Rotate provides options for rotating an image or a shape and for flipping an object horizontally or vertically to change its orientation.

Working with pen input

Also on the Draw tab is a gallery of pens and highlighters that you can use to handwrite notes. In the Tools group on the Draw tab, click a pen color, and then start writing your notes. Use the ScreenTips for the different pen tools to identify color, type (pen or highlighter), and thickness. (To type notes after you activate a pen, click Select & Type.)

You can work with additional pens and highlighters by clicking the Color & Thickness button. This command opens the Color & Thickness dialog box. In the dialog box, select

Pen or Highlighter, and then choose the line thickness you want. Under Line Color, select the color for the pen or highlighter.

At the bottom of the pen and highlighter gallery is the Pen Mode command, which displays a set of options to let you control how OneNote interprets pen input:

- **Create Both Handwriting and Drawings** This is the default setting. It converts handwritten notes to text when you add input with a pen. To convert the input, click Ink To Text in the Convert group on the Draw tab.

- **Create Drawings Only** This setting disables the Ink To Text command. Handwritten text that you add to a page is represented as a drawing and cannot be converted to text.

- **Create Handwriting Only** This setting prevents OneNote from misinterpreting your handwriting as a drawing.

- **Use Pen As Pointer** This setting converts a pen to a pointing device (to select items on page, for example) so you don't need to switch to the Select & Type mode.

TIP The Advanced page of the OneNote Options dialog box includes settings for working with pens. These options let you control whether the "scratch out" gesture deletes portions of handwritten notes or drawings and control whether you switch automatically between inking, selecting, typing, and panning.

Adding audio and video recordings

Like Lync (see Chapter 6 for details), OneNote lets you make audio and video recordings (provided you have the necessary hardware, such as a microphone and a webcam). If your team is meeting in a conference room instead of online via Lync, you can use One-Note to add recordings of the proceedings to a notebook.

For audio-only recordings, click Record Audio on the Insert tab and start speaking into the microphone (or toward your computer if it has a built-in mic). OneNote displays the Audio & Video Playback contextual tab on the ribbon. Use the controls on this tab to pause or stop the recording, to play it back when you want to review it later, and to rewind or fast forward through it.

When you click Record Video, OneNote opens a small window showing the video output. A video recording also includes a sound recording. Like for an audio recording, use the commands on the Audio & Video Playback tab to pause, stop, rewind, or fast forward a video recording.

You can add notes and perform other operations in OneNote while recording. For example, you can attach files or insert links. OneNote keeps track of the actions you take while you record, which lets you follow the path of a conversation, for example, when you replay a recording. If you select See Playback (in the Options group on the Playback tab) when you replay a recording, OneNote highlights notes and other additions to the page so that a note is highlighted at the point in the recording when the note was made. If you highlight a note that was inserted during the recording, a small Play button appears next to the note. Click Play to replay the point in the recording that corresponds to when the note was made.

OneNote's search feature can locate words that are part of an audio or video recording. To set this option (and other options for audio and video recordings), click Audio & Video Settings on the Playback tab, and then select the option under Audio Search in the OneNote Options dialog box, as shown in Figure 7-5.

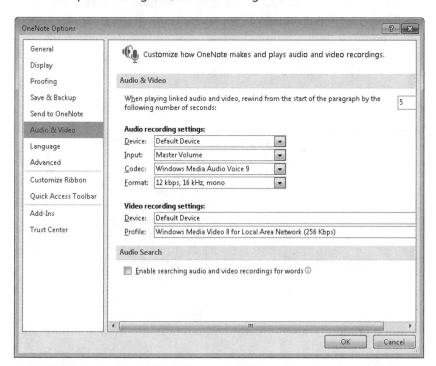

FIGURE 7-5 Click the option under Audio Search to include recordings in OneNote search results.

Working with tables

Information that's best displayed in a table often takes a little time to prepare. You may need to tweak the dimensions of columns and rows or edit the wording of entries to make them consistent. But tables don't always need this level of attention, and the variety of ways you can add tables to a notebook make them a useful format for quickly listing items such as tasks, dates, and assignments, for example, or information like a supplier, a product, and the order quantity.

You can add a table by using the Table command on the Insert tab, but perhaps the most direct approach is to type the text for the table's first entry (the first column heading, for example), and then press Tab to create another column. Press Tab again to create a third column (you don't need to type any text in the previous cell), and so on. Press Enter to start the next row.

When you insert a table (or when you select a table), OneNote displays the Table Tools Layout tab, which you can use to select the entire table or specific columns, rows, or cells; insert or delete columns and rows; hide the table's borders; and align the contents of table cells. Figure 7-6 shows the Table Tools Layout tab.

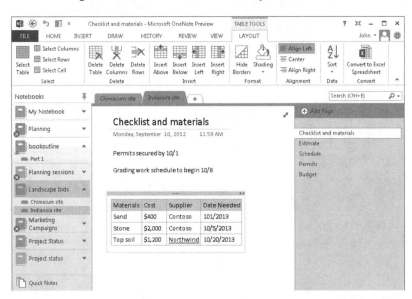

FIGURE 7-6 Insert a table in OneNote to capture information about schedules, tasks, products, and so on.

TIP You can also access the table layout commands by right-clicking in a table and choosing Table from the shortcut menu.

If you first start a table by using the keyboard, you can continue to build it by using the following key combinations to modify the layout:

- To create a new column to the left or right of the current column, press Ctrl+Alt+E or Ctrl+Alt+R, respectively.

- To create a new row below the current one, even if the cursor is in the middle of the row, press Ctrl+Enter.

- To create a new row above the current row, move the cursor to the beginning of the row and press Enter. (This does not apply to the first row in a table.)

- To begin a new paragraph in the same cell, press Alt+Enter.

Editing and formatting text in OneNote

Much of the information you add to OneNote can remain raw and essentially unformatted. But you can format and edit notes by using a variety of tools, many of which appear on the OneNote ribbon's Home tab. Applying styles and formatting to notes (as for other types of content) helps emphasize important items and adds structure to them.

OneNote includes Format Painter, common to other Office applications. OneNote also provides 11 built-in styles that you can apply to the text in a notebook. You cannot create your own styles or modify the styles that come with OneNote, but the Styles gallery provides six levels of headings, a style for page titles, styles for citations and quotations, a style for programming code, and the Normal style. If you need to remove text formatting that's been applied in a notebook, select the text and then click Clear Formatting at the bottom of the Styles gallery. You can also select the text and press Ctrl+Shift+N to remove formatting and apply the Normal style.

Adding links and linked notes

As your team uses OneNote to record ideas and compile information, you can connect pages, sections, notes, and whole notebooks to avoid repeating information and to navigate to data you need with greater ease.

You can also connect notes to information in other applications—to Microsoft Word documents, PowerPoint presentations, or webpages, for example. Linking notes to pages, sections, or notebooks and linking notes to files created in other applications are two ways you can deepen the associations between the content you include in a notebook.

Linking pages to other OneNote pages

By linking one page to another, you can navigate through a notebook, create relationships between pages, and reduce redundant information. The Copy Link To Page command appears when you right-click a page in the page tabs bar. (You'll see a similar command—Copy Link To Section—when you right-click a section title in the Navigation bar.) Click this command, display the page you want to add the link to, and then paste the link.

 **TIP** If you click the Paste button on the Home tab, it's best to choose the Keep Source Formatting or Merge Formatting option. If you use one of these options, OneNote uses the page title for the link's display text. If you choose Keep Text Only, the link will work, but the link's display text will be the lengthy ID OneNote uses to refer to a page.

By default, links to pages are shown in a blue font with a solid underline. Links to subpages are displayed in a blue font with a dashed underline. You can apply other formatting to a link by selecting it and then applying a style or by using the basic text formatting tools on the Home tab.

To modify a link, right-click it, and choose Edit Link. This opens the Link dialog box. (See "Linking to files" earlier in this chapter for more information.) Here you can choose a different page or section for the link. You can also use this dialog box to modify the display text. Use the Copy Link, Select Link, and Remove Link commands on this shortcut menu to manage the link as necessary.

Linking notes to pages, sections, and notebooks

In addition to using the Copy Link To Page command to link one page to another, you can use variations of this command to link notes to pages, sections, and notebooks.

To link a note to a page, section, section group, or notebook, right-click the item in the page tabs bar or the Navigation bar, and then choose one of the Copy Link To commands. The command's full name reflects the item you are linking to—Copy Link To Page, Copy Link To Section, Copy Link To Section Group, and Copy Link To Notebook.

 TIP Right-click a paragraph in a note container and choose Copy Link To Paragraph to create a link to a specific note.

After copying the link to the destination, display the note (which could be a note you added previously or a new note) in which you want to include the link, and press Ctrl+V to paste the link. Right-click a link you've added to edit, copy, format, or remove the link. (The Edit Link command on the shortcut menu opens the Link dialog box, which, as mentioned previously, you can use to change the display text for the link or to select another location.)

CREATING A WIKILINK

Enclosing text in a pair of square brackets, such as [[text]], links a note to a page or to a section in the current notebook or in another notebook. Just type the name of the notebook, page, or section between the brackets. (This technique is also used to create links in some wiki pages on websites.) If the page or section is in a closed notebook, OneNote opens the notebook when you click the link.

You can also use the wikilink syntax to create a page and a link to that page at the same time. To do this, type the text you want to use as a page title (which can't duplicate an existing page) between the brackets. OneNote creates the page in the current section.

Working with linked notes

You can use linked notes to connect notes to specific locations in OneNote, as well as to Word documents, PowerPoint presentations, and webpages you view in Internet Explorer. The advantage of using linked notes is that the link between a note and its reference or location is created automatically when you enter a note in the docked OneNote window (assuming that you haven't turned off linked notes). With linked notes, you can do research in one application (reviewing the content on a webpage, for example), type a note in the docked window, and then later use the link to open the page you were using for research.

See Also For detailed information about creating linked notes in Word, PowerPoint, and Internet Explorer, see "Linking notes to other applications" later in this chapter.

On the View tab, click New Docked Window to dock a second OneNote window (which displays the current page) along the right side of the screen. (If you use keyboard shortcuts, press Ctrl+Alt+D to dock the OneNote window.) This command also enables linked notes, which is indicated by the link icon at the top of the docked window. In the docked window, click the ellipsis to display the ribbon. You'll see that the configuration of the

OneNote ribbon changes in the docked window. The Insert, History, and Review tabs are no longer included, and the Home, Draw, and View tabs include a subset of their regular commands.

To create a linked note that refers to another page in a OneNote notebook, display the page you want to add the linked note to in the docked window. Then, in the main One-Note window, open the page you want the linked note to refer to. When you start typing a note in the docked window, you'll see the OneNote program icon displayed to the left of the note container. Point to this icon to see which page the linked note refers to. Click the icon to activate the link and jump to the page.

To work with linked notes, click the down arrow below the linked note icon (in the top-left corner of the docked OneNote window) to display a menu that lets you open a linked file, delete one or more links on the linked note page, stop taking linked notes (and resume taking linked notes again), and set linked note options. Right-click the OneNote icon or the program icon that appears with linked notes you create in Word, PowerPoint, or Internet Explorer (see the next section) to open a menu and open the linked file, copy the link, change the destination of the link, remove the link, or set linked note options.

TIP Linked note options appear on the Advanced page of the OneNote Options dialog box. Clear the Allow Creation Of New Linked Notes check box to turn off the linked notes feature. Clear the check box for the document snippet option if you don't want OneNote to include identifying text with the linked note. Click Remove Links From Linked Notes to remove links from the current notebook. (OneNote prompts you to confirm this operation before the links are removed.)

Linking notes to other applications

Linked notes are also supported in Word, PowerPoint, and Internet Explorer. In each of these programs, the steps to create linked notes are generally the same.

■ **IMPORTANT** You can create linked notes only to saved Word documents and PowerPoint presentations.

Linking notes in Word and PowerPoint

To start using linked notes in Word, click Linked Notes in the OneNote group on the Review tab in Word. The first time you start taking linked notes in a document, OneNote displays the Select Location In OneNote dialog box. Use this dialog box to specify the OneNote page on which you want the linked notes to appear. You can also choose a section, in which case OneNote creates a new page to store the linked notes. After you create linked notes in a document, the page associated with the linked notes is opened automatically in OneNote.

When you start typing a note in the docked OneNote window, OneNote adds the Word icon to the left of the note to indicate that the note is linked to the document. When you point to the icon, OneNote displays a ScreenTip that includes a short passage of the text near the cursor, as shown in Figure 7-7. To associate a specific passage of text with a linked note, select the text in Word, and then type the note in OneNote.

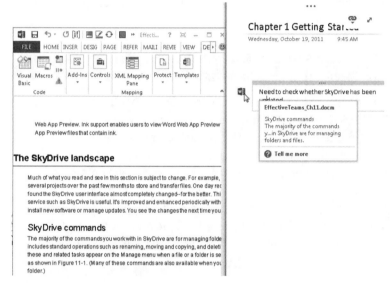

FIGURE 7-7 Use the Linked Notes command in Word to open a OneNote window. Add notes to a page that you can use to navigate back to the Word document to revise and review it.

You follow essentially the same steps to create notes linked to a PowerPoint presentation. In PowerPoint, open the presentation you want to work with, and then click Linked Notes in the OneNote group on the Review tab. Select a location (using the Select Location In OneNote dialog box) if this is the first time you've created linked notes for this presenta-tion. If you have created linked notes previously, OneNote opens the associated page.

Display the slide you want to link a note to, and then type a note in the docked OneNote window. OneNote adds the PowerPoint icon to the left of the note container to indicate that the note is linked.

Linking notes in Internet Explorer

In Internet Explorer 9, you can find the OneNote Linked Notes icon on the command bar. (Right-click to the right of the address box, and then choose Command Bar to display the icon.) Go to the webpage you want to link to a note, and then type the note in the docked OneNote window. This note could be as simple as the title of an article on the page or the name of the site, but it can be more detailed, of course, and indicate the reason you are creating the link, the relationship to your current task, and so on.

To see details about the link, point to the Internet Explorer icon that OneNote adds to indicate that the note is linked. The ScreenTip shows the URL for the webpage and the webpage's title. To open the page, click the icon.

ADDING WEB CONTENT TO ONENOTE

If OneNote isn't running, you can send the content on a webpage to OneNote by choosing Send To OneNote from the menu that appears when you right-click the webpage in Internet Explorer. (The location of this command may vary depending on which version of Internet Explorer you are using.) You can send the entire page or elements (images or text) that you select on the page. By default, the Select Location In OneNote dialog box opens after you choose Send To OneNote. Specify where you want the content to appear, and select the check box at the bottom of the dialog box if you want to set the location as the default location. (Not all the formatting on the webpage will be preserved in OneNote.)

Managing changes and additions to shared notebooks

Sharing notebooks with your team brings with it a few management needs, such as identifying who contributed a recent note and knowing what notes have been added since you last opened the notebook. The commands on the History tab in OneNote let you find notes by different authors, see recent changes to a notebook, hide author initials, and mark other users' notes as read or unread.

Marking coauthor edits as read or unread

When you open a shared notebook, notes added by other users since the last time you opened the notebook are highlighted. In addition, OneNote displays the names of pages with unread notes in bold (see Figure 7-8). Use the commands in the Unread group on the History tab to navigate to pages that contain unread notes and to mark notes as read or unread.

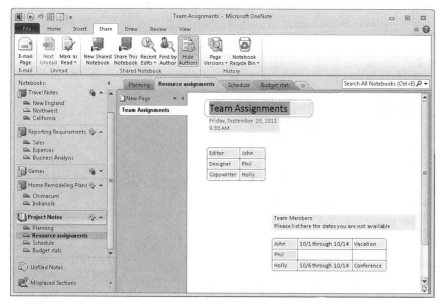

FIGURE 7-8 Unread notes are highlighted, and the names of pages with unread notes appear in bold. Use the Mark As Read menu to manage unread notes.

To move to the next page in a notebook with notes you haven't read, go to the History tab and click Next Unread. Using the commands on the Mark As Read menu, you can do the following to indicate that you've read notes entered by others since the last time you opened a notebook:

- Click Mark As Read (or press Ctrl+Q) to show you have read notes on a page. The notes on the page are no longer highlighted, and the page's name is no longer bold. You can choose Mark As Unread (or press Ctrl+Q) again to revert to showing the highlighting.

- Click Mark Notebook As Read to show you've read all new notes in a notebook.

- Clear the Show Unread Changes In This Notebook check box if you don't want to track the status of new notes.

Viewing recent edits

The Recent Edits menu in the Authors group on the History tab lets you choose an option for seeing the edits made to a notebook over a specific period of time. You can choose Today, for example, to see the most recent changes, or Since Yesterday to review any additions or changes made since the previous day. You can also specify a period of time, such as the last seven days or a span as long as the past six months, or choose All Pages Sorted By Date to see a list of pages organized by time period, as shown in Figure 7-9.

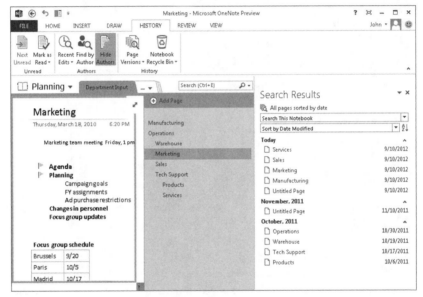

FIGURE 7-9 Click a command on the Recent Edits menu to locate notes added within the timeframe you specify.

When you view recent edits, OneNote opens the Search Results pane and lists sections and pages that match the option you selected. In the Search Results pane, the search scope is set to Search This Notebook by default. You can choose an alternative from the search scope list to search only the current section, search the current section group, or search all open notebooks.

TIP To switch to a different search scope by using the keyboard, press Ctrl+E, press Tab, and then press Space to display the list of options.

Click Sort at the right of the Sort By list to change the order from ascending to descending. Clicking Recent Edits specifies that the Search Results pane is sorted by date modified. After the Search Results pane opens, you can use the Sort By list to organize results by section, title, or author.

Finding notes by author

You can also use the Search Results pane to find notes added or changed by a specific author. Click Find By Author in the Authors group to display the Search Results pane with Sort By Author selected in the list of sorting options.

You can expand and collapse the entries for a particular author by using the arrow to the left of an author's name. Click an entry in the list to jump to that page. Click Sort to sort the entries in ascending or descending order.

> **TIP** You can use the Search Results pane independently of the commands on the History page. You can select a different sorting option, for example, or select a different search scope.

Hiding author initials

In a shared notebook, OneNote identifies the person who inserted or edited a note by displaying that person's name or initials next to the note. You can see more details—the person's full name and the last modified date and time—by pointing to the initials to reveal a ScreenTip.

If you want to see the page without the identifying initials, click Hide Authors in the Authors group on the History tab. To reveal authors again, click Hide Authors a second time. OneNote doesn't identify notes or other content that you add yourself.

Working with page versions

OneNote maintains earlier versions of a page that has been changed by more than one user. To view these versions, on the History tab, click the Page Versions button in the History group, and then choose Page Versions. An entry for each previous version, labeled with the modification date, is added to the page tabs bar, as shown in Figure 7-10.

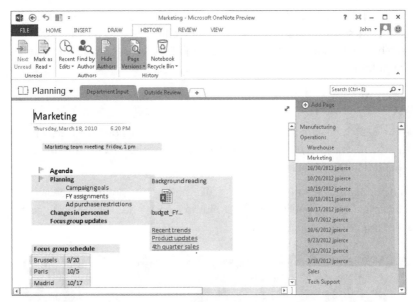

FIGURE 7-10 When you display page versions, you can see when a page was modified and who modified it.

Other options on the Page Versions menu let you delete all previous versions in the current section, section group, or notebook. You can also select Disable History For This Notebook if you don't want OneNote to track previous versions.

When you click a previous version in the page tabs list, a OneNote notification indicates that the page is a previous version, that it will be deleted over time, and that you can click the notification if you want to restore that version to the notebook. The menu that appears when you click the notification includes the commands available on the Page Versions menu as well as commands for deleting that version, copying the earlier version to another location in OneNote, and hiding the list of earlier versions.

Searching notebooks

When a notebook or a set of notebooks are full of information, how do you find the small nuggets of importance that you want to look back on and consider some more? In OneNote, you can search a page, a section or section group, the current notebook, or all open notebooks. OneNote's search feature instantly filters results as you type information in the search box. If you want to work with results in a separate task pane, you can display the Search Results pane, where you can sort results by date or title, for example, and also change the scope of your search.

Searching notebooks, sections, and pages

To search for a word or phrase on the current page, press Ctrl+F to activate the search box. Type the word you are looking for, and OneNote highlights each instance of the word. To the left of the search box, OneNote shows how many instances of the term appear on the page. Move from the first instance to the next (and back) by using the arrows next to the search box, or use F3 and Shift+F3 to move through the page.

 **TIP** You can use the AND and OR operators (use the uppercase characters) to perform more complex searches. Use quotation marks around a term to restrict the results to a specific phrase. For example, type Contoso AND August to find notes that contain both of those terms. Type Contoso OR Adventure Works to find notes related to either company.

To find a note in the current notebook, press Ctrl+E to activate the search box. OneNote displays a list of open notebooks, and as you type your search text, OneNote quickly filters the contents of the list to show you relevant notes.

To change the search scope, click the arrow to the right of the search box and click This Section, This Section Group, This Notebook, or All Notebooks. You can choose Set This Scope As The Default at the bottom of the menu to specify the current scope as the one you want OneNote to use each time you start a search.

OneNote provides a set of keyboard shortcuts you can use to conduct searches and move through results, as summarized in the following table:

TO DO THIS	PRESS
Move the cursor to the search box to search all notebooks.	Ctrl+E
While searching all notebooks, preview the next result.	Down Arrow
While searching all notebooks, go to the selected result and dismiss Search.	Enter
Change the search scope.	Ctrl+E, Tab, Space
Open the Search Results pane.	Alt+O after searching
Search only the current page.	Ctrl+F
While searching the current page, move to the next result.	Enter or F3
While searching the current page, move to the previous result.	Shift+F3
Dismiss search and return to the page.	Esc

Displaying the Search Results pane

Instead of working in the results list, you can open the Search Results pane by clicking the link at the bottom of the results list. In this pane, search results are initially sorted by the date modified. You can also sort by section or by title, and you can use the sort order button to arrange results in ascending or descending order.

By default, the Search Results pane shows search results for the current notebook. To change the scope of the results shown in the Search Results pane, open the list at the top of the pane, and choose Search This Section, Search This Section Group, or Search All Notebooks. The Search pane updates results immediately when you change the search scope or the sorting arrangement.

Tagging notes

Many notes added to a notebook have common attributes. They may pertain to the same event or project, for example, or all be items on the team's to-do list. You can use the tags feature in OneNote to identify and categorize notes. After notes are tagged, you can use the tags to search for and locate certain types of notes or to group notes on a summary page.

To apply a tag to a paragraph, select the paragraph, open the Tags menu on the Home tab, and then select the tag you want to apply. You can apply one or as many as nine tags to each paragraph in a note container. (If you select a note container and apply a tag to it, the tag is applied to each paragraph in the container.) You can also apply a tag as the first step in creating a note by clicking a page, choosing the applicable tag from the menu, and then typing or writing the note. To remove a tag from a paragraph, select the paragraph, open the Tags menu, and then click Remove Tag—or simply right-click the tag, and then choose Remove Tag from the shortcut menu.

Setting up a group of common tags

The default set of tags in OneNote serves as an example of the types of tags you can apply. Teams might use some of the built-in tags from the start, but tagging becomes more useful when you customize the list, removing tags you won't use, modifying those you want to keep, and defining custom tags that the team adopts to identify notes related to its projects, work assignments, and products.

At the bottom of the Tags menu, click Customize Tags to begin defining the set of tags you want to use. Select any tag that you don't need, and then click the Remove button (the delete icon) below the Move Tag Up and Move Tag Down buttons. After you have a list of built-in tags you want to keep, you can use the Move Up and Move Down buttons to reorder the tags, and then define new tags and modify built-in tags to better suit your needs.

To create a new tag, follow these steps:

1. In the Customize Tags dialog box, click **New Tag**.

2. In the New Tag dialog box, type a name for the tag.

3. Using the Symbol, Font Color, and Highlight Color controls, define the visual properties for the tag.

   ■ Under Symbol, click **None** or one of the many choices that OneNote provides.

   ■ You can select from 40 font colors and from 15 highlight options.

   The selections you make are shown in the Preview area of the New Tag dialog box. (You don't need to use each of these formatting options.)

To modify a tag, select the tag and then click Modify Tag in the Customize Tags dialog box. The Modify Tag dialog box contains the same set of controls as the New Tag dialog box, as shown in Figure 7-11. You can update the display name for the tag you are modifying and also make changes to the symbol that represents the tag, the font color, and the highlight color.

FIGURE 7-11 Use the New Tag and Modify Tag dialog boxes to create a custom set of tags that team members use to identify the content in a notebook.

■ **IMPORTANT** Note the statement just above the OK and Cancel buttons in the New Tag and Modify Tag dialog boxes. If you change the appearance of the built-in To Do tag, for example, the tag's appearance doesn't change for existing tagged notes. You'll see the modified tag when you apply the tag from this point forward.

Custom notes become part of the local OneNote profile of the person who creates or modifies the note. For all team members to have access to a common set of tags, each member needs to customize his or her own list. This means that you might need to write down the name and formatting specifications for each tag you want to use, and then each member can work in OneNote to compile those tags.

Even though some team members don't have a specific tag saved in their respective profiles, they will see the tags when they open a notebook that uses them. At this point, team members can copy a custom tag (one at a time) to their profiles by right-clicking the custom tag's symbol and clicking Add To My Tags.

Finding tagged notes

When you click Find Tags in the Tags group on the Home tab, OneNote displays the Tags Summary pane and lists each tagged note in any open notebook under a heading for the tag—all To Do notes are grouped together, for example, as are all the Important notes. You can collapse and expand the tag groups to make your view of the notes in a group more concise. To display the page that contains a tagged note, click its entry in the tag groupings.

TIP To change the view and the results shown in the Tags Summary pane, in the Group By list, change Tag Name (the default view) to Section, Title, Date, or Note Text.

In the Search list below the tag groupings, specify the scope and the time period for locating notes. For the search scope, you can choose from This Page Group, This Section, This Section Group, This Notebook, and All Notebooks. The time period options include Today's Notes, Yesterday's Notes, This Week's Notes, Last Week's Notes, and Older Notes. Click Refresh Results after changing the setting in the Search list to update the results in the Tags Summary pane.

Creating a tag summary page

A tag summary page displays all tagged notes in a section on their own page. Click Create Summary Page in the Tags Summary pane to collect tagged notes on this page. OneNote adds a page to the end of the current section (in a single note container) where you can check off to-do items, for example, or review notes with other types of tags.

The entries on the tag summary page are copies that are linked to the original notes. When you point to a tagged note on the summary page, a OneNote icon appears. Click the icon to display the original note. Although the summary notes are linked to the originals, they are not synchronized copies. This means that if you remove a tag on the summary page or select the check box for a tagged note, the action you take does not change the original note. In addition, notes you add to a section are not automatically added to the summary page.

TIP Click Create Summary Page a second time to create a second summary page. Doing so does not update a summary page already in the notebook.

A few options for configuring how OneNote displays original tags when you create a tag summary page appear on the Advanced page in the OneNote Options dialog box. With the default setting, Leave Original Tagged Notes Unchanged, OneNote shows tagged notes as you see them when you first apply the tags—in other words, tagged notes are displayed the same on the tag summary page and on the pages that contain the original notes. The Show Original Tagged Notes As Dimmed setting displays the tagged notes as they normally appear on the tag summary page, but the tagged notes are dimmed on the original pages. The Show Dimmed Tagged Notes In The Tags Summary Task Pane option includes dimmed tags from the original page and the normal tag from the tag summary page. By selecting this option, you essentially create duplicate entries for tags.

Doing more with OneNote

This section provides an overview of other features you'll find useful from time to time when you work with OneNote on your own or as a team.

Saving the current page as a template

In Chapter 4, "Building team templates," you learned about working with templates in Word, Excel, and PowerPoint. Templates are also a feature of OneNote, which comes with a number of page templates and also lets you define a template of your own. You can review these templates—organized under five default headings (Academic, Blank, Business, Decorative, and Planners)—by clicking Page Templates on the Insert tab.

TIP You can use one of the standard OneNote templates or a page template you create as the default page template for the current section. Open the Templates pane (click Page Templates in the page tabs bar), and then choose the template you want to use from the list under Choose Default Template.

The first step in creating your own page template is to set up the page with the text, images, or other elements you want to work with. If you examine a few of the built-in templates, you can see the types of elements they contain. For example, the Project Overview template, which is included in the Business category, has placeholders for information such as the project name, the project goals, team members, and the schedule.

When the page is ready, follow these steps:

1. In the Templates pane, click **Save Current Page As A Template**.

2. In the Save As Template dialog box, type a name for the template.

3. To use this template as the default template for new pages in the current section, select that option, and then click **Save**.

When you save your own page template, OneNote creates a new category called My Templates and displays the templates in this group at the top of the Templates pane.

Research and references

In OneNote, as in other Office applications, you can look up word definitions and find suitable synonyms in a thesaurus by using the Research pane. (In OneNote, you open the Research pane from the Review tab.) Enter the term you want to look up, and then choose the reference source you want to work with. For example, choose Encarta Dictionary to find a definition, or choose Bing to find additional information about a topic or term. You can navigate through recent searches by using the Back (the ScreenTip refers to this button also as Previous Search) and Next Search buttons.

Sending pages in shareable formats

You can use the Email Page command in the E-Mail group on the Home tab to send a OneNote page via e-mail to recipients you designate. For example, you might do this to share the page with an absent team member or with a partner, vendor, or manager who doesn't meet regularly with the team and doesn't have access to the notebooks you use.

Click Email Page to add the contents of the page, including the page title and the date and time stamp, to a message window in Outlook. OneNote inserts the page's name in the message window's subject line. Add addresses for recipients, update the subject line (if necessary), and then send the message. You can also edit the message's body as necessary.

Other options for sharing the content of a notebook via e-mail appear on the Send page in Backstage view, as shown in Figure 7-12.

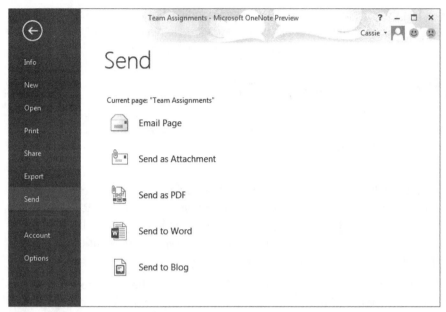

FIGURE 7-12 To distribute a page from a notebook to someone who doesn't have OneNote, open the Send page and select the format for how to send the page in e-mail.

The Send page lists three options for the format of a page you send in e-mail. The Email Page option produces the same result as when you click Email Page on the Home tab. The content of the page appears in the message body. Complete the message by adding e-mail addresses for recipients and making any modifications to the subject line and message body.

The Send As Attachment option attaches the page to the message in two different formats. The page is attached in the .one format as a OneNote section and also in the .mht format, which lets recipients who don't have OneNote open the page in Internet Explorer, Word, or the Word viewer application. (OneNote adds instructions about viewing the .mht file as a webpage to the message's body.)

■ **IMPORTANT**   The .mht file name extension is associated with the MHTML format. (MHTML is an abbreviation for MIME HTML.) The page's contents, including text and images, are saved along with formatting in a single file. You cannot directly open MHTML files in browsers other than Internet Explorer or Opera, but you can install an add-on to work with .mht files in browsers such as Firefox or Safari.

To attach the current page as a PDF file, click Send As PDF. OneNote displays a progress bar to show that the page is being converted to PDF and then displays an Outlook message window with the attachment in place and the name of the page in the subject line. The page name is also used for the file name, with "as PDF" added to identify the format.

Use the Send As PDF option to distribute pages to people who don't have Microsoft Office installed on their computers, for example. Recipients do need at have Adobe Reader or another compatible application installed to open and read a PDF file.

Using the notebook Recycle Bin

Each notebook includes a built-in Recycle Bin where pages and sections are stored when you delete them. OneNote preserves content in the Recycle Bin for 60 days. The content in the Recycle Bin is read-only. You can't edit notes or insert new content when you view pages in the Recycle Bin.

To view the Recycle Bin, right-click a notebook in the Navigation bar, and then click Notebook Recycle Bin. You can also click Notebook Recycle Bin on the History tab. To restore a page or section, right-click the item in the Recycle Bin, and then click Move Or Copy. In the Move Or Copy dialog box, select the location where you want to place the item—in the current notebook or in a different one.

To clear items from the Recycle Bin, click Empty Recycle Bin on the Notebook Recycle Bin menu on the History tab, and then click Yes when OneNote prompts you to confirm the action. If you click Disable History For This Notebook, OneNote displays a message box that prompts you to confirm whether you want to delete page versions and empty the Recycle Bin.

Opening backup notebooks

OneNote maintains backup copies of notebooks on your computer, which it stores in a hidden folder in your user profile. When you need to refer to a backup, click File and then click Open Backups on the Info page. In the Open Backup dialog box, notebooks are organized in folders, and within each folder you can see the backed-up section files with the date the backup was made. Double-click a backup file to open a read-only copy of the page or section in OneNote. The page is displayed under Open Sections, an entry that OneNote adds to the Navigation bar. From the Open Sections area, you can drag sections to any open notebook or right-click a section tab or a page tab and use the Move Or Copy command to add the backed-up page to a notebook.

You control backup settings in the OneNote Options dialog box on the Save & Backup page. You can clear the automatic backup option—which means you run more of a risk of losing data—and also set the backup time period. The intervals range from one minute to six weeks. (All notebooks are affected by these settings.) Click Backup Changed Files Now or Backup All Notebooks Now to create backup copies you can refer to later.

CHAPTER 8

Working on shared documents in Word

TEAMS OFTEN PRODUCE and distribute the content they use internally—such as meeting summaries, task lists, and status reports—without formal reviews. However, the documents, spreadsheets, and presentations that teams share with clients, partners, executives, and others need to meet a high bar. That means additional care is required to ensure that the content is accurate and persuasive and that the formatting is clear and well designed.

In Chapter 4, "Building team templates," you saw how you can incorporate many of the formatting options in Office programs into templates you create in Microsoft Word, Microsoft Excel, and Microsoft PowerPoint. Formatting options like themes can be applied with preset attributes or modified to amplify the goals, capabilities, and accomplishments of a team.

Just as much effort is required to create convincing content, so team members generally don't work in isolation when they are responsible for a work product that will reflect on the team as a whole. It's most often the case that documents of this sort, after they are drafted, will be revised and reviewed more than once by members of the team and possibly by outside reviewers.

In this chapter, you'll learn about the sharing and collaboration features in Word. In Chapter 9, "Collaborating in Excel," I'll describe how teams can collaborate in Excel, and in Chapter 10, "Preparing a presentation as a group," I'll outline a way teams can work together to prepare a presentation in PowerPoint. As you'll see, the collaboration features in Word, Excel, and PowerPoint have a lot in common. In each program, for example, you can annotate a file with comments. You can also merge two or more versions of a file to see changes that reviewers have made to the original. Word, Excel, and PowerPoint (along with Microsoft OneNote) also support coauthoring, a feature that lets more than one person work on a single file at the same time.

> **NOTE**   Coauthoring in Word and PowerPoint is supported only if a document is stored on SharePoint or SkyDrive. Also, each contributor to the document must be using Office 2010, Office 2013, or Word for Mac 2011. You can also coauthor a document using Office Web Apps. To learn more about working with the Web Apps, see Chapter 11, "Working with Office Web Apps on SkyDrive."

Teams can make use of this range of collaborative tools to create, review, and share documents in Word. The specific tools that a team member or a reviewer uses depends on a number of factors, including the following:

- Will all team members working on the document be updating every section, or do some sections require expertise provided by different disciplines, such as finance, design, or legal? Do you need to apply restrictions to some sections of a document so that only the people designated can edit them?

- Where is the document in its life cycle? Is it in draft form, or is it ready for revisions and final proofreading?

- Does everyone who needs to review the document have access to a single copy, or do some reviewers need to work on separate copies for logistical reasons?

You'll learn how the collaboration features in Word can address each of these situations in the sections that follow.

Controlling the editing of a document

When you upload a document to your team site in SharePoint, place it on a network share, or add it to a folder in SkyDrive, you need to consider who can access the document in the location where you store it—and also what restrictions you want to place on the document itself. For some documents, you want to protect specific areas of the content or control how formatting can be applied. For example, should any team member with access to your team site be able to open and edit a contract or a proposal that includes legally binding language as well as financial assumptions and descriptions of complex engineering or design specifications? These documents might contain information that a majority of team members need as context for their work, but you want only some team members to update all or part of them. To manage cases like these, you can share a document with team members in a location that's accessible and then restrict what operations can be performed on the document and who can perform them.

To control how a Word document can be formatted and edited, you specify options and settings in the Restrict Editing pane, which you open by clicking Restrict Editing on the Review tab. Figure 8-1 shows the pane with the options to restrict formatting and editing selected.

FIGURE 8-1 Options in the Restrict Editing pane let you control who can edit specific sections of a document and how the document can be formatted.

You can choose from several options for editing restrictions, including one that allows no changes. You can apply this option generally and then define exceptions that apply to sections of the document and grant access to specific people or to everyone. Formatting restrictions allow you to control which styles can be applied to a document. By choosing only a select group of styles, you can keep the appearance of documents more uniform, avoid unnecessary formatting, and preserve styles that are compatible for working with a document in a more advanced desktop publishing program.

Follow these steps to specify formatting restrictions:

1. In the Formatting Restrictions area, select the check box to limit formatting to a specific set of styles.

   Selecting this option also prevents users of a document from modifying styles and from applying local formatting such as bold and italics.

2. Click **Settings** to open the Formatting Restrictions dialog box, shown below.

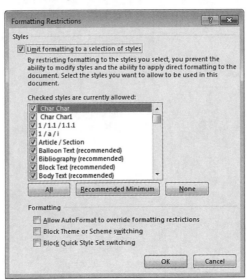

3. In this dialog box, specify the set of styles you want to have available in the document.

   All styles are selected by default. Click **Recommended Minimum** to use a subset of styles that includes standard heading, list, and emphasis styles. To select a specific set of styles, click **None** to clear the check boxes, and then select each style you want to include. For example, you can select only the styles defined for a template associated with the document.

4. In the Formatting area, select the check boxes if you want to allow formatting that Word applies automatically, to block users from switching themes, or to prevent users from changing the group of styles in the Quick Styles gallery.

5. Click **OK** to return to the Restrict Formatting And Editing pane.

6. If the current document contains styles or formatting that aren't allowed by the settings you specified, Word displays a message box that gives you the option to remove the styles and formatting. If you click Yes, Word converts styles that aren't allowed to the default Normal style and removes restricted local formatting.

If you are setting up only formatting restrictions, click Yes, Start Enforcing Protection at this point, and then go to step 7 in the following procedure for more information. To continue by adding editing restrictions, use the following steps:

1. In the Editing Restrictions area, select **Allow Only This Type Of Editing In The Document**.

2. In the list box, choose an option to control the types of changes users can make to the document. The choices are as follows:

    ■ **No Changes (Read Only)**   This prevents users from making revisions, although you can set up exceptions that allow specific users to edit all or certain sections of the document, as you'll see in the steps that follow.

    ■ **Tracked Changes**   Revisions made to the document are indicated by revision marks. Tracked changes cannot be turned off without removing protection.

    ■ **Comments**   Users can add comments to the document, but they can't make revisions to the document's content itself. For this option as well, you can set up exceptions for specific users. (For more information about adding comments in Word, see "Annotating a document" later in the chapter.)

    ■ **Filling In Forms**   This option lets you restrict input to filling in forms that are part of a document.

    If you select No Changes (Read Only) or Comments, use the Exceptions area to specify users who can edit all or sections of a document. Exceptions apply to the complete document by default, but you can also apply exceptions to a particular section of a document by selecting that section and then designating the people who can edit it. (You can also allow everyone to edit specific sections.) You can apply different exceptions to different sections of a document. For each section you want to define exceptions for, select that section and then follow steps 3 and 5.

3. Click the **More Users** link.

4. In the Add Users dialog box, type the names of users, using the format DOMAIN\username or using an e-mail address, as shown below:

5. Click **OK** in the Add Users dialog box. In the Restrict Editing pane, select the check box beside the user's name. You can use the down arrow at the right side of the list box to open a menu that provides options for locating sections the user can edit and an option to remove editing permissions for the user.

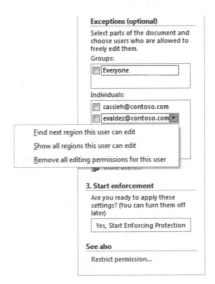

6. Click **Yes, Start Enforcing Protection**.

7. In the Start Enforcing Protection dialog box, type a password that users need to enter to remove protection from the document, or choose **User Authentication** so that only users who are authenticated on the network can remove protection. By choosing this option, you also encrypt the document.

> **TIP** If Information Rights Management isn't already set up, choosing the User Authentication option prompts you to enroll in this service. For more information, see Chapter 3, "Managing access and preserving history." In addition, when you specify User Authentication, the user account you select to manage Information Rights Management for the document is added as an individual with access to the editing exceptions you define.

When a user opens a document that formatting and editing restrictions have been applied to, he or she can use the Restrict Editing pane to find sections that can be edited or stop protection by providing the password. This version of the pane is shown in

Figure 8-2. In addition, in the document, sections that can be edited are highlighted by default.

FIGURE 8-2 Find the editable regions of a document by using the buttons in the Restrict Editing pane.

If editing and formatting restrictions have been protected with the User Authentication option, a user is likely to see the message shown in Figure 8-3 when he or she opens the document. If the user's credentials are verified with the Information Rights Management service, Word opens the document and displays a notification indicating that access is restricted. In the notification, click Change Permission to open the Permission dialog box, which you can use to provide Read and Change permissions to other users and to set other options to control the use of the document.

FIGURE 8-3 Click OK in this message to open a restricted document that is protected with Information Rights Management.

Basic collaboration tools: comments and revision marks

Comments and revision marks provide some of the basic mechanics of working with shared documents. When circulating a draft, for example, team members writing the document can use comments to provide context and guidance to reviewers. When reading the draft, reviewers can insert comments to point out missing or inaccurate data or to call attention to sections that need further revision.

Revision marks (also called tracked changes) create a record of how the text and other content in a document is changed during reviews and updates. Word tracks each revision, highlighting the text that authors and reviewers insert, delete, or move, and also indicates changes in formatting. Revisions (like comments) are identified so that teams know who made a revision and when.

The purpose of both comments and revision marks is to facilitate feedback. Comments appear beside the document's content (or can be read in the Reviewing pane or as ScreenTips). Someone reviewing the document can reply to a comment and, as needed, update the text to address the issue the comment raises. The original comment and replies to it are shown together in the Comments pane, which lets you see the thoughts and actions a comment generates.

Revision marks are integrated into the text and identified by formatting such as underlining or strikethrough. You can switch views to temporarily hide revision marks to see clearly how a revision changes the text and then accept or reject revisions to produce an updated version of the document.

Annotating a document

Comments provide a simple way to review and annotate a document. Teams can use comments to do the following:

- Highlight text or other content that needs to be revised or reformatted
- Pose a question or seek clarification
- Describe decisions to other reviewers of the document
- Provide context or instructions for users of the document

To insert a comment, select the text or object (such as an image or a table) you want to tie the comment to, and then click New Comment on the Review tab. (You can also right-click and choose New Comment from the menu that appears.) Word identifies each comment that's inserted in a file with the name of the user who inserted it. You can see more information—such as when the comment was inserted (which might be a few minutes ago or some days or months in the past)—by pointing to a comment. Right-click the picture or user icon for the person who entered the comment to open a menu that lets you contact that person by instant message, a call, a video conference, or e-mail.

> **TIP** ✓ The user name that identifies comments (and revisions) is specified on the General tab in the Word Options dialog box. For some documents, you might want to be identified by your role or by a different user name. For example, you might want to associate revisions with the user name Engineering if you are reviewing a document on behalf of that department. You can change your identity by clicking File, Options, and then updating the User Name text box on the General tab. (You can also click Change User Name in the Track Changes Options dialog box, shown later in Figure 8-4.) You also need to select the option Always Use These Values Regardless of Sign In To Office. Otherwise, comments will always be identified using the name associated with your account. Any change you make is carried over to other documents. You should revert to your standard user name as necessary.

Depending on the current view (Page Layout or Draft, for example) comments appear in a pane along the side of a document, in the Reviewing pane, or in ScreenTips. Comments are displayed in a pane in the Print Layout, Read Mode, and Web Layout views. In Draft and Outline views, comments are displayed in ScreenTips when you point to the highlighted text. In any view (except Read Mode), you can open the Reviewing pane to see comments. In Read Mode view, comments appear initially as comment icons. Click an icon to read the comment. Choose Show Comments from the Tools menu in Read Mode view to see the text of a comment instead of the icon.

Move from one comment to the next by using the Previous and Next buttons in the Comments group on the Review tab. To reply to a comment, click in a comment balloon and then click New Comment. Word identifies this comment by user name and indents it under the comment above. Use the Delete button in the Comments group to remove a comment or to remove all comments from a file.

If you want to emphasize the text in a comment, you can apply a limited range of font formatting from the Home tab or the mini toolbar. For example, you can apply bold or italic to text in a comment, highlight a comment, and change the font and font color. You cannot, however, change the size of the font.

Tracking changes

Tracking revisions that you and other users make to a document can be straightforward. For example, if three team members are responsible for updating a document, they can in turn check out the file from SharePoint (or open it from SkyDrive or another shared location), turn on the Track Changes option (only the first person to open the file needs to take this step), revise text and other content in the file, and then check the file in. If all the team members who are involved have set an alert in SharePoint, they'll see that the file is available, and the next in line can add his or her revisions to the file. When revisions are complete, the designated team member (the team's lead or maybe one of the reviewers) opens the file, reviews the changes, and accepts or rejects them.

To keep track of revisions in a file, click Track Changes on the Review tab. This setting is preserved when you save the file. The next time someone opens the file, Track Changes is already enabled. With Track Changes turned on, insertions, deletions, and text moves made in the document are highlighted. Changes to formatting and changes made in ink (with pen input) are also tracked by default.

> **NOTE**   If you are working with a document in compatibility mode, text moves are not tracked with distinct highlighting. They are treated as deletions and insertions.

You can also create a password that prevents other users from turning off Track Changes. On the Review tab, click Track Changes and then click Lock Tracking. In the dialog box Word displays, enter and confirm the password.

Setting track changes options

You can set a number of options to modify how Word tracks changes and displays revisions. You manage basic settings for the types of revisions to show—insertions, deletions, formatting, and ink, for example—in the Track Changes Options dialog box, shown in Figure 8-4. In this dialog box, you can also choose a setting for what balloons show in the All Markup view and a display setting for the Reviewing pane. (You'll learn more about the All Markup view and related views later in this section.) To open the Track Changes Options dialog box, click the dialog box launcher in the bottom-right corner of the Review tab's Tracking group.

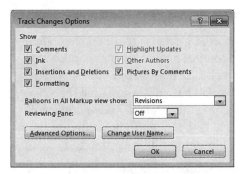

FIGURE 8-4 The default settings for tracking changes provide a clear picture of the revisions made to a document, but for personal preference or for specific documents, you can update the options in the Track Changes Options dialog box.

For more control over the display of revisions, click Advanced Options in the Track Changes Options dialog box. You'll see the dialog box shown in Figure 8-5.

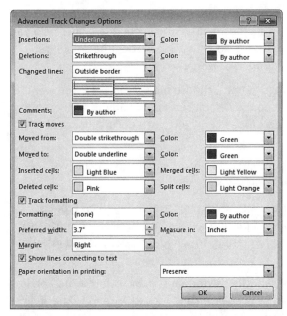

FIGURE 8-5 Advanced settings let you choose options for how insertions, deletions, and other elements of track changes are displayed.

In the Advanced Track Changes Options dialog box, you can do the following:

- Specify formatting for insertions and deletions. By default, insertions are underlined and deletions are shown with strikethrough. Some of the other options for showing insertions are Color Only, Bold, and Italic. For deletions, you can choose formatting options such as Color Only, Bold, and Italic or use a special character (either a carat or an asterisk) to mark where text is deleted. If you choose one of the symbols, the symbol replaces the original text, so you see only where text was deleted (not text with strikethrough as you do with the default setting).

  The settings for insertions and deletions are by user (as are other settings in this dialog box). They do not carry over when another user opens the document on his or her computer. For example, if you choose Bold to mark deletions, that setting is preserved for your use of the document, but if another team member has maintained the default Strikethrough setting, that team member sees deletions with the strikethrough formatting, not in bold.

- Use the Changed Lines list to specify where Word places a line that indicates where a change has been made. In a lightly revised document, these lines help you locate revisions. In the Changed Lines list, keep Outside Border (the default setting) or choose Left Border, Right Border, or None.

- In the Color lists for insertions and deletions, choose the specific color you want to use to identify your changes, or keep the default setting By Author to have Word assign a color to you. Revision marks for each reviewer of a document are displayed in a different color.

- Under Comments, choose a background color that identifies comments you insert, or keep By Author and let Word assign a color.

- When Track Moves is selected, Word applies specific formatting to text that is moved by dragging or by cutting and pasting the text. If you clear the check box for Track Moves, Word applies the formatting specified for deletions and insertions to text that is moved.

  Use the lists under Track Moves to specify the formatting and colors Word applies to identify text that's been moved (Moved From and Moved To) and to specify options for how changes to the layouts in a table are marked. You can manage settings separately for inserted, deleted, merged, and split cells.

- Keep Track Formatting selected to see changes to a document's formatting. In long documents with extensive local formatting (italics, for example), clear this option if you don't need to see each formatting change. By not tracking formatting, you reduce the number of items listed in the Reviewing pane and the number of balloons displayed, which can make reviewing changes more manageable.

- Use the Preferred Width list to control the size of the markup pane. You can also specify a different unit of measure (Measure In) and whether the pane appears along the right or left margin.

- If you expect to print a heavily revised document with a large number of comments, you might consider changing the setting for Paper Orientation In Printing from Preserve (which uses the orientation specified on the Page Layout tab) to Force Landscape, which provides more room for comments along the side of the page.

Reviewing a file

Reading through a heavily revised document that also includes a number of comments and annotations—something like you see in Figure 8-6—can be time-consuming. You want to understand the effect of each revision by seeing how the original text was changed. The additional formatting and the gaps in the readable text can hinder your comprehension.

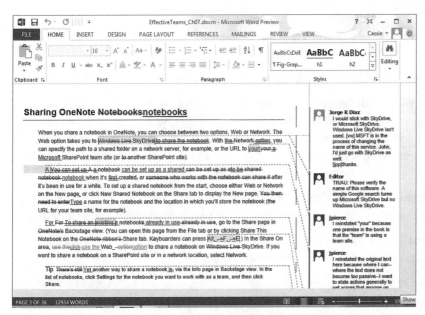

FIGURE 8-6 A heavily revised and annotated document can be difficult to review. Word provides options for temporarily hiding revision marks to make reading easier.

To adjust the view of how revisions are shown in a document, select one of the views available in the Display For Review list at the top of the Tracking group to temporarily show or hide revisions:

- **Simple Markup** The default option, shows the document as though revisions have been accepted. Comments are shown as icons that you can click to read the comment. Word marks areas of the document where revisions occur with a line along the side of the window. You can go to a revised section and then switch views to see the details for each change.

- **All Markup** Shows insertions and deletions in the colors assigned to reviewers. The full text of comments are shown along the side in Print Layout view.

- **No Markup** Shows the document with insertions, deletions, and other revisions accepted, but without any cues to where revisions have been made. No comment icons are displayed either. Use this view to read the document in its current edited state.

- **Original** Shows how the original document appeared without any revisions (as the document would appear if all revisions were rejected).

In addition to switching views, you can use the Show Markup menu to control and filter the types of revisions you see. Here are the options you can choose from:

- **Comments** Shows or hides comments. Clear this option if you want to view the document without comments showing.

- **Ink** Shows or hides any annotations or revisions made in ink.

- **Insertions And Deletions** Clear this option to hide revision marks. If you are revising a document, clearing this option is often helpful because you can read the text and see the effect of your changes without seeing the revision marks themselves. Word still tracks changes and shows them when you select this option again.

- **Formatting** Clear the check mark for Formatting to suppress the corresponding balloons or other highlighting in a document that indicate formatting changes.

- **Balloons** Controls whether Word shows revisions in balloons or inline or shows only comments and formatting changes in balloons.

- **Specific People** Word shows changes by all reviewers of a document by default. If you want to see the changes made by a specific reviewer or a particular set of reviewers, click Specific People, click All Reviewers to remove the check mark, and then open the menu again and select the reviewer or reviewers whose work you want to inspect. This option is particularly helpful when you want to see revisions made by someone with a specific perspective on a document—for example, a product's marketing manager. You can choose that reviewer from this list and then scan the document to find the changes and comments this individual made.

If you want to work with revisions in a separate pane, click Reviewing Pane and choose the location where you want Word to display it (in a horizontal or vertical layout). The pane shows you the collection of revisions made to a document and also displays a set of statistics about how many of each type of change the document contains.

Accepting and rejecting changes

When you need to accept and reject changes, you have a couple of choices for how to do this work. In the Reviewing pane, you can right-click an insertion or a deletion and then accept or reject it. Working in the Reviewing pane can be cumbersome, however, so you might prefer to work in the document itself. Close the Reviewing pane by clicking the X in the pane's upper-right corner or by clicking Reviewing Pane on the Review tab.

When the Reviewing pane is closed, you can use commands in the Changes group to navigate from change to change (by clicking Previous or Next) and to accept or reject the changes showing in the document. The Accept and Reject menus have similar sets of commands, such as Accept And Move To Next, Accept All Changes Shown, Reject Change, and Reject All Changes In Document. You can also choose Accept All Changes And Stop Tracking (or the comparable command for rejecting changes) to manage changes at once and no longer track changes.

The Accept (or Reject) All Changes Shown command is active only when you select an option other than All Reviewers from the Show Markup menu described in the previous section. By filtering which reviewers' changes are showing, you can accept or reject revisions made by a particular reviewer or set of reviewers. To do that, follow these steps:

1. On the Review tab, in the Tracking group, click **Show Markup, Specific People**.

2. Clear the check mark next to All Reviewers, and then repeat step 1 and select the first (or only) reviewer whose revisions you want to see. Repeat step 1 again to select any other reviewer.

3. In the Changes group, click the arrow under Accept (or Reject) and then click **Accept All Changes Shown** or **Reject All Changes Shown** to work with this group of revisions all at once.

TIP   You can also right-click a change and then click Accept Insertion or Reject Insertion, for example.

Comparing and combining documents

When each team member involved in producing a document can work on the same copy, tracking changes is a good approach. (You can also use coauthoring to share a single copy of a file. Coauthoring is described later in this chapter.) In cases when reviewers need to work on separate copies of a document, you can distribute copies of the file to reviewers, collect the copies, and then use the Combine command to produce a single document that displays and identifies revisions.

In other cases, you might simply want to compare two versions of a document to see how the versions differ. You aren't as concerned about who made revisions; you simply want to know how the content in one version compares to content in the other.

The Compare and Combine commands provide similar results, but you apply them in different circumstances. Use Compare when you want to see the differences between two documents. Use the Combine command to merge revisions in two or more versions of a document and to identify who made the revisions.

Comparing documents

Let's say you're the team member in charge of preparing a proposal. On the team's SharePoint site you find two documents, both in the proposal template, that you want to use as the basis of the proposal you need to compile. One document was sent to the same client you're working with, but it was created two years ago, before you joined the team. The second document is dated three months ago, and you know the proposal process changed just before that document was prepared. You can compare these documents to see how they differ.

When you compare two documents, the differences between the original document—in this case, the proposal given to your client two years ago—and the revised document—the one the team prepared more recently—are shown in the original document (or in a new document) as tracked changes. For the best results when you use the Compare command, the original and the revised documents should not contain any revision marks. If either document does, Word treats the documents as though the changes have been accepted.

Here are the steps you follow to compare two documents:

1. On the Review tab, click the **Compare** button, and then click the **Compare** command.

2. In the Compare Documents dialog box, shown below, click the More button if you don't see the Comparison Settings and Show Changes areas. (The More button becomes the Less button shown in the screen shot.)

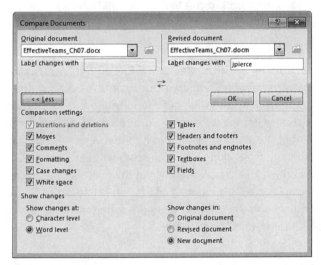

3. In the Original Document list, select the original document or click the folder icon to browse to the file.

4. In the Revised Document list, select the document you want to compare with the original.

5. By default, all the options in the Comparison Settings area are selected. You can clear the check box for any option other than Insertions And Deletions. If you don't need to see formatting differences, for example, clear the **Formatting** option. If you are interested chiefly in comparing the differences in the main body of each document, you might also clear the check boxes for Comments, Case Changes (whether a character is lowercase or uppercase), White Space, Headers And Footers, and Fields.

6. Under Show Changes, Word Level is selected by default. Select the **Character Level** option to show when a change is made to a few characters of a word, such as when only the case of the first letter is changed. At the word level, the entire word is shown as a revision; at the character level, only the letter is shown as a revision.

7. Under Show Changes In, select **Original Document** to display the differences there (although you might not want to alter the original document in that way). Select **Revised Document** to add changes to that document, or select **New Document** (which is always a safe choice) to create a document based on the original with the differences shown with tracked changes.

8. Click **OK**.

Revisions in the comparison document are attributed to a single author and are displayed in a document window with the title Compared Document. You can use the Previous and Next buttons in the Review tab's Changes group to move from change to change, view them, and accept or reject the differences. You can also view the compared, original, and revised document at the same time—if that isn't the view Word provides when it completes the comparison—by clicking Show Source Documents on the Compare menu and clicking Show Both. (An example is shown in the next section in Figure 8-7.) Other options on the Show Source Documents menu include Hide Source Documents (which removes the original and the revised document from the view, keeping the compared document), Show Original, and Show Revised.

Combining documents

You're still in charge of creating a proposal, but in this case you need to send a draft to three outside firms who will be your team's partners in this project. You need their comments on the sections you wrote about the work they'll provide and about the sections that detail work you'll do together. When you get the documents back, you want to merge them with the original draft you're working on to see the changes each firm inserted. In a case like this, you need to combine the documents. You can combine more than one document, but you combine each document with the original one at a time.

When you combine documents, differences between the original and revised documents are shown as tracked changes. If a revised document includes tracked changes, these changes are also displayed in the combined document as tracked changes. Each reviewer is identified in the combined document as well.

To combine two or more documents into a single document, follow these steps:

1. Open a blank document in Word. (You can also start with the original document or one of the revised documents open.)

2. On the Review tab, click **Compare**, and then click **Combine**.

3. In the Combine Documents dialog box, shown below, select the original document. (It might be selected already.)

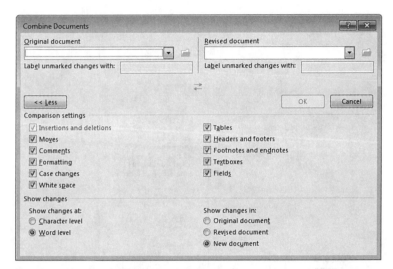

4. Select the revised document you want to combine with the original document. You can combine only one document at a time with the original document. To combine additional documents, you need to repeat this procedure.

5. In the Comparison Settings area (click **More** if this area is not displayed), clear the check boxes for any settings that you don't need to account for. For example, clear **Headers And Footers** if that aspect of the document is not significant to the combined result.

6. In the Show Changes At area, choose the option to show changes at the character level or the word level.

7. In the Show Changes In area, choose an option for where Word will show changes: in the original document, the revised document, or a new document.

When you click OK in the Combine Documents dialog box, Word is likely to display a message box telling you that only one set of formatting changes can be stored in the combined document. You need to choose between the changes in the original document and the revised document to continue combining the documents.

Word can display the results of combining documents in a set of windows that shows the combined document in a central pane and the original and revised documents in smaller panes at the right. To set up this display, point to Show Source Documents on the Compare menu and then choose Show Both. To facilitate your review of the combined document, Word also displays the Revisions pane along the left side of the window, as you can see in Figure 8-7.

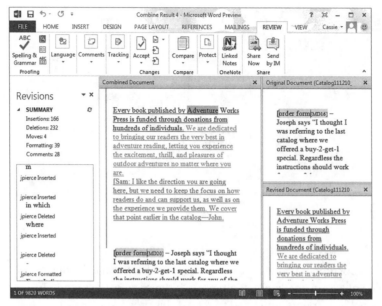

FIGURE 8-7 To review a combined document, you can display the original, revised, and combined documents in a single view.

If you need to merge another version of the document, choose Combine from the Compare menu again. Select the combined document (Combined Document in Figure 8-7) as the original document, and then select the next file you want to combine.

To save the combined result, click Save on the Quick Access Toolbar (or click File, Save) and then name the combined document. You can then open the combined document and work through the variations (indicated by revision marks), accepting and rejecting them as necessary, to achieve a final document.

REVIEWING A COMBINED DOCUMENT

When you have the combined document and both source documents displayed (as in Figure 8-7), you can scroll through the combined document and the original and revised documents at the same time. Your location in each document is synchronized, which lets you refer to any of the documents as you need to.

Coauthoring documents in Word

This section introduces coauthoring, a feature that's available in several of the Office programs. Coauthoring gives team members the ability to work simultaneously on documents—in other words, more than one team member can be writing or editing the file at the same time. This doesn't mean, however, that team members who are working on a coauthored document always need to schedule a time to work together. Although these occasions will occur—and coauthoring sessions might be scheduled—the broader purpose of coauthoring is that team members can work on the document when they need to. No team member who's contributing to the document needs to wait for another team member to save and close the file before he or she can start working on the file.

The requirements for coauthoring are that you store the file on a SharePoint site or on SkyDrive and that each team member who needs to work on the document uses Word 2010, Word 2013, or Word for Mac 2011. Coauthoring works the same whether the file is saved on SharePoint or SkyDrive, but you get additional options for comparing and managing versions of a shared file by storing it in SharePoint. You'll learn more details about working with versions of a coauthored document later in this section.

Word coauthoring basics

In Word, if the document isn't already in SharePoint or on SkyDrive, start by using the Save As page in Backstage view to save the document to a shared location. (You can, of course, also upload the document when you are working in a SharePoint document library or add it to a SkyDrive folder when you're signed in and working in SkyDrive.) For the team site, you can choose a library from the list of recent folders or click Browse to find the library you want to use. If you are storing the file on SkyDrive, you might need to sign in with your Microsoft account user name and password before Word lists available folders.

OPTIONS FOR SHARING AND EXPORTING DOCUMENTS

As you'll see in Chapter 9 and Chapter 10, the Share and Export pages in Excel and PowerPoint, as well as in Word, provide several options that are designed for sharing files. For example, the Share page provides commands for sending a file as an e-mail attachment and for making an online presentation. In Chapter 9, you'll see how to apply some of these commands in more detail, and in Chapter 10, you'll learn about commands designed specifically for your work in PowerPoint.

■ **IMPORTANT**   **If your team is using a SharePoint document library as the location for sharing a file you want to work on as coauthors, you (or another team member) should not check out the file before you open it. You need only to open the file from Word or from the shared library or folder where it's stored.**

When another team member opens the file when you are already working in it, you'll see a notification like the one shown in Figure 8-8. The status bar also indicates that the document is being shared, and you can find this information on the Info page in Backstage view as well.

FIGURE 8-8 Word displays a notification when a coauthor starts editing a shared document.

When a team member starts editing a section of the document, Word blocks other users working on the file from making changes to that section. On your screen, Word brackets the paragraph and displays a ScreenTip indicating who is working in that section and telling you the section is blocked. Figure 8-9 shows an example. As you can see, coauthoring is also integrated with Microsoft Lync. By pointing to the coauthor's name, you can display a small contact card that tells you about your coauthor's status and provides buttons for contacting the coauthor by instant message, a call, or e-mail. You can also start a video call to share ideas.

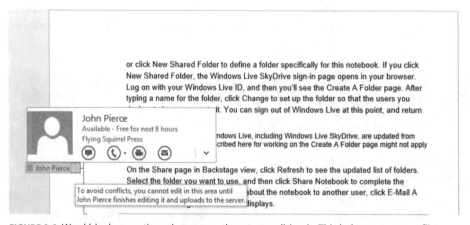

FIGURE 8-9 Word blocks a section when a coauthor starts editing it. This helps prevent conflicts.

The section remains blocked until the person editing the section saves the file. Saving the file refreshes the copy that's stored in SharePoint or on SkyDrive and alerts you and other users that an updated copy is available. The alert appears on the status bar (where you'll see the notification Updates Available) and on the Info page in Backstage view. To retrieve the updated copy, you also need to save the file. Areas where changes were made are highlighted in green.

Blocking authors

As I mentioned in the last section, Word automatically locks the section of a document a coauthor is working on. You can also reserve sections to yourself by blocking other authors manually. By blocking other authors, you can work on portions of a document and then save changes without freeing the section for use by coauthors. This lets you complete and preserve the writing or revisions you have underway without running into potential conflicts. (You'll learn more about resolving conflicts in coauthoring later in the chapter.)

To block authors, follow these steps:

1. Select the paragraph or paragraphs you want to edit exclusively.

2. On the Review tab, in the Protect group, click **Block Authors**.

   Word brackets that section and displays an icon to the left of it to indicate that you blocked other authors from editing this section. Other coauthors will see a notification such as shown below. Notice that in this notification, Word indicates that the section is blocked until the person editing it unblocks the section.

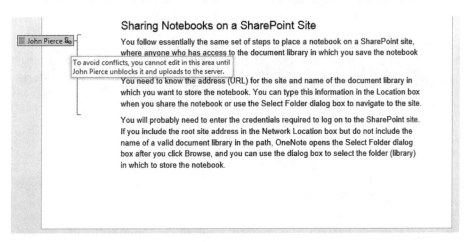

3. With the section blocked, make the changes you want. You can save the file without releasing the sections you reserved.

4. When you're ready to make the section available for others to edit again, click
   Block Authors, Release All Of My Block Areas.

5. Save the file to refresh the copy on the server so that coauthors can update the
   copy they're working on.

After you release blocked sections and save the file, other team members working in the
file are notified that updates are available. They need to save the file to refresh their copy
with your updates. When the file is updated, Word highlights changes you entered so
that others can see them.

Resolving conflicts

Word is quick to recognize when a coauthor starts editing a section of a shared document, and Word then blocks other authors from editing that section to avoid conflicts.
But conflicts will occur when team members share a document. Two people working on
the document can simply start editing the same paragraph at the same time and make
conflicting changes before Word can lock that section. Conflicts can occur as well when
one team member updates a document while working offline and then saves the document to the server (where the current version contains conflicting changes that were
made by other users online).

If conflicts occur, Word displays a notification when you save the document, as shown
in Figure 8-10. You then need to work with the Conflicting Changes pane (which lists
conflicts) and the Conflicts tab (which provides commands you use to accept or reject
conflicts) to resolve conflicts before you can save the document to the shared location
again.

> **NOTE**   Changes in the document are saved on your computer even though the
> document contains conflicts, but the changes aren't saved to the server
> until the conflicts are resolved.

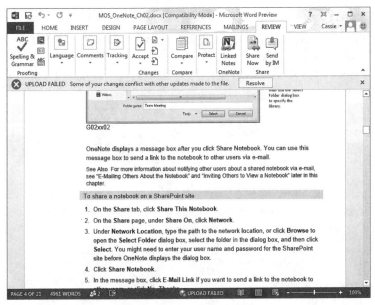

FIGURE 8-10 When conflicts occur, Word won't upload the shared document. You need to resolve conflicts before you save to the server again.

To resolve conflicts, follow these steps:

1. Click the notification in the message bar, and then click **Resolve**.

2. In the Conflicting Changes pane, click a conflicting change. Word highlights the conflicting text in the document.

3. On the Conflicts tab, click **Accept My Change** to preserve the change you made, or click **Reject My Change** to preserve the conflicting change.

4. Use the Conflicts tab to add a comment to the file if you can't resolve the conflict without consultation with others.

5. When all conflicts are resolved, you'll see the notification shown below. Click **Save And Close View** to update the file in the shared location.

Comparing versions

As you've seen in this section, when you work on a file set up for coauthoring, saving the file saves your changes to the file on SharePoint or SkyDrive and updates the file you are viewing with changes made by coauthors. If the file is stored on SharePoint, saving it also stores the previous version.

> **NOTE**   You can view previous versions of a file on SkyDrive, but not when working in Word, as you can for files stored on SharePoint.

You can view and compare earlier versions of a shared file by switching to the File tab and working with the list of versions shown on the Info page. You can also work with options on the Manage Versions menu, as shown in Figure 8-11.

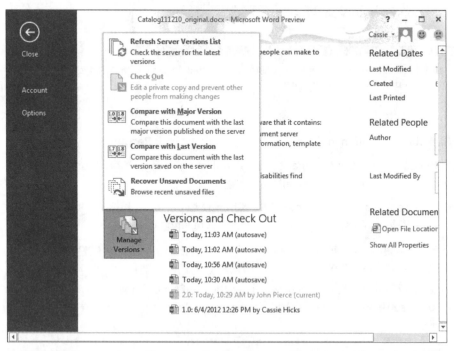

FIGURE 8-11 When you store a file on SharePoint, you can use this menu and the version list to manage, compare, and restore versions.

To view a specific version, double-click a version in the list (for example, version 1.0, shown in the figure), or one of the interim versions Word saved automatically. Word opens the version you selected and also displays a notification indicating that you are viewing a previous version. In the notification, click Compare to compare the previous version with the current version. Changes are shown in a new compared document, with the original and revised documents displayed in smaller windows, as in Figure 8-7, earlier in this chapter. You can scroll through the compared document to see changes shown in revision marks and use the commands in the Changes group on the Review tab to accept and reject changes. The document Word creates to show the comparison is not tied to the file in SharePoint. If you save this document to keep as the current version, you need to save it to the library again.

The other option Word provides when you view a previous version is Restore. When you click this option in the notification, Word makes the previous version the current version in the library.

You can use the Manage Versions menu on the Info page to compare the current document with the last major version published to the library or with the last version saved to the library. You can also use this menu to refresh the version list and to recover any versions of the document that have not yet been saved.

See Also   To learn more about managing versions in SharePoint, including publishing major versions of a document, see Chapter 3.

CHAPTER 9

Collaborating in Excel

A GLANCE AT the categories of Microsoft Excel templates listed on the New page in Backstage view or available on *www.office.com* shows you the assortment of information that can be managed in Excel—budgets, calendars and schedules, lists, reports, and timesheets are just a few examples. And as you'll see in this chapter, when teams use Excel in collaborative scenarios, team members can work independently and together in a variety of ways, from distributing all or a portion of a workbook as an e-mail attachment to sharing a workbook so that more than one person can work on the file at the same time.

Most teams will use a mix of the collaborative features in Excel to set up, review, and maintain data. Which techniques a team uses depends in part on the type of information stored in the workbook, as well as on requirements and processes that your team or organization needs to follow. Here are some situations and questions that can serve as a guide:

- Does the workbook contain proprietary information such as your profit margin, markup, or tax calculations? If you answer yes to this question, you probably want to restrict who can see formulas and other assumptions that underlie the information in the workbook. In this case, you might not want to distribute or share the workbook itself, but distribute a snapshot or static copy of the data it contains.

■ Does the workbook contain confidential information, such as salaries or human resource data? Perhaps a workbook such as this should not be shared at all, but if it is, changes to the workbook should be tightly managed.

■ Is everyone on the team responsible for information in a workbook or only one or two individuals? If only a few team members are responsible for maintaining a workbook, but the team at large provides feedback on workbook data, you can distribute separate copies of the workbook and then review and merge changes.

■ Is the workbook suitable for simultaneous editing? For example, you can share a workbook that's designed as a status report or task list so that team members have access to it and can add and update information even when another member has it open. If you do enable simultaneous editing, you need to decide how to manage conflicts between changes that users enter, which you'll learn about later in this chapter.

■ Does your team's configuration or its work habits require that a workbook be accessible on the Internet, outside an organization's domain? If so, you can store a workbook on SkyDrive. Teams can use the Excel Web App in these situations to update a workbook as coauthors.

See Also   For more information about coauthoring in the Excel Web App, see Chapter 11, "Working with Office Web Apps on SkyDrive."

Making use of file formats and annotations

One regular aspect of collaboration is simply getting information to other people, who might be everyday members of your team, colleagues in other departments, company executives, prospective customers or clients, or business partners. In some cases, the systems you put in place, like a SharePoint team site, aren't easily accessible to everyone in these groups, or, perhaps more to the point, you don't want everyone you involve in the scope of your activities to participate in that system for reasons of simplicity of process, limitations on administrative resources, or the need to keep at least some information more confidential.

Another issue you need to address from time to time is how to provide context, emphasis, and explanations for information and analysis that might be clear to you and other members of your team but isn't familiar to people you want to inform and consult with about decisions you've made or about the status of your work. This need can also arise within a team. For example, perhaps financial experts or people in other roles who use Excel frequently need to identify information in a fairly complex spreadsheet so that other team members can understand what's relevant to their work.

Distributing Excel files in other formats

To save Excel files in different formats—which you might do when you distribute the files for review or informational purposes—you can use options on the Export page on the File tab. Figure 9-1 shows the Export page with the Create PDF/XPS Document option selected.

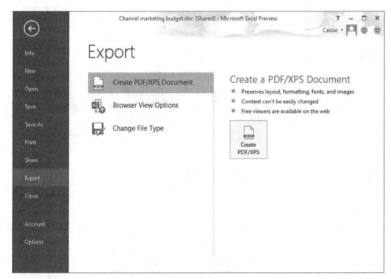

FIGURE 9-1 To distribute a workbook to others, you can create a PDF file or change the file type, including to earlier versions of Excel.

See Also   You'll learn more about the Browser View Options command later in this chapter, in the section "Sharing Excel files on SkyDrive or SharePoint."

Creating a PDF/XPS document

When you want to provide information to others but don't want to attach the Excel file itself, you can create a PDF or XPS document. (If you aren't familiar with XPS, it is a portable document format designed by Microsoft that lets you view a file in a web browser or an XPS viewer.) Files you distribute in either of these formats show the workbook's data (and retain formatting applied in Excel), but recipients can't see how the workbook was put together by viewing formulas, data validation ranges, or conditional formatting rules, for example. The information in the file is not easily editable, and any changes that can be made aren't made to the workbook itself.

You also gain access to publishing options when you use the Create PDF/XPS Document command, as you can see in Figure 9-2. Click Options in the Publish As PDF Or XPS dialog box to specify a page range or whether to create a file of the entire workbook, the active sheet, or a portion of a worksheet that you've selected. The Selection option might be particularly helpful when you are in the middle of compiling a spreadsheet but want feedback from someone else on a particular portion. Select the rows and columns you want the other team member to review, create a PDF or XPS file that shows just that selection, and then attach that file to an instant message in Lync.

> **NOTE**   If you don't want to include document properties (such as the workbook's author), clear the Document Properties option. Keep the Document Structure Tags For Accessibility option selected if you want to include tags used by screen readers and other technologies designed for accessibility. The PDF/A format is designed for archiving electronic files. Select the check box under PDF Options if you are creating a file you want to maintain in an archive.

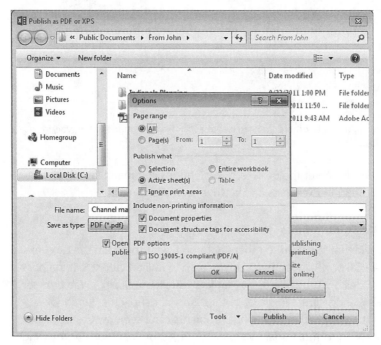

FIGURE 9-2 When you create a PDF or XPS version of a workbook, you can specify a page range and also choose to publish the full workbook, the active sheet, or a cell range you've selected.

TIP   If you want to view the PDF or XPS file when you save it, select the Open File After Publishing option in the Publish As PDF Or XPS dialog box.

Saving files in different formats

Within your team (especially if you all work for the same company), it's likely that you all use the same version of Microsoft Office. If that's not the case, or when you need to send a workbook to a partner or another person outside your team, you can save the file in a different workbook file type (the Excel 97-2003 Workbook format, for example) or one of several other formats, included as a text file, as you can see in Figure 9-3.

FIGURE 9-3 Convert a workbook to a different file type to share it with people who don't use Excel, use an earlier version of the program, or need to import Excel data into a database.

One example of a file type you can choose is the OpenDocument Spreadsheet format, which saves the workbook in an XML-based format that's readable by programs that aren't Office programs. A tab-delimited text file or comma-separated value file (not shown in Figure 9-3) are often compatible formats when data in Excel needs to be imported into a database such as Microsoft Access or Microsoft SQL Server.

QUICK SHARING WITH LYNC

Chapter 6, "Working together in Lync," describes how you can share a program (or your whole desktop) during a conference call or online meeting so that participants can review and update a file as they meet. You can also share information in Lync directly from Excel by using the Present Online command on the Share page.

To share the current workbook in Lync, click Present Online, and then click Share. (If you aren't signed in to Lync, you're prompted to do so at this point.) In the Share Workbook Window, shown in the following screen shot, you can choose a meeting that's already scheduled (including one you're already attending) or initiate a new meeting. Invite team members to join you, and then start a conversation via instant message, a Lync call, or a video conference. If you're the one who shares the workbook, Lync notifies you that you are presenting. Participants you invite to the meeting can accept the sharing request and then see the shared file on their computers.

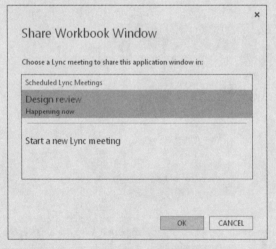

See Also For more details about sharing programs, see the section "Collaboration tools" in Chapter 6.

You can also share a workbook as an attachment to an instant message you send in Lync. When you are signed in to Lync, the Send By Instant Message command appears on the File tab's Share page. Click this command, address the instant message, replace the default subject line (which is initially simply the name of the workbook), type a message, and then click Send IM.

The Share group on the Review tab in Excel includes similar commands (assuming that Lync is installed). Use Share Now to invite Lync contacts to an online conference that features the open worksheet. Click Send By IM to attach the workbook to an instant message session. Lync must be running for you to use these commands.

Sending an Excel file in e-mail

You can distribute a workbook via e-mail by using the Email command on the File tab's Share page. Click Send As Attachment to open a Microsoft Outlook message item with the current workbook added as a file attachment. Address the e-mail message, provide some context in the message's body, and send it.

Taking this step poses no special issues if the recipients of the workbook know about the data it contains and you aren't concerned that the file you attached is editable and that people viewing it can see not only the data but also any formulas used for analysis or calculations. If you want to convert the workbook to a less revealing format before you send your message, choose Send As PDF or Send As XPS. Choosing either of these commands opens an Outlook message item with the current workbook attached in the format you select. As you saw earlier in this chapter, you can also use the Create PDF/XPS Document command on the Export page to convert a workbook to one of these formats. Save a copy of the workbook as a PDF or XPS file, instead of sending it directly as an attachment, when you want the option to save a selected cell range, for example, or only the active worksheet.

Annotating and reviewing worksheets by using comments

On complex worksheets and on any worksheet to highlight specific information, you can use comments to identify the data that a certain cell requires, provide context, and explain assumptions.

Comments are also useful when team members are reviewing a workbook. Comments allow a reviewer to ask questions and suggest changes without affecting the structure of the worksheet or changing the data.

A comment in Excel is attached to a particular cell. A small triangle at the top-right corner of a cell indicates the cell contains a comment. Nothing prevents you from associating a comment with a range of cells, but even if a range of cells is selected when you add a comment, the indicator appears only in the cell that is at the top left of the range.

You'll find the Comments group on the Review tab. Select a cell and then use the New Comment button to insert a comment. (The name of the New Comment button changes to Edit Comment when a commented cell is selected.) The other commands in the group let you delete a comment that's no longer needed, navigate from comment to comment (Previous and Next), and control whether comments are displayed. Click Show All Comments to display the full set of comments in a worksheet. Use the Show/Hide button to display or hide a comment in the selected cell. Use the Show Ink button to show or hide comments written with a pen device.

When you point to a commented cell, Excel shows a ScreenTip that identifies who made the comment and displays the text of the comment itself. A simple example is shown in Figure 9-4.

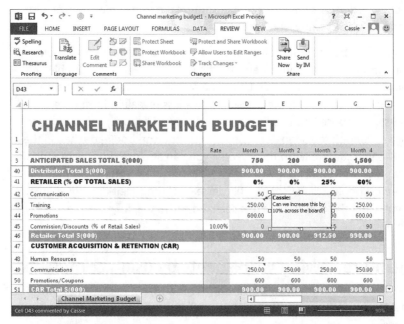

FIGURE 9-4 Reviewers of a worksheet can use comments to raise questions or suggest changes. Comments can also be used to provide context and directions to people who use a workbook.

All comments won't have equal importance, and that's where you can make use of simple comment formatting. (You aren't limited to simple formatting in a comment, as you'll see next.) To draw attention to a comment, you can use a different font or font color, for example. Here are the steps you follow to change the standard font formatting in a comment:

1. Right-click a commented cell, and then click **Edit Comment**. (Or select the cell, and then click **Edit Comment** on the ribbon).

2. In the comment container, select the text you want to format.

3. Right-click the comment container, and then click **Format Comment**, which displays the Format Comment dialog box, shown here:

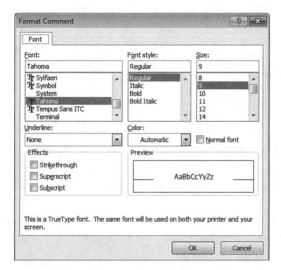

4. Use the controls on the dialog box's Font tab to change fonts, apply bold or italic (or a combination), change the font size or color, and apply other formatting effects.

 TIP When a comment is open and available for editing, you can also select text in the comment and apply formatting by using the formatting controls on the Home tab.

Applying a variety of font properties is not where comment formatting leaves off. To open an expanded version of the Format Comment dialog box, right-click a commented cell, choose Edit Comment, right-click on the border of the comment container, and then choose Format Comment. The Format Comment dialog box now includes eight tabs. The Colors And Lines tab is active in Figure 9-5.

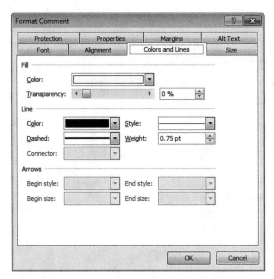

FIGURE 9-5 For comments that need a variety of formatting for emphasis or effect, you can apply colored lines, change margins, and adjust the size of the ScreenTip, among other formatting changes.

Explore the tabs in this version of the dialog box to see the range of formatting you can apply. Here's a list of what you can do in addition to changing the font properties of a comment:

- **Alignment tab** Set the horizontal and vertical alignment of the text (Left, Center, Right, Top, Bottom, Justify, and Distribute are the options), change the orientation of the text, and change the text direction.

- **Colors And Lines tab** Apply a different background color to a comment container, add fills, and change properties of the comment container's lines.

- **Size tab** Set the height and width of a comment container. Use the Scale area on this tab to change the relative proportions of the container's height and width. (You can also change the size of a comment by dragging the handles on the comment's border.)

- **Protection tab** If you have applied protection to a worksheet, use the Protection tab to lock the comment container and the comment text. For details about protecting worksheets in Excel, see Chapter 3, "Managing access and preserving history."

- **Properties tab** Use the options on the Properties tab to control whether a comment container changes size or position when you move or resize the cell it is associated with.

- **Margins tab**   If you don't want to use the default margins set for a comment container, clear the Automatic option on this tab and then specify the margins you want to use.

- **Alt Text tab**   Alt (for alternative) text is used by web browsers in lieu of a missing image and for user assistance and by search engines to locate a webpage. You can consider changing the default alt text (the text of the comment and the name of the person who inserted the comment) if you are planning to post a worksheet on the web.

Distributing and merging multiple workbooks

As I mentioned at the start of the chapter, how a team works together in Excel is influenced in part by the degree to which the information in Excel needs to be controlled. Controlling information means, among other things, determining who can make changes to a shared worksheet: a single team member, a handful of team members, or all team members. You can control through permissions who has access to a SharePoint document library and what operations individuals and groups can perform on a file. That's a very workable approach in many cases—and you'll learn more about sharing a workbook on SharePoint and on the web later in this chapter.

See Also   For more information about managing permissions in SharePoint, see Chapter 2, "Building a SharePoint team site."

But there's another scenario that comes into play. How do you manage a workbook that needs input from multiple people (team members and others) when for reasons of control you don't want to post the file to a location that's generally accessible—when, in this instance, you don't want the group to work in a single file? One solution is to distribute copies, collect them, and merge them.

To implement this solution, you first need to set up the workbook to be shared. Here are the steps:

1. Open the workbook. (For a new workbook, save the workbook before continuing with these steps.)

2. Click the Review tab, and then click **Share Workbook**.

3. On the Editing tab of the Share Workbook dialog box, select the option to allow changes by more than one user, and then click **OK**.

4. When you are prompted to save the workbook, click **OK** to continue.

You can now distribute this workbook, by e-mail or by other means, to the individuals you want feedback from. Instruct the users to update the workbook and then save and return it to you. Store these copies in the location that contains the shared workbook, and be sure to use a unique file name for each so that you don't unintentionally over-write changes from anyone.

The command you use to compare and merge workbooks isn't on the ribbon by default. You can add it to a custom group you create on the ribbon or to the Quick Access Tool-bar. To add the command to the Quick Access Toolbar in Excel, follow these steps:

1. Click the arrow to the right of the Quick Access Toolbar, and then click **More Commands**.

2. On the Quick Access Toolbar page of the Excel Options dialog box, from the Choose Commands From list, select **Commands Not In The Ribbon**.

3. Scroll down the list to locate the Compare And Merge Workbooks command. Select it and click **Add**.

4. Click **OK** to close the Excel Options dialog box.

Now, to review the changes in the workbooks, follow these steps:

1. Open the copy you want to maintain as the master copy.

2. On the ribbon or the Quick Access Toolbar, click **Merge And Compare Workbooks**.

3. Click **OK** in the message that prompts you to save the workbook.

4. In the Select Files To Merge Into Current Workbook dialog box, select one or more of the copies of the workbook you want to review, and then click **OK**. (To select multiple copies of the workbook, press **Ctrl** or **Shift** and then select the files.)

   After you click OK to close the Select Files To Merge Into Current Workbook dialog box, Excel highlights each of the cells in the master copy that contains a change. (If changed cells aren't highlighted, click Track Changes on the Review tab and then choose Highlight Changes. Clear the When option—so that it is set to All—and then click OK.) Point to a cell to display a comment container that shows the revision.

5. In the Changes group on the Review tab, click **Track Changes** and then select **Accept/Reject Changes**.

6. In the Select Changes To Accept Or Reject dialog box, shown below, select the option from the Who list for the changes you want to review. You can choose a specific person, Everyone, or Everyone But Me, for example. Click **OK**.

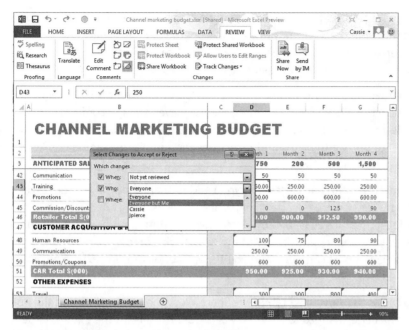

7. Use the Accept Or Reject Changes dialog box to move through the worksheet and accept or reject changes. The dialog box shows you who made a change and what change was made, as you can see here.

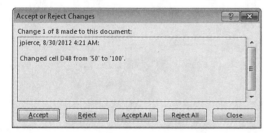

Repeat steps 2 through 6 to merge other copies of the workbook. Once you have incorporated the changes into the master copy of the workbook, you can return to the Review tab, select Share Workbook again, and then clear the option to allow changes by more than one person.

Sharing workbooks on a network

Some of the workbooks your team uses will best be maintained if they are shared so that each team member who needs to add or edit data in the file uses the same copy. You can use your team site to manage this process, but when one person opens the file from the library where it's stored, the file is locked and not available to someone else who wants to use it at the same time. Often, you want this degree of control because letting more than one user edit a file at the same time can introduce conflicts. In Excel, conflicts occur if more than one user updates the same cell or group of cells.

Another approach is to share the file on a network location (not on SharePoint), which can make the file available for simultaneous editing. Even though conflicts can occur, making a file available for simultaneous editing provides a distinct advantage—no one needs to wait to update the file—and Excel offers options for managing conflicts when you need to.

To implement this sharing arrangement, you need to share the workbook in Excel, specify options for how to manage changes and conflicts, and store the workbook in a network location that's available to the members of your team (you can't keep this workbook on your SharePoint site). With the workbook stored in an accessible network location, team members can open and edit the workbook as they do with any local copy of an Excel file.

Figure 9-6 shows the Advanced tab of the Share Workbook dialog box and the options that let you manage changes to a shared workbook. You'll learn the details of these options in the procedure that follows.

FIGURE 9-6 One important option you set for a shared workbook is how to manage conflicts that multiple users can introduce. By default, Excel asks you which changes should "win."

To set up a shared workbook, follow these steps:

1. With the workbook open, click **Share Workbook** on the Review tab.

2.   In the Share Workbook dialog box, select the option **Allow Changes By More Than One User At The Same Time**.

3.   Switch to the Advanced tab, and then set the following options:

■ **Track Changes**   Specify the time period (30 days is the default) for saving the change history—a record of who made changes to the workbook and the data that was changed. If you don't want to keep this history, select that option.

■ **Update Changes**   Choose when you want Excel to save changes. The default setting is When File Is Saved, but for a finer degree of control, select Automatically Every and set the time period (if you want to change the default period of 15 minutes). If you choose to update changes automatically, two other options are enabled. By default, when Excel updates changes at the time interval you specify, changes you make are saved, and you see changes made by others. The other option is to just see the changes other users have made.

■ **Conflicting Changes Between Users**   If updates to a shared workbook result in a conflict, Excel by default prompts you to review those changes to determine which should be incorporated. (You'll learn more about how to resolve conflicts shortly.) Instead of this option, you can choose The Changes Being Saved Win. With this option selected, you won't need to administer conflicts in data, but you have less control over which changes are incorporated.

■ **Include In Personal View**   With these options selected (they are selected by default), you see print area settings and settings for filters that other users have applied when you open the shared workbook.

WHAT YOU CAN'T DO IN A SHARED WORKBOOK

Some features are restricted or limited in shared workbooks. For example, you cannot create a table, delete a worksheet, or merge or split merged cells in a shared workbook. You can, however, insert rows and columns. In Excel Help, search for the topic "Features a shared workbook doesn't support" to find a table that lists the features that aren't available in a shared workbook and related features that are. If you plan to share complex workbooks, review the limitations outlined in this table.

TIP   You can see a list of users who have a shared workbook open by clicking Shared Workbook on the Review tab and selecting the Editing tab.

Protecting a shared workbook

You learned about protecting workbooks and worksheets in Chapter 3, and shared workbooks often need protection as well, especially if you need to maintain a record of changes to the workbook's data. To protect a workbook that you've shared, click Protect Shared Workbook on the Review tab. In the dialog box that Excel displays, select Sharing With Track Changes. This protects change tracking, but someone with access to the workbook can turn off protection.

You can add an extra level of security by specifying a password that someone sharing the workbook must provide to remove protection, but you can do this only for a workbook that you haven't already shared. Open the workbook, and click Protect And Share Workbook on the Review tab. In this version of the Protect Shared Workbook dialog box, the Password text box is enabled when you select Sharing With Track Changes. Type a password to add the extra level of protection to change tracking.

Keep in mind that when someone enters the password required to remove protection from the shared workbook, that step not only removes protection but also turns off sharing.

TIP   If you have already shared the workbook, click Share Workbook, and then clear the sharing option on the Editing tab of the Share Workbook dialog box.

Tracking changes in a workbook

Tracking changes in Excel works only for workbooks that are shared using the steps outlined earlier in this section. (If you have not shared the workbook before you choose the Track Changes, Highlight Changes command on the Review tab, selecting the Track Changes While Editing option shares the workbook.) Excel keeps a history of changes to a shared workbook, which can show you the following information:

- Who made the change
- What type of change was made
- When the change was made
- What cells were affected
- What data was added or deleted

By default, Excel uses a different color to highlight changes by each user of a shared workbook. You can view details about a change in a comment container that Excel associates with the updated cell. As you'll learn in the section "Viewing change history," you can also direct Excel to compile the history of changes on a separate worksheet. You can print this list or save it in its own workbook.

You can adjust settings in the Highlight Changes dialog box, shown in Figure 9-7, to view changes according to when, who, and where.

- In the When list, choose All or choose an option to see changes since a specific date, only the changes you haven't yet reviewed, or only changes made since you last saved the workbook.

- Under Who, choose Everyone, Everyone But Me, or a specific user.

- For Where, you can select a cell range you want to review.

- The Highlight Changes On Screen option is selected by default. Select List Changes On A New Sheet if you want to document changes on a separate worksheet.

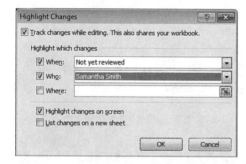

FIGURE 9-7 When you want to review changes on the screen, apply selections from the When, Who, and Where lists to specify which changes you want Excel to display.

When the team member responsible for the data in the workbook is ready to accept or reject changes, click Track Changes on the Review tab and select Accept/Reject Changes. In the dialog box that Excel provides, you can set options for who, when, and where (as described earlier). You can then use the Accept and Reject buttons to move from change to change, using the change history that Excel displays to determine whether to incorporate a change or not.

Resolving conflicts

When you share a workbook so that more than one person can work on it simultaneously, you create the possibility of a conflict. Conflicts can occur when two people working in the workbook try to save changes that affect the same cell.

As mentioned earlier, on the Advanced tab of the Share Workbook dialog box, you can set an option for how to manage conflicts. The default option is Ask Me Which Changes Win. The alternative is the option The Changes Being Saved Win. With the default option, you maintain more control over conflicting changes, so when a user saves a workbook that contains conflicts, Excel displays the Resolve Conflicts dialog box, shown in Figure 9-8.

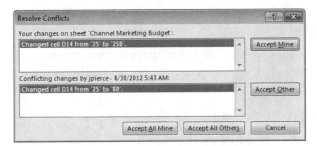

FIGURE 9-8 Excel displays conflicts in a shared workbook in the Resolve Conflicts dialog box. You can then review which change you want to preserve.

To manage conflicts, follow these steps:

1. In the Resolve Conflicts dialog box, read the information about each change and the conflicting changes made by the other user.

2. To keep your change or the other user's change, click **Accept Mine** or **Accept Other**. Excel then moves to the next conflicting change.

TIP

To keep all of your remaining changes or all of the other user's changes, click Accept All Mine or Accept All Others.

Viewing change history

Another of the advanced options you can set for a shared workbook is how long Excel maintains a history of the changes that users have made. (The default period is 30 days.) You can adjust this setting, but increasing it also increases the size of the workbook file. To maintain an efficient file size and preserve changes over a longer period of time, you can print the change history or save it in a separate file.

The change history that Excel maintains will prove useful if you need to look back and determine which cells were changed when (and by whom). Excel can compile the change history on a separate worksheet in a workbook, and you can print this worksheet (or save it in its own file) to maintain the change history as part of your team record.

To work with the history of changes to a shared workbook, follow these steps:

1. On the Review tab, in the Changes group, click **Track Changes**, and then click **Highlight Changes**.

2. In the When list, select **All**, and clear the check boxes for the Who and Where lists if necessary.

> **TIP** If you just want to see the changes on the screen, keep Highlight Changes On Screen selected, and then click OK in the Highlight Changes dialog box.

3. Select the option **List Changes On A New Sheet**, and then click **OK**.

Excel creates a worksheet named History that lists details such as the date and time of a change, who made the change, the type of change, and in which cell range the change occurred. As Figure 9-9 shows, you can also see the new and old values and, for conflicts, which change won. If the worksheet had any conflicts, the changes that were kept show Won in the Action Type column. The Losing Action column shows row numbers that identify the rows with information about the conflicting changes that were not kept, including any deleted data.

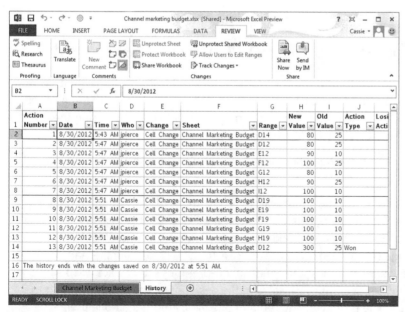

FIGURE 9-9 When you stop sharing a workbook, Excel erases the change history. To preserve a record of changes, print the History worksheet or copy it to a separate workbook.

Clearing the sharing option

Sharing a workbook can often be a temporary measure that teams use to compile and refine information the workbook's designed to hold. You might gather input to define a project's preliminary budget or a series of sales forecasts by using a shared workbook. You can then turn off sharing, have the team leads meet and refine the data, save the workbook, and then post it to a SharePoint site, where it can be maintained as needed.

Here are the steps you follow to stop sharing a workbook:

1. Click **Share Workbook** on the Review tab.

2. On the Editing tab of the Share Workbook dialog box, check which users have the workbook open.

3. If you need to remove a user, select that user and then click **Remove**, but be sure to read the warning that Excel displays, describing the consequences of this action—any user you remove might lose unsaved work. (Use Lync to call a user you are about to remove to be sure that you won't create a problem.)

4. Clear the option to allow more than one user to make changes.

■ **IMPORTANT** If you protected the shared workbook, you must first remove protection before you can clear the option that shares a workbook. For more information, see "Protecting a shared workbook" earlier in the chapter.

Sharing Excel files on SkyDrive or SharePoint

To conclude this chapter, I'll cover options for sharing Excel files on a SharePoint site and on SkyDrive. You can save files to either SharePoint or SkyDrive from the Save As page (it's likely that one or both options are included on the Places list) or by using the Invite People command on the File tab's Share page.

See Also For more information about the Invite People command, see Chapter 1, "Collaboration basics."

Saving a file to SkyDrive or SharePoint makes the file accessible to you and other people via the Internet or your network and lets you edit the file in Excel Web App or the Office desktop version of Excel. Storing a workbook on SkyDrive is a solution that virtual teams can take advantage of. It provides common access to the file, for example, and no one person on the team needs to host the file on an on-premises server. Excel Web App does not provide the full set of features available in the desktop application, but among the features it does provide is simultaneous editing of a file by more than one user.

See Also You'll learn more details about working on SkyDrive in Chapter 11.

When you select the SkyDrive option on the Save As page, Excel displays a list of current and recent folders available on that site. Select the folder you want to save the file to, or click Browse to view other folders on the site. You'll see a similar list of recent folders if you choose the option to store the file on your team site.

| TIP | Click New Folder in the Save As dialog box if you want to create a folder for the purpose of storing the current workbook. |

With the file stored in SkyDrive or SharePoint, you can open it in Excel by selecting it from the Recent Workbooks list or via the Open dialog box. The file is also accessible from your SkyDrive location or the team site itself, of course, where you have the options to view the file in your browser, edit the file in Excel Web App, or open the file in Excel. (On SharePoint, not all these options will be available for files not stored in the most recent Excel format.)

Excel Web App won't open files that you have set up for sharing in the desktop version of Excel, but teams can use Excel Web App to work together on a file at the same time (a feature that Microsoft refers to as *coauthoring*). Excel Web App indicates the number of people working on a file in the lower-right corner of its window, as you can see in Figure 9-10.

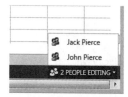

FIGURE 9-10 One way to enable simultaneous editing is to share a workbook on SkyDrive or SharePoint and edit the file in Excel Web App.

■ **IMPORTANT** Some features in Excel are not compatible with editing a workbook in the Excel Web App. Comments and shapes are two examples. The web app notifies you if a workbook contains elements that aren't compatible and lets you save a copy for editing.

Setting browser view options

Excel Services is a feature that lets you display all or portions of a workbook in a web browser. You can, for example, show only selected sheets or other elements of the workbook (such as charts and tables) that users without permission to edit the file can view in their browser. (People with edit permission see these elements in their browser as well, but can take the next step to edit the file.) You might use this feature to make a chart of regional sales or a table that shows revenue by product available to users outside the team, who you don't want to set up as members of your team site, for example, and who don't need to see the entire workbook. Excel Services also lets you specify cells that are the only cells that users viewing the file can edit. By specifying editable cells—which Excel refers to as parameters—you can have users modify or input data that you need for further analysis and additional calculations.

To define which portions of the workbook you want to make available for viewing in the browser and to designate editable cells, you work with the Browser View Options dialog box, shown in Figure 9-11. To open this dialog box, select Browser View Options on the File tab's Export page, and then click the Browser View Options button.

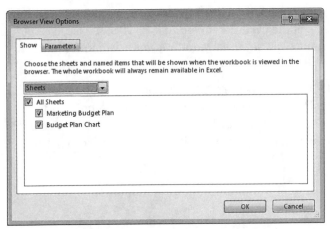

FIGURE 9-11 Before you publish a workbook to SharePoint or SkyDrive, you can specify which portions will be visible in the browser for viewing. Use the Parameters tab to make named cells editable.

On the Show tab of the Publish Options dialog box, use the drop-down list to specify elements of the workbook (one or more worksheets or items such as a table or a chart) you want to display in the browser. The settings you make here affect only what users see when they view the workbook in their browsers—when, for example, they open the file from SkyDrive in the Excel Web App or choose View In Browser in SharePoint. (The entire workbook is stored on SkyDrive, for example, and the full workbook is available when a user chooses Edit In Browser to use the Excel Web App or opens the file for editing in Excel.)

To make a cell editable, you first need to assign a name for the cell. (To name a cell, select it and then click in the cell reference box to the left of the formula bar in Excel. This box shows cell references such as A5, for example. Type a name for the cell, and then press Enter. Cell names do have some restrictions. For example, they cannot include spaces. Search Excel Help for more information about naming cells.) You can then add that defined name as an item on the Parameters tab in the Browser View Options dialog box.

When a user views the workbook in a browser, any parameters you've defined are listed along the right side of the window, as shown in Figure 9-12. Users can enter new values for a parameter and then click Apply to cause calculations or update other data. Portions of the workbook that are viewable but not defined as a parameter are not editable unless a user (with adequate permissions) chooses Edit In Excel Web App or Open In Excel.

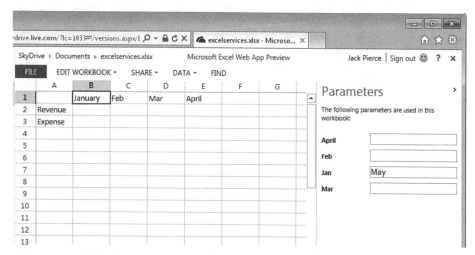

FIGURE 9-12 Only the cells defined as parameters are editable in this view.

Here the detailed steps for specifying browser view options:

1. On the Export page, select **Browser View Options**, and then click the **Browser View Options** button.

2. In the Browser View Options dialog box, on the Show tab, use the drop-down list to specify whether you want to publish the full workbook, only one or more selected worksheets (as shown in Figure 9-11), or specific items (such as tables or charts).

3. On the Parameters tab, select cells you want to enable for editing in the browser. Again, you can specify only single cells here and only cells to which you've already assigned a name.

   Of course, be careful that you don't define parameters in areas of the workbook that you don't select on the Show tab.

4. Click **OK** in the Browser View Options dialog box, and then save the file.

CHAPTER 10

Preparing a presentation as a group

IN THIS CHAPTER, I'll outline a path that teams can follow to develop a presentation using Microsoft PowerPoint. In the approach I describe, team members work independently on some tasks and collaboratively on others. You'll see that PowerPoint easily supports both modes of working.

To facilitate the development of presentations as a team, you can follow the general steps described next. Of course, a lot of detailed work creating slide content and defining presentation effects is associated with each stage.

1. Set up and populate a slide library in SharePoint. The steps you follow to create a slide library are described in Chapter 2, "Building a SharePoint team site." In this chapter, you'll learn how to add slides to the library and how to use slides stored in the library in your presentations. Some of the work required to build the content of a slide library might take place before you start creating any particular presentation. For example, team members might spend time creating slides they know they want to include in multiple presentations, which the use of a slide library facilitates. The content of a slide library will grow over time as well, as presentations are developed and new slides are added to it.

2. Designate a specific team member (a project manager, for example) who will build the framework of the presentation by selecting the relevant slides from the slide library. Post the framework file to your team site or to SkyDrive for shared access.

3. Select the team members who have the most knowledge about the subject matter of the presentation, as well as the team members who have the greatest range of PowerPoint skills, and have them work as coauthors to develop the framework into a complete draft.

4. Meet as a team (possibly using Microsoft Lync) and review, refine, and annotate the draft. In Lync, teams can use the annotation tools that Lync provides through its PowerPoint sharing feature. (See "Sharing a PowerPoint presentation" in Chapter 6, "Working together in Lync," for more details.) You can also use the comments feature in PowerPoint to annotate slides.

5. Distribute the file to key reviewers who don't have access to the file in the shared location. Ask these reviewers to make changes, add suggestions, and return the file, and then have the team member with overall responsibility for the presentation use the Compare command in PowerPoint to merge accepted changes into the master file.

6. Inspect the document for any lingering comments or personal information and mark the file as final. Marking the file as final creates a read-only copy of the file and lets team members know it is ready to be presented.

In the sections that follow, we'll look at each stage in more detail.

Working with a slide library

As you saw in Chapter 2, one of the elements you can include on a SharePoint team site is a slide library. A slide library has many of the features of a standard document library (check in and check out, version management, and so on), but specific features tailor its support for slides you want to maintain and use in multiple presentations.

Having a library of standard slides means that team members don't need to prepare every presentation from scratch or search through e-mail attachments or folders to locate a presentation that was given last month and contains a slide you need for next week's presentation as well. Building presentations through ad hoc searches and the re-creation of slides is not only an ineffective use of time, but it can introduce inconsistencies into the information you present. You don't want slides that contain your team's mission statement, for example, or an organizational chart or financial information to vary or be inaccurate. You want to present this information uniformly in any presentation you give.

Using a slide library also supports a helpful division of labor. Departments and specialists that manage specific types of information can take on the responsibility for creating slides, adding them to the library, and updating them when necessary. And, as you'll see in the sections that follow, you can select an option so that PowerPoint notifies you when a new version of a slide in your presentation is available in the library. You don't need to search the contents of the library to see whether slides have been updated.

Building the library

You can add slides to a slide library from PowerPoint or when you are working in the library in SharePoint. PowerPoint provides a default name to slides before you add them to a library and uses a slide's title to describe it. Whoever adds slides to a library should update the default name and description so that the content and purpose of the slide are clearly identified for team members who want to include the slides in a presentation.

Adding slides from PowerPoint

In PowerPoint, the option you use to publish slides to a library is on the Share page in Backstage view. Open the presentation that contains the slides, display the Share page, and then follow these steps:

1. In the list of options under Share, click **Publish Slides**.

2. Click the **Publish Slides** button to open the Publish Slides dialog box, shown below.

    The file names and descriptions shown in this screen shot are the default values that PowerPoint provides. Default file names appear something like Project Update_001, and the slide's title is used as the description.

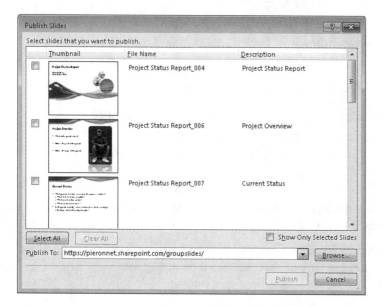

3. In the Publish To box, type the address of the slide library, or click **Browse** to open the Select A Slide Library dialog box and select the library.

4. To rename a slide, click in the File Name column and type the name. To change the default description, click the entry in the Description column and then update the text for that field.

5. Select the slide or slides you want to add to the library (or click **Select All**), and then click **Publish**.

   If you are not signed in to your team site (or the site where the library is located), you are prompted for your user name and password. After you are connected to the site, you'll see a progress bar in the status bar in PowerPoint indicating that the slides are being published.

Adding slides from the team site

In a slide library, the New Document command is not available on the SharePoint ribbon. Slide libraries aren't designed for creating new slides. Instead, you add selected slides or full presentations to the library by using the Upload command on the menu bar above the list of slides.

■ **IMPORTANT** **To upload slides to the library, you must be using Internet Explorer 5.5 or later to work with the SharePoint site.**

Follow these steps to upload slides to the library:

1. In the menu bar above the list of slides, click **Upload**, and then click **Publish Slides**, as shown below:

2. In the Browse dialog box, open the presentation that contains the slide or slides you want to upload to the library.

3. In the Publish Slides dialog box (shown in the previous procedure), use the check boxes to select the slide or slides you want to add, update the file names and descriptions for these slides, and then click **Publish**.

You can update the title (file name) and description for a slide in the library by pointing to the right of the name, clicking the arrow, and then choosing Edit Properties. The properties dialog box for a slide also shows you the presentation that originally contained the slide. As the number of slides in the library grows, use the New Folder button on the library's Files tab to create folders for related slides, such as folders for departments, projects, product lines, and the like.

Another way to organize a library with a large number of slides is to create or modify a view that groups slides. For example, you could create a custom column named Department and then edit the properties of each slide to indicate which department created and maintains the slide. Add the Department column to a custom view or modify the All Slides view to include the Department column and choose Department as the group-by field. You could also use the Department field to sort the library.

See Also   For details about how to create columns and work with views in a SharePoint library, see "Creating and modifying views" in Chapter 2.

Reusing library slides

After you and others populate a slide library, you can add slides to a presentation either from PowerPoint or from the library itself. We'll first look at the steps you follow when you're working in PowerPoint.

To insert a slide from PowerPoint, open the presentation you want to work with, and then follow these steps:

1. On the Home tab, click **New Slide,** and then click **Reuse Slides** in the list of options below the gallery.

    PowerPoint displays the Reuse Slides pane at the right side of the window.

2. In the Reuse Slides pane, click **Open A Slide Library**, and then select the slide library in the dialog box that PowerPoint displays.

    PowerPoint refreshes the content in the Reuse Slides pane with the slides contained in the library.

    TIP   You can select a library you used recently from the Insert Slide From list at the top of the Reuse Slides pane.

In the Reuse Slides pane, shown below, you can use the Search box to find slides. PowerPoint searches the text in the body of slides and slide titles and descriptions for slides that match the text you type. Use the Group By list to organize slides by date modified, by presentation, or by editor.

3. Before you insert a slide, select **Keep Source Formatting** if you want to use the slide's current formatting. If you don't select this option, slides take on the theme and other attributes applied to the current presentation.

4. If you want to be notified when an updated version of a slide is available, select **Tell Me When This Slide Changes**. You'll learn more about this option later in this chapter.

5. To insert a slide, click its thumbnail image in the Reuse Slides pane, or right-click a slide, and then click **Insert Slide**.

   The menu that appears when you right-click a thumbnail also contains commands you can use to apply a theme to all or selected slides or to edit the slide before you insert it.

Inserting slides from SharePoint

By sorting, grouping, and applying views and by referring to the titles, descriptions, and other properties of the slides in a library, a team member can essentially build the framework for a presentation from SharePoint. If you want to add slides to a PowerPoint file that's already in progress, open that file before you begin these steps.

■ **IMPORTANT**   To copy slides from the library, you must be using Internet Explorer 5.5 or later to work with the SharePoint site.

To insert slides into a presentation when you are working in SharePoint, follow these steps:

1. In the slide library, use the column headings to sort and filter the list of slides to help locate the slides you need. To apply a different view to the library, click the **Library** tab, and then select the view from the Current View list.

2. In the list of slides, select the slides you want to insert.

3. On the library's menu bar, click **Copy Slide To Presentation**. You'll see the Copy Slides To PowerPoint dialog box, shown below.

4. In the top section of the dialog box, select the option to add the slides to a new presentation or to a presentation that is currently open. (If more than one presentation is open, select the presentation from the list.)

5. At the bottom of the Copy Slides To PowerPoint dialog box, select the options you want to use: keep the source formatting and whether to be notified when an updated version of a slide is available in the library.

    In many cases, you will want the slides you're inserting to use the formatting applied to an open presentation, so don't select Keep The Source Presentation Format in these cases. Setting the notification option doesn't update slides automatically. As you'll see in the next section, you can choose to ignore an updated slide if you want to.

6. Click **OK**, and the slide or slides are inserted at the end of an open presentation (or the end of the current section).

    For a new presentation, the slides appear in the order in which they're listed in the slide library. You can reposition the slides if necessary in PowerPoint.

Updating slides

Selecting the Tell Me When This Slide Changes option in the Reuse Slides pane or in the Copy Slides To PowerPoint dialog box creates a link between the slide in the presentation and the slide library. Choosing this option is especially important for slides that you know are still being developed by others, for example, and for slides that contain information that's likely to be updated frequently—such as sales data or a list of new investors.

When you open a presentation that contains slides with the Tell Me When This Slide Changes option set, PowerPoint displays the Check For Slide Updates dialog box. At this point, you can cancel the dialog box and not check for updates, click Disable to no longer check for updates, or click Check to see whether any slides have been updated. If you click Check, PowerPoint displays either a message box telling you no slides in the presentation have been updated (just click OK to close the message box) or the Confirm Slide Update dialog box, shown in Figure 10-1. This dialog box lists the slides in your presentation with updated versions in the slide library. You can replace the slide in your presentation with the updated version, append the updated slide to your presentation (and then examine the new content in the full context of the presentation), or skip the update.

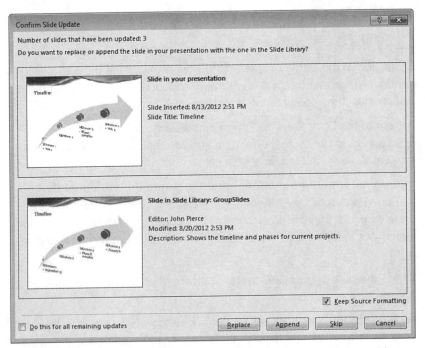

FIGURE 10-1 Keep the slides in your presentation up to date by replacing them with current versions from the library.

TIP   In PowerPoint, slides from a slide library are marked with a small refresh icon in the slide list. Right-click the icon to display a menu with commands that let you check for updates to that slide or all slides in the presentation or to stop checking for updates.

BACKSTAGE COLLABORATION

In PowerPoint (as in other Office programs), the Backstage area provides a number of options that can be useful in collaborative projects. You can find details about some of these sharing options in Chapter 1, "Collaboration basics."

In PowerPoint, review the options that appear on the Export, Save As, or Share page in Backstage view. As you learned in Chapter 9, "Collaborating in Excel," these options let you save an Office file as a PDF or an XPS document, for example, attach a file to distribute it via e-mail, or save a file in an earlier version of a program or a different format. (For PowerPoint, you can save presentations as PNG or JPEG image files as well as in other PowerPoint formats.)

Among the commands on the Export page are the following:

- **Create Handouts**   This command produces a Microsoft Word document with the slides and any presenter notes. You can edit this file in Word and distribute it for reference during a live presentation.

- **Package Presentation for CD**   This command creates a version of the presentation that can be viewed on computers that don't have PowerPoint installed, for example.

- **Create a Video**   Use this command to produce a video of the presentation. The video includes animations and other effects defined for the presentation.

On the Share page, choose Present Online to present a slide show to people attending a meeting via Lync or to make a presentation by using the free Office presentation service, which lets you broadcast a presentation over the Internet. The presentation is displayed in a web browser. To connect to the Office presentation service, you need to sign in with a Microsoft account. To set up a broadcast in PowerPoint, follow these steps:

1. On the Share page, select **Present Online**, choose Office Presentation Service from the list of services, and then click the **Present Online** button.

2. When prompted, sign in with a valid Microsoft account.

3. The Present Online dialog box appears and displays a link to the broadcast, as you can see in the following screen shot. Send the link via e-mail or an instant message, or simply copy it to the Clipboard. (If you aren't signed in to Lync, the Send In IM option isn't available.) You can send an invitation to as many as 50 people.

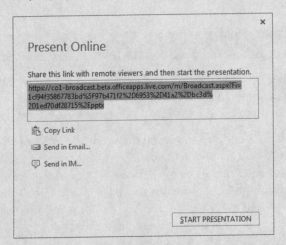

4. When you've notified your audience, click **Start Presentation**.

The presentation appears in the web browsers of people who click the link you send. You don't automatically get audio capabilities through the Office presentation service option, but you can set up a Lync call or converse over regular phone lines as needed. If you are the presenter of an online slide show, you can use the Present Online tab in PowerPoint to share meeting notes via OneNote, send invitation to others (with the same meeting link), and manage the pace of the slide show.

Coauthoring a presentation

At this point in the process I've outlined, one or more team members have assembled the foundation for an upcoming presentation by inserting relevant slides from the team's slide library. The next step is for the team members who are closest to the presentation's subject matter (and perhaps someone on the team who's a skilled PowerPoint user) to work together to develop and refine the presentation. The team members involved can collaborate on this work in a number of ways, from sharing the presentation in Lync, to meeting together, or simply by taking turns editing the file.

Coauthoring in PowerPoint, which lets more than one person work on the file at the same time, is another option. To enable coauthoring, you need to store the presentation on a SharePoint site (such as your team site) or in a SkyDrive folder. (Each team member who wants to contribute to the presentation must be using PowerPoint 2010 or PowerPoint 2013. You can also coauthor by using the PowerPoint Web App. You'll learn more about using Office Web Apps in Chapter 11, "Working with Office Web Apps on SkyDrive.")

To save a presentation to a shared location, use options in the Places list on the Save As page. When you choose SkyDrive, for example, you need to sign in (if you aren't already), and then you'll see a list of folders where you can save the file.

Team members working on the presentation can open the file from PowerPoint or from the shared location (by using the Edit In Microsoft PowerPoint command). When more than one person is working on the file, PowerPoint displays a notification to other users. You can keep track of who is editing a file by periodically checking the status bar in PowerPoint or by switching to the Info page in Backstage view, as shown in Figure 10-2. In addition, in the slide list, PowerPoint displays a small icon below the slide number to indicate that a team member is editing that slide. Click the icon to see who in particular is working on it.

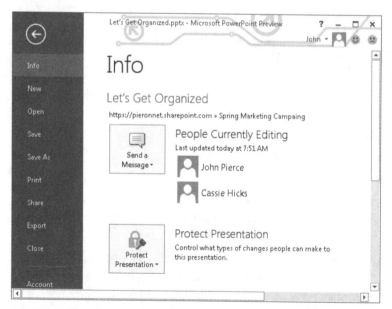

FIGURE 10-2 The Info page is one of the places in PowerPoint where you can see which team members are currently working on a file. Click Send A Message to contact other users via e-mail or with an instant message in Lync.

When team members complete their work and save changes (including formatting changes, inserting or deleting slides, or changing the content of specific slides), the shared version of the file is refreshed. If you still have the file open, you can review the changes other team members made and accept those you want to merge into the file.

TIP Team members can add comments to slides to provide context for changes and additions they make. Having this context helps the team member who reviews changes understand other team members' decisions and preferences. For details about adding comments, see "Adding annotations and comments" later in this chapter.

Follow these steps to review and merge changes:

1. Switch to the Info page in Backstage view

2. Under Document Updates Available, click **Save**, and then click **Save And Review**.

   You'll see the following dialog box, which tells you that a coauthor has made changes, and directs you to the File tab if you want to compare the current presentation with a previous version.

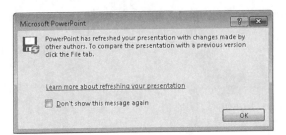

3. Click **OK** in the message box.

Notice that the PowerPoint window has changed its configuration. The File tab remains, but the standard tabs on the ribbon are replaced by the Merge tab and the Revisions pane, which are shown in Figure 10-3.

As you can see, the Revisions pane is organized in two tabs, Details and Slides. On the Details tab, the Slide Changes area lists elements on the current slide (for example, Content Placeholder 4) that contain text or formatting changes. The Presentation Changes area lists slides that were inserted, deleted, or moved.

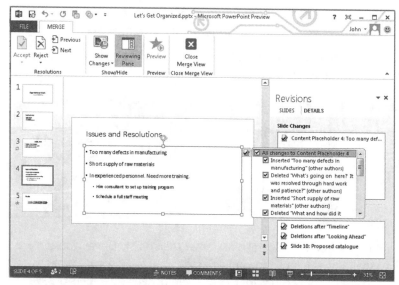

FIGURE 10-3 Changes made by other authors are accepted by default. Clear the check box next to a detailed change to reject that revision.

When you click an entry in the Slide Changes area on the Details tab, a small window opens in the main pane with a list of the changes on that slide. (The changes made to Content Placeholder 4 are shown in Figure 10-3.) The selected check box beside each change indicates that the change has been accepted at this point. (You can also see this in the content and formatting shown on the slide.) Clear the check box beside a change to reject that change, and you'll see that the text and formatting of the slide is updated. You can also use the Accept and Reject buttons in the Resolutions group to manage changes.

TIP   Some types of changes, for example changes to slide animations, will be labeled "non-mergable." You might see this notification if you click an entry in the Details pane for Slide Properties, for example.

You review changes listed under Presentation Changes in a similar manner. When you click an entry in this list, PowerPoint displays the window describing the change at the relevant location in the slide list. Clear the check box to reject any changes to the order of the slides, to reinstate slides that were deleted, or to remove a slide that was inserted.

On the Slides tab on the Revisions pane, you can look over changes by reviewer. For a slide that contains changes, you'll see a thumbnail image on this tab. Otherwise, Power-Point indicates that the selected slide has no changes and directs you to the next slide with changes. Point to the thumbnail, and then click the arrow that appears to open a menu that lets you accept or reject changes made by the selected reviewer.

When you finish reviewing the presentation and have decided which changes to accept and which to reject, click Close Merge View, and then save the file.

TIP In the PowerPoint Options dialog box, you can set an option to always review changes when you work with others on a presentation. Open the dialog box from the File tab, and then click Save in the list of categories. Under File Merge Options For Shared Document Management Server Files, select the Show Detailed Merge Changes When A Merge Occurs check box.

If the shared presentation is stored on SharePoint (rather than on SkyDrive), you can use the Manage Versions menu on the Info page in Backstage view to work with versions of the file. PowerPoint shows a list of versions that were saved by team members or saved automatically. Each version is identified by date and time and indicates whether the version was saved automatically or by an individual.

You can open a previous version by clicking its entry in the list. You'll see a notification below the ribbon stating that you are viewing a previous version and that a newer version is available. Click Restore if at this point you want to view the most recent version on the server.

Adding annotations and comments

At any step in developing a presentation, team members can make use of comments to suggest changes to slides, to approve the work that's been done, and to explain revisions and additions they make to a file they're sharing. Comments can be used as well by people outside the team, who might receive the file as an e-mail attachment instead of accessing it through SharePoint or SkyDrive.

To annotate a presentation and manage comments in PowerPoint, start on the Review tab by clicking New Comment. This opens the Comments pane along the right side of the PowerPoint window, as shown in Figure 10-4. Type your comment in the text box that PowerPoint displays.

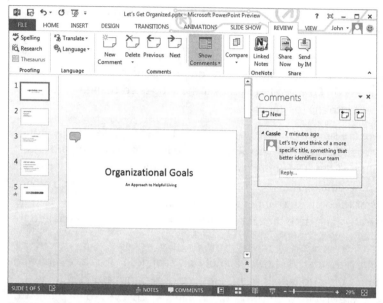

FIGURE 10-4 Annotate a presentation with comments. Click Reply to respond to a comment another team member made.

As you can see, PowerPoint identifies who adds a comment and how long ago the comment was inserted. Click New in the Comments pane to insert a comment, or click in the Reply prompt to add to a comment already in the file. To review the comments in a presentation, use the Previous and Next buttons in the Comments pane or in the Comments group on the Review tab. You can also remove a comment by clicking Delete on the Review tab or by clicking the Delete icon in the upper-right corner of a comment in the Comments pane.

Click the Show Comments button to hide comments temporarily. Click the button again to display them.

Comparing presentations

With a presentation nearing its final state, you can post it for review by interested team members and other colleagues. You might do this in a meeting and use Lync to share the presentation and have one of the meeting's presenters annotate the slides with final changes.

See Also   For details about sharing a presentation in Lync, see "Sharing a PowerPoint presentation" in Chapter 6.

If some reviewers don't have access to a shared file, you can distribute the presentation to these reviewers, have them mark up the file with comments and revisions, and then use the Compare command in PowerPoint to go over the suggested changes, merging those you want to accept into the master file.

The steps you take here are similar to those you use to review and merge changes for a file that is set up for coauthoring. They are also similar to how you can compare and merge Excel workbooks (see the "Distributing and merging multiple workbooks" section in Chapter 9 for more details), but in PowerPoint, you can compare only one other file at a time. If you want to compare changes from a number of people, you need to go through each file separately and each time merge the changes you want to keep into the master file.

Comparing versions of a presentation shows you not only changes that a reviewer made to the text of slides but changes to details such as font color and formatting. Both text and formatting changes are visible when you compare files, which gives you a preview of how the final slide will look.

Here are the steps you follow to compare two PowerPoint files:

1. Open the master copy of the presentation.

2. On the Review tab, click **Compare**.

3. In the Choose File To Merge With Current Presentation dialog box, browse to the folder where the review copies are stored. Select the copy you want to merge, and then click **Merge**. (Remember that you can merge only one version of the presentation at a time.)

   At this point, you'll be working with commands and tools very similar to the tools on the Merge tab that PowerPoint displays when you review changes made to a coauthored presentation. (See "Coauthoring a presentation" earlier in this chapter for details.) The Compare group on the Review tab lets you move from change to change, accept or reject changes, and show or hide the Revisions pane. The Revisions pane displays detailed changes to slides as well as changes to the overall presentation—slides that were deleted, inserted, or moved, for example. In the coauthoring approach, changes made by other authors are selected (accepted) by default. When you compare presentations using the Compare command, however, changes have not been incorporated. You need to accept any changes you want to apply.

4. Select a check box beside a detailed change to accept it. The change is reflected on the preview of the slide, and you can undo the acceptance of a change simply by clearing the check box again.

5. To see how a slide would look with all of a reviewer's changes incorporated, switch to the Slides tab on the Revisions pane, and then browse to that slide in the list of slides. Point to the thumbnail, and then click the arrow to open a menu with commands that let you accept or reject all changes made by a reviewer on this slide.

6. When you finish reviewing changes, click **End Review**.

■ IMPORTANT   Be sure to go through each change and specify whether to accept or reject it before you click End Review. Any changes that haven't been applied are rejected, and changes you accept aren't fully merged until you end the review and save the file.

A few final steps

After the presentation is complete, you can take the following steps to check for any issues PowerPoint might find in the file and then mark the file as final.

1. Click the File tab, and then display the Info page.

2. Click **Check For Issues**, and then click **Inspect Document**.

    The Document Inspector dialog box lists several categories (such as Comments And Annotations, Document Properties And Personal Information, and Invisible On-Slide Content) that PowerPoint examines to determine, for example, whether the file contains any comments or whether a document property such as Author is filled in. A stray comment that someone forgot to delete is generally harmless if only team members are looking at the file, but you should know whether any comments remain before you share a file because the comment probably wasn't intended for everyone to read.

3. Click **Inspect** in the Document Inspector dialog box. Depending on which categories you selected and what PowerPoint discovers in the file, you'll see results such as the following:

4. In the results view, click **Remove All** for any categories you want to clear.

5. On the Info page, click **Protect Presentation**, and then click **Mark As Final**.

6. Click **OK** in the message box, and then you'll see the following dialog box:

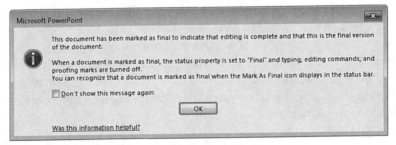

Marking the presentation final is mostly an informative step. It doesn't prevent someone with access to the file from turning off this setting and making changes. But any team member who opens the presentation is notified that file has been marked as final and must remove this setting to make changes to the file.

TIP You can apply the steps in this section to other types of Office documents as well. Inspecting a document is an especially important step for any file you distribute outside your organization. For more details, see Chapter 3, "Managing access and preserving history."

CHAPTER 11

Working with Office Web Apps on SkyDrive

COAUTHORING DOCUMENTS, storing files in a shared repository, sharing calendars, applying permissions, restoring a previous version. In earlier chapters, you've seen examples of how these capabilities and others like them facilitate the work teams do in Microsoft Office. For the most part, the examples have shown how you work with these features in the Office desktop programs. In this chapter, you'll cross a boundary and examine what you can do with Office Web Apps—web-based versions of the Office programs that render documents in your browser, where you can view and edit the documents using many of the same commands and features.

Office Web Apps are supported on a number of devices and platforms, including mobile phones and Microsoft SharePoint. The focus of this chapter is how you use the web apps from SkyDrive, the service that provides cloud storage and, with a Microsoft account, access to e-mail, calendars, and contacts as well.

Most teams will likely use Office Web Apps to complement the work team members produce using the desktop versions of the programs. A team member on the road working at a computer kiosk or at home with a computer without Office installed can create an Excel spreadsheet in Excel Web App, set up the column and row headings, input some of the data, and then share it with team members via SkyDrive. Team members with access to the file can update it in the web app or open it in Excel and add more data and charts and perform more advanced analysis. With so many virtual teams operating these days, and with many workers traveling and performing their jobs from multiple computing devices, tools like Office Web Apps can quickly become essential.

Before exploring how you work with Office Web Apps, I'll describe how SkyDrive can facilitate collaborative work within a team. The material covered here should be of particular interest to people like me, who work independently, often on teams with other self-employed individuals under contract with a larger business. I don't have much in the way of at-home IT infrastructure. For example, I rely on hosted services for SharePoint, don't have a company network, and often need to work remotely. Freelance workers will find much they can take advantage of in SkyDrive, but SkyDrive's services are equally geared toward groups of friends with common activities, small businesses, families, and not-for-profit organizations. As you'll see, Office Web Apps have some limitations when compared with the full desktop versions of the programs, but they let people you work with create files, share them in variety of ways (including on social media sites), and quickly gain access to the desktop programs if Office is installed on the computer you're using.

WHAT'S NEW IN THE LATEST OFFICE WEB APPS

If you've worked with Office Web Apps before, you might be interested to learn about updated features in a recent iteration. For example, you can now open documents with tracked changes in Word Web App. You can't see the changes or mark changes, but you *can* open the documents. You can also insert comments in files you open in Word Web App or in PowerPoint Web App. Coauthoring is now enabled in Word Web App and PowerPoint Web App. The ability to embed content in a website that you can view in a web app is new in Word Web App, Excel Web App, and OneNote Web App. You can also now view ink objects in Word Web App and OneNote Web App.

The SkyDrive landscape

Much of what you read and see in this section is subject to change. For example, I've used SkyDrive on several projects over the past few months to store and transfer files. One day recently I signed in and found the SkyDrive user interface almost completely changed—for the better. This is one reason that a service such as SkyDrive is useful. It's improved and enhanced periodically without you needing to install new software or manage updates. You see the changes the next time you sign in.

SkyDrive commands

The majority of the commands you work with in SkyDrive are for managing folders and files. This includes standard operations such as renaming, moving and copying, and deleting. Commands for these and related tasks appear on the Manage menu when a file or a folder is selected in the Files list, as shown in Figure 11-1. (Many of these commands are also available when you right-click a file or a folder.)

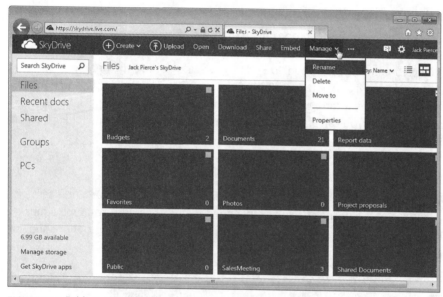

FIGURE 11-1 Folders such as Documents, Favorites, Photos, and Shared Documents are provided by default. Use the Create menu to define folders of your own, which you can keep private or share with others.

Other commands you use regularly include Create, Open, Upload, and Download. The Create command leads you to the four Office Web Apps (for Word, Excel, PowerPoint, and OneNote). When a file is selected, the Open menu provides options for opening the file in the web app or in the related Office desktop program. Upload and Download let you transfer files between SkyDrive and your computer.

See Also To set up SkyDrive to use with a team, you use the Share command to make documents and folders accessible to others. I'll cover the details of sharing files and folders in the next section.

The Embed command creates HTML (inside an iframe tag) that you can copy and paste to add the content to a webpage or to a blog. You could use the Embed command to add a PowerPoint slide show to your team blog or to your team's website.

In addition to Rename, Delete, and other utility commands, the Manage menu includes the Properties command. Choose this command if you want to see details about a file or a folder. In the Properties pane, you can add a description or click Share to share the file or folder. You'll also see details like the type of folder, when it was added and last modified, and the size. When you have a folder open, the Folder Actions menu includes commands such as Download Folder and Delete Folder.

Sharing documents

In this section, I'll use an Excel workbook in an example of how you can share a file from SkyDrive. You can do this in a couple of ways—using commands in SkyDrive or from the web app when you have the file open. In SkyDrive, you don't have the degree of control over access to a shared file as you do in SharePoint, for example. You can assign either the Can View or Can Edit setting to a file or a folder. Files inherit the permission you set for a shared folder, but you can also set permissions for particular files in a folder that you've shared.

Sharing from SkyDrive

When you share a document from SkyDrive, by default a link to the document is sent via e-mail to the recipients you specify. You simply need to add the addresses, type a message to provide some context, and then select one or both of the sharing options shown in Figure 11-2.

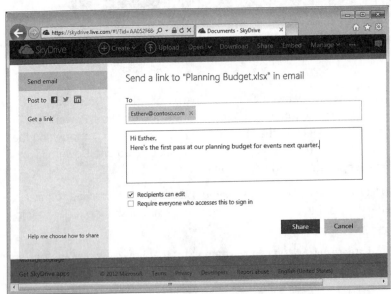

FIGURE 11-2 By default in SkyDrive, you share a file with others via e-mail and recipients can edit the file.

The option Recipients Can Edit grants direct access to the document (signing in isn't required) and lets recipients edit the file and save changes. Select Require Everyone Who Accesses This To Sign In to share the file but require others to sign in with a Microsoft account to start working with the file.

The people you share the document with receive the e-mail message and can click the link to first view the file in the related web app's Reading view. (They'll need to sign in if you select that option.) They can edit the file in the Office desktop app (if Office is installed) or edit the file in the related web app in their browser. Remember that editing rights are granted by default, so if your intent is to share the document but not let recipients make changes, be sure you clear the Recipients Can Edit option before you send the message. By clearing this option, you grant rights to view the document only. In this case, when a recipient opens the file using the link (or from the Shared folder on the recipient's SkyDrive), the document opens in the web app's Reading view. The recipient can't open the file to edit it in the web app. If a recipient opens the file in the desktop version of the program (Excel in this example), the file is opened as read-only.

You have other options for sharing a file as well. You can post it to a social network such as Facebook, Twitter, or LinkedIn once you connect your Microsoft account with your account on the social network. In the sharing window shown in Figure 11-2, select the Post To option, and then click the link Add Services. You'll then need to sign in and connect to the service, as shown in Figure 11-3 on the next page. You can use the link provided to read about what connecting accounts means. Keep in mind that you can remove the connection later if you want to stop sharing with the social network you chose. To update that setting, sign in to SkyDrive. Click your account name, and then choose Account Settings. You'll be required to sign in again before you see the Account Summary page. Click Permissions in the navigation pane and then click Manage Your Accounts.

The Get A Link option (also shown in Figure 11-2) reveals three choices for sharing a file: View Only, View And Edit, and Public. Click Create to generate a link that you can copy into an e-mail message, for example, and send to people you want to share the file with, granting them permission to only view the file or to view and edit it. Click Shorten if you want a shorter URL. Click Make Public to create a link that makes the file available publically. The Public link grants view-only permissions to the file, but it also allows people to find the file through a search on the Internet.

After you share a file or a folder, you can adjust the permissions granted by right-clicking the file and choosing Properties. In the Properties pane, under Sharing, you'll see a list of people who have access to the file. Use the menu beside a person's name to switch between Can View and Can Edit, as shown in Figure 11-4 on the next page.

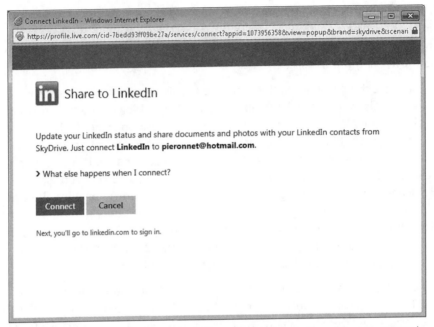

FIGURE 11-3 From SkyDrive, you can share files and other information with your contacts in a social network.

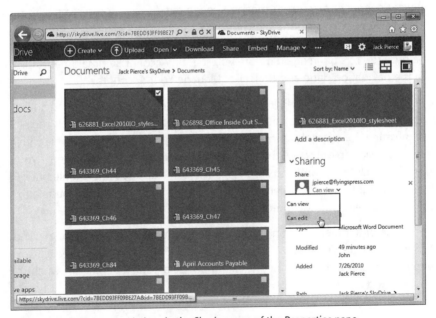

FIGURE 11-4 Manage permissions in the Sharing area of the Properties pane.

Sharing a file from a web app

If you are working on a file, editing it in one of the web apps, you can also share it. Click the File tab and then click Share. On the Share page, click Share With People. You'll then see the same window as shown in Figure 11-2 in the previous section. Address the e-mail message, post the file to a social media site your account is connected to, or click Get A Link to generate links you can copy to send to others.

Sharing SkyDrive folders

The same options are available for sharing folders. Select the folder in the list under Files and then click Share, or open the folder and then click Share Folder. You'll see the sharing options shown earlier in Figure 11-2. As you can for a file, you can change the sharing permissions for a folder in the Properties pane.

Using the SkyDrive Application

Keeping all or the majority of the files you and other team members use on SkyDrive means at least one trip to your browser to sign in so that you can upload, download, and otherwise manage files. You can also do some of the work of managing files stored on SkyDrive from your desktop by installing the SkyDrive app designed for your operating system or device. The SkyDrive app keeps files synchronized between your computer and SkyDrive. In other words, you can open a file from the SkyDrive folder the app creates on your computer, update the file, and then save it. The SkyDrive app will synchronize the file to SkyDrive.

When you install the SkyDrive app, files already stored in your SkyDrive are downloaded to the SkyDrive folder and synchronized. The SkyDrive app also lets you connect to another computer from the device you're using. For example, let's say you're away from the office, working on your laptop or tablet, and need a file that's on your main computer at the office—a file that isn't stored on SkyDrive or in another shared location. If your office computer is turned on and you're logged in, you can connect to it via SkyDrive and retrieve the file you need.

One limitation of the SkyDrive app is that it doesn't provide access to files that another person has shared with you from his or her SkyDrive. You need to sign in to SkyDrive with your browser to gain access to those files.

■ **IMPORTANT** SkyDrive for Windows, the SkyDrive app discussed in this section, requires Windows 8, Windows 7, or Windows Vista with Service Pack 2 and the Platform Update for Windows Vista. You can also use SkyDrive for Windows on recent versions of Windows Server.

Setting up the SkyDrive app

To install the SkyDrive app, click Get SkyDrive Apps at the bottom of the navigation bar in SkyDrive. You'll see links to versions for Windows desktop, Mac, Windows Phone, iPhone and iPad, and Android. For the Windows desktop version, click Download The App.

Work through security messages to allow the installation. After the application downloads, click Get Started in the Welcome To SkyDrive window. You'll then need to sign in with your Microsoft account. By default, the SkyDrive folder is set up in your user profile at C:\Users\ *YourName*\SkyDrive. You can direct the app to a different folder by clicking Change on the page titled Introducing Your SkyDrive Folder. The next page provides the option that lets you access files on the current computer from other devices. That option is selected by default, so clear the check box only if you don't want to enable this feature. (You can set up the computer to let you retrieve files later if you clear the option at this point.)

Once the installation process is complete, you'll see a SkyDrive icon in the notification tray in the Windows task bar and the welcome message shown in Figure 11-5. To open the folder, right-click the icon in the notification tray and then click Open Your SkyDrive Folder. You'll also see the status of synchronization.

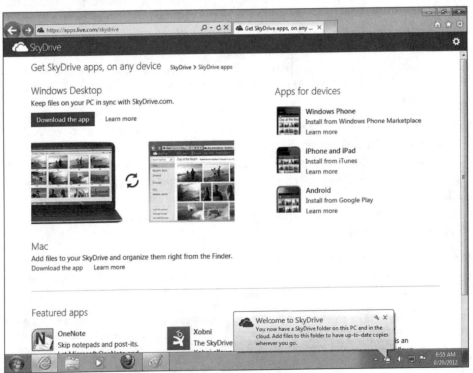

FIGURE 11-5 You can access your local SkyDrive folder by right-clicking the SkyDrive icon in the notification tray.

Connecting remotely from SkyDrive

As mentioned in the previous section, you can connect remotely to another PC from SkyDrive (provided that the remote computer is turned on and you're logged on). If you did not enable remote connections when you set up the SkyDrive app, you can use the Settings dialog box to enable the feature.

To open the dialog box, right-click the SkyDrive app icon in the notification tray and then click Settings. In the Settings dialog box, select the option Make Files On This PC Available To Me On My Other Devices, as shown in Figure 11-6.

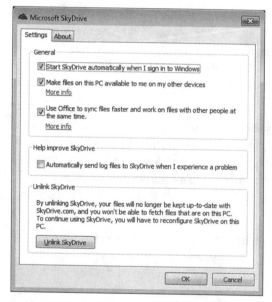

FIGURE 11-6 In the Microsoft SkyDrive dialog box, select Make Files On This PC Available To Me On My Other Devices to gain access to files you need that aren't stored on SkyDrive.

With remote connections enabled, you'll see an entry for each of your trusted computers in the PCs list in SkyDrive. Click a computer to connect to it.

Using Mail, People, and Calendar apps

Beyond storage, file sharing, synchronization, and access to Office Web Apps (which I'll cover in detail in the next section), when you sign in to SkyDrive using your Microsoft account, you gain access to three apps that assist group collaboration—a web-based e-mail client, a contact application, and a calendar. To switch between these tools, point to the SkyDrive label in the upper-left corner of the window and then choose Mail, People, or Calendar.

> **NOTE** Microsoft periodically changes the user interface and configuration for SkyDrive and its associated services. The descriptions in the following sections are based on a Microsoft account related to my Hotmail.com e-mail address. With other accounts, you might not see the same features. For example, when I signed in to SkyDrive using an account that's also tied to an Office 365 subscription, I could not access the Mail app.

Mail

You probably won't come to rely on the Mail app as your only e-mail application. It doesn't provide the range of commands in Outlook, for example. But for times when you need to contact someone and don't have access to any of your day-to-day PCs, the Mail app serves the purpose. If you think you'll use the Mail app regularly, you should definitely take steps to add contacts to the People app. You'll find that you get more use from the Mail app that way.

The Mail app comes with a default set of folders that's displayed along the left side of the window. Click New to write a message and send it. A list of frequent contacts is displayed for you to choose from (or you can simply type a name or address), and you can format text, check spelling, save a draft, set priority, and choose a message format (Rich Text, Plain Text, or Edit In HTML). To create additional folders, right-click Folders and type the folder's name.

The Quick Views area of the navigation pane lets you see messages by category, such as messages with photos attached, shipping updates, and flagged messages. Click New Category at the bottom of the list to define a custom category, which can come in handy if you create rules to help organize your e-mail messages.

If you're using the Mail app for work purposes, rules help you manage messages related to specific projects or events by applying actions to the messages you receive from specific senders or messages that contain specific words in their subject lines. Setting up a rule involves just a few steps. Start by right-clicking Folders, and then click Manage Rules. In the next window, you'll see a list of rules (if any are already defined). To set up a rule, click New.

In the first step, you specify criteria to identify the messages a rule applies to. Choose from a list of options that includes Sender's Address, Sender's Name, To or CC Line, Subject, and Attachments. Next you choose a filtering operator—such as Is, Contains, Does Not Contain, or Begins With. The operators you can choose from depend on the item you select in the first list. Use the third text box in step 1 to define the value for the criteria—a sender's name or text you want the rule to act on in the subject line. The Create Rule page at this point should resemble Figure 11-7.

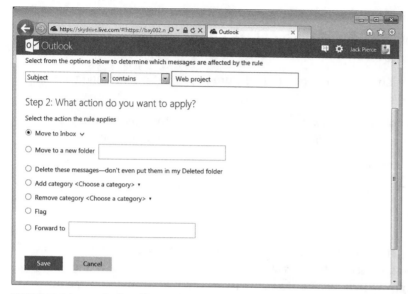

FIGURE 11-7 In step 1 of creating a rule, you specify criteria to identify messages. In step 2, you choose an action.

In step 2, you define the action that the rule applies. You can choose from the options shown in Figure 11-7. For example, you can delete all messages from a specific sender, move messages to a folder, forward them, flag them, or add them to a category. Among the built-in categories are Documents, Groups, and Travel. Although you can't create a category when you set up a rule, you can do this on the main Mail page in the Quick Views area of the navigation pane. Also, you can't apply more than one action to a rule— you can't, for example, add a category and move a message to a different folder.

People

Without overlooking too many of the features in the People app, which lets you add contacts from various social media sites and invite contacts to converse using instant messaging, I'll highlight what I think teams can benefit from most here. That's groups. By creating a group, you can send a single message from the Mail app to all the members of the group.

In the People app, add a new contact item for each person on your regular team (or teams) and then follow these steps:

1. In the menu bar, click **Manage**, and then click **Manage Groups**.

2. On the Manage Groups page, click the plus sign next to Group.

3. Type a name for the group, and then click **Apply**.

4. Go through your list of contacts and select each person you want to make a member of this group.

5. On the menu bar, click **Groups**, select the group you just created, and then click **Apply**.

6. Above the contact list, click the arrow next to All, and then choose the group. You'll see that the list of contacts is filtered to show only group members.

7. Click **Send Email**.

You'll switch to the Mail app with a message addressed to each member of the group.

Calendar

Clicking Calendar in the group of apps (SkyDrive, Mail, and People being the others) opens a Hotmail calendar. Use the tabs along the top of the calendar to change views (Day, Week, Month, Agenda, and To-Do List). Use the commands above the tab to schedule an event, add an item to your to-do list, and to delete calendar entries. You can create a calendar by clicking New, Calendar, and then giving the calendar a name, assigning a color to identify entries, selecting a charm (an identifying icon), and describing it.

The Subscribe and Share commands will be useful to teams using Calendar to keep track of meetings, events, deadlines, and the like. The next two sections cover these features in more detail.

Subscribing to a calendar

Coordinating time among the members of a virtual team can be trickier than for a team that shares a common domain and especially a common workplace. Creating a project or team calendar, publishing it online, and then having each team member subscribe to the calendar maintains a live calendar that each team member can see in its up-to-date form.

Keep in mind, however, that not everyone who subscribes to a calendar can update it. In other words, five team members can subscribe to a calendar that a sixth team member owns and updates. That keeps the five subscribers current about activities, but it does make work for the individual in charge of maintaining the calendar.

See Also   For information about publishing an Outlook calendar to the Internet so others can subscribe to it, see Chapter 5, "An integrated Outlook."

Before you can subscribe to a calendar, you need the URL that points to the calendar. The person who publishes the calendar should have this URL and can send it to you in an e-mail message.

Click Subscribe in the Calendar toolbar. On the Import Or Subscribe To Calendar page, keep Subscribe To A Public Calendar selected, and then paste the URL into the Calendar URL box. Type a name, choose a color to identify the calendar, and select a charm if you want to use one. Click Subscribe To Calendar.

You won't see updates to the calendar instantaneously. The server where the calendar is hosted will update the file at some regular interval.

Sharing a calendar

Sharing a calendar with team members can take the burden off having any single team member be responsible for updating the schedule for meetings, events, milestones, and tasks. If you work with a shared calendar, you can also provide an e-mail address where you'll receive notifications when the calendar is updated.

To share a calendar with other people, follow these steps:

1. Click **Share** and then choose the calendar.

2. Select **Share This Calendar**.

    In the options that appear, the default selection is Share Your Calendar Privately With Friends And Family. You can also choose Send People A View-Only Link To Your Calendar or Make Your Calendar Public. Stick with the default selection for now, but if you choose one of the other options, you need to click Get Your Calendar Links to generate the address where people can find the calendar. When you select Make Your Calendar Public, you can also specify whether other people can view calendar details or just free and busy times.

3. Click **Add People**. Type e-mail addresses or names in your list of contacts or use the check boxes in the contact list to select people.

4. In the lists under Choose How Much These People See And Do, choose one of the following options, which start with full privileges and work down to a limited view of the calendar.

    - Co-owner

    - View, edit, and delete items

    - View details

    - View free/busy times, titles, and locations

    - View free/busy times

5. Use the Who Can See To-Dos list to specify the permission level at which people can see tasks entered on the calendar's to-do list.

6. Click **Preview Invitation** under the name of someone you're sharing the calendar with to see the e-mail message that will accompany the sharing invitation. The following screen shot shows an example:

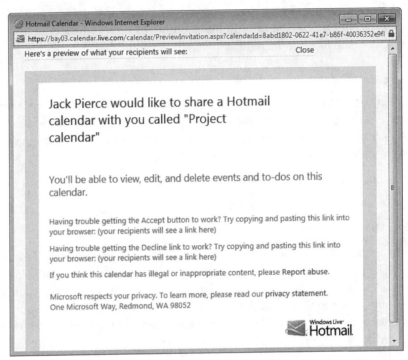

7. Click **Save**, and then click **OK** in the Sharing Confirmation message box to send the invitations.

When recipients receive the message, they need to accept (or decline) the sharing invitation. When recipients accept a sharing invitation, they see a page where they can type a description for the calendar, specify how often to be notified about updates to the calendar, and choose whether to receive a daily e-mail message that summarizes the schedule for the calendar.

As you can see, for team members spread far and wide who need to coordinate time, travel, and tasks, setting up a simple shared calendar such as this will save hours of time.

Creating and editing documents in Office Web Apps

The four Office Web Apps—Word, Excel, PowerPoint, and OneNote—should look familiar, with the Office ribbon above the document window and commands organized in groups on several tabs. The web apps don't provide all the commands that the desktop versions have, but you can perform a broad scope of work, and when necessary open a file in the full desktop version (assuming the relevant program is available on the computer you're using).

In SkyDrive, use the Create menu to start a new document in the associated web app. To open a document already on SkyDrive, right-click the file and then choose to open the file in the web app or in the related desktop application. As you saw earlier, you can share documents directly from a web app (or by using the commands in SkyDrive). The web apps also support coauthoring, letting more than one person work in the same file simultaneously. The coauthoring experience in each of the web apps is different from coauthoring in the desktop apps and also varies among the web apps. In the following sections, I'll describe how to coauthor in the web apps and also briefly touch on other capabilities the web apps have, including the commenting feature in the Word and PowerPoint Web Apps.

Using Word Web App

When you open a document in Word Web App (and this applies to the web apps for PowerPoint and Excel as well), the document opens in Reading view. You can't make changes to the text in a document in this view, but you can perform some operations. Across the top of the document is the File tab and, left to right, commands named Edit Document, Share, Find, and Comments. Use Edit Document to open the document for editing in either the web app or in Word. Click Share to open the SkyDrive window (see Figure 11-2 earlier in the chapter) that lets you share the file, post it for contacts to see, or generate a link to the file. Click Find to open a pane along the left side of the window where you can search for information in the file. Click Comments to open a pane on the right where you can read, insert, reply to, and manage comments. Opening a document in Reading view is really all someone outside the team who's responsible for reviewing a document needs to do. He or she can use this view to insert comments and never need to open the document for editing.

Editing in Word Web App

To open the document for editing, click Edit Document and then choose Edit In Word or Edit In Word Web App. If you choose the web app, you'll see the ribbon appear with five tabs: File, Home, Insert, Page Layout, and View. The Home tab has most of the formatting tools included in the desktop version of Word, including options for applying font and paragraph properties and styles. You can't create or modify styles in the web app.

The Insert tab has fewer options than in the desktop version of Word. Absent, for example, are commands for several types of illustrations and objects such as text boxes. The commands that are present let you insert tables, pictures, clip art, and links (to websites, for example). On the Page Layout tab, you can change margins, page orientation, and page size and also adjust indentation and line spacing in paragraphs. On the View tab, you can switch between Editing view and Reading view.

You can manage a document you have open in Word Web App by displaying the File tab and clicking Save, Save As (to download a copy), Print (to create a printable PDF), or Share to share the file (as you saw earlier). On the Info page, you can open the document in Word or see a previous version.

Although you can coauthor a document in Word Web App and add comments, you don't have access to all the collaboration features included in the desktop version of Word. For example, in Word Web App you can open a document in which Track Changes is turned on, and changes to the document will be tracked (and visible in Word), but the web app doesn't display insertions or deletions (in colors or in other formatting). You can't turn on Track Changes in the web app either. Furthermore, if a document's editing is restricted (see "Controlling the editing of a document" in Chapter 8, "Working on shared documents in Word," for details), the web app won't open the document for editing. Instead, you'll see the message shown in Figure 11-8.

In addition, you can't edit certain types of document objects in the web app. If a document contains SmartArt or a watermark, for example, you won't be able to remove or edit those objects. You need to open the file in Word before you can work with those elements.

Coauthoring in Word Web App

When more than one person has the file open for editing in Word Web App, a notification is displayed in the status bar. Open the notification to see who's editing the file. Like the desktop version, Word Web App locks a paragraph when a coauthor starts making changes to it. Point to the icon to the left of the paragraph to see who's editing it. You can see a coauthor's changes after that person saves the file and you're notified that an update is available. Save the document yourself at that point to see the updated version. When the updated document is displayed, the changed text is highlighted to indicate that it was changed, as shown in Figure 11-9.

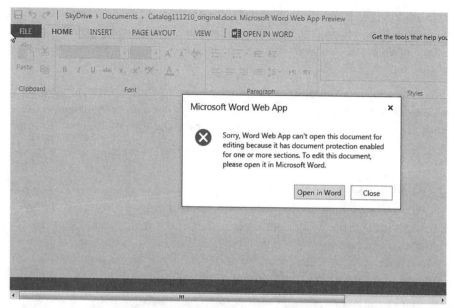

FIGURE 11-8 When editing restrictions are applied to a document, you can't open it in Word Web App.

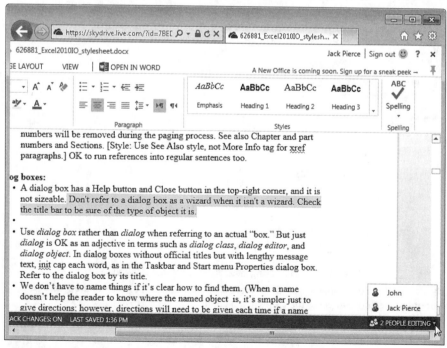

FIGURE 11-9 Check the status bar to see who's editing a document. Updates made by a coauthor are highlighted in green.

During a coauthoring session in the web app, if one of the coauthors opens the document in the full version of Word, the coauthoring session is maintained. If you do open the document in Word, you can switch back to the browser window and close the web app.

If conflicts occur during a coauthoring session in the web app, the web app notifies you and opens a window in which you can choose to keep your changes or the changes of the coauthor. Select the option for which change to retain, and then click Submit to save the document.

Taking notes in OneNote Web App

A notebook you create by using OneNote Web App appears as shown in Figure 11-10. Initially, the notebook contains a single, untitled section, which you can name by right-clicking the label, choosing Rename, and then typing the name. To start taking notes, type a title for the default page that's provided and then click in the body of the page. In the web app, you won't see a note container as you do in OneNote.

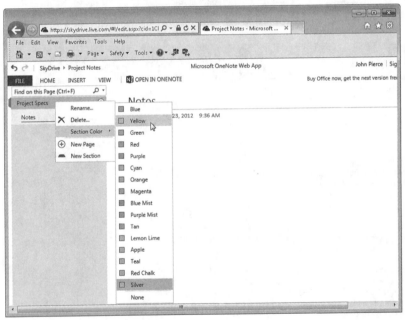

FIGURE 11-10 Use this menu to rename a section, create a new page or section, delete the section, or choose a background color to apply to the pages in a section.

To add a new page, click the plus sign beside the section name. Right-click a section name and then choose New Section to add a section to the notebook. You can use this menu to select a section color as well.

Use the Home tab to work with the Clipboard, format a note, apply a style or a tag, or check spelling. In the web app, you can't create or modify tags. (See "Tagging notes" in Chapter 7, " Keeping track of discussions and ideas," for more details.)

On the Insert tab you can add a page or a section to the notebook, insert a table or images, and add links to websites. In the web app, you can still create a table by using the keyboard (one of the handiest OneNote shortcuts, I think). Type the first column heading, press tab, type another column heading, and press enter to create a new row. On the ribbon, contextual tabs appear when you select objects such as a table or a picture. Use these tabs to modify the layout, sizing, and other properties of the object.

The View tab provides two notebook views: Editing view and Reading view. When you switch to Reading view, the Home, Insert, and View tabs are replaced by the Edit Notebook command, the Share command, and the Show Authors command. Use the File tab or the Edit Notebook command to switch back to Editing view in the web app or open the notebook in OneNote.

The Show Authors command also appears on the View tab, along with the Page Versions command. Click Show Authors to see which team member added a note. Click Page Versions to display a list of previous versions of a page under the page's name in the navigation bar. Refer to the date and author information to determine which version you want to see. Select it, and OneNote displays that version in read-only format with a notification above the page. Click the notification to hide versions, restore the version you selected, or to delete that version.

Coauthoring in OneNote Web App is straightforward. More than one person can open a notebook in the web app, but you won't see the type of notifications that you do in Word Web App, for example. You don't need to save changes to see a coauthor's updates. Changes are saved automatically by the web app, and eventually you'll see the changes that other authors made, but you might experience a delay.

Working together in Excel Web App

Team members can work as coauthors on an Excel workbook when they edit the file in Excel Web App. You'll see the same type of notification that Word Web App displays, shown earlier in Figure 11-9. In fact, this notification appears even when only one person is editing a file.

Unlike Word Web App, Excel Web App has no Save button. Edits to a worksheet are saved automatically, so you'll see a coauthor's changes in the copy you have open as soon as a change is made. The last value saved in a cell is the value that persists in the file.

A coauthoring session in Excel Web App moves along smoothly until one of the coauthors clicks Open In Excel, which displays the message shown in Figure 11-11. That coauthor is prevented from opening the file if another team member also has the file open. Clicking OK in this message doesn't send a notification to other coauthors, which would be helpful. Coauthors need to close the file before it can be opened in Excel.

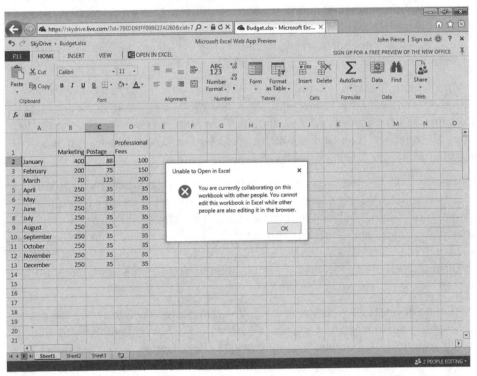

FIGURE 11-11 You can't open a workbook in Excel if more than one person is editing the file in Excel Web App.

Excel Web App does not support features that you might otherwise apply to workbooks you use collaboratively. For example, Excel Web App can't open a shared workbook or a workbook whose worksheets are protected. Also, you can't work with PivotTables in the web app at the same level of detail as you can in Excel.

The File tab in Excel Web App—as in the other Office Web Apps—lets you save a copy of the file, download the file, display a "print friendly view" (something like print preview), and share the file. You can also view earlier versions of a document via the File tab.

Click File, and then click Previous Versions. You'll see a window such as the one shown in Figure 11-12. Click an entry under Older Versions to display it. You can then restore that version for editing or download that version.

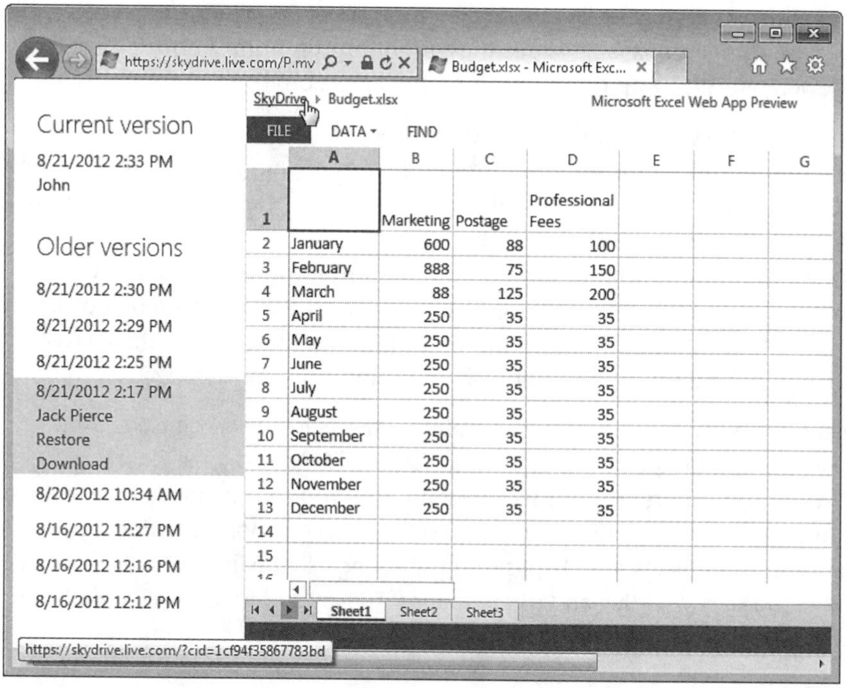

FIGURE 11-12 Office Web Apps give you access to previous versions of a file. Click Restore to make the selected version the current version on SkyDrive. Click Download to create a copy on your computer.

Building and editing presentations in PowerPoint Web App

Like Word Web App, PowerPoint Web App opens a file in Reading view, where you can open the file to edit it or share the file, view a slide show, or add or view comments.

Of the four Office Web Apps, PowerPoint Web App provides more of the features that are available in the desktop version. For example, PowerPoint Web App is displayed with seven standard tabs, including Animations and Transitions.

Coauthoring in PowerPoint Web App has some similarities with the experience in Excel Web App and some with Word Web App. A notification reporting that more than one person is editing the file is displayed in the status bar. Like Excel Web App, PowerPoint Web App has no Save button, so changes are saved automatically, and your view of the presentation is refreshed periodically. But as in Word Web App, you can use the desktop version of PowerPoint to open a presentation that you're coauthoring in the web app and continue editing the file.

If you have the file open in the desktop version of PowerPoint, you receive notifications when another author changes the file, even when that author is working in the web app. You can then click Updates Available to see the current version from SkyDrive. Coauthors working in PowerPoint Web App don't receive such notifications.

You can view a slide show in the web app, or switch back to Reading view to scroll through the slides and add comments. The process for developing a group presentation outlined in Chapter 10, "Preparing a presentation as a group," includes a stage in which outside reviewers are provided with the file, and they can then suggest changes and annotate the presentation with comments. For this stage, instead of sending a presentation via e-mail, which can be problematic for especially large files, post the presentation on SkyDrive, share it with outside reviewers with the Can View setting, and let the reviewers watch and annotate the file in PowerPoint Web App using only Reading view.

You also have more editing capabilities for graphical objects in PowerPoint Web App than you do in Word Web App, for example. You can modify the text in a SmartArt diagram, or switch to a different SmartArt layout entirely. You can change fills and colors as well. You also get access to context tabs such as the Drawing Tools tab, which lets you work with drawing objects and shapes. You can change shape fill and outline, move shapes forward and back in order, and rotate shapes. The level of functionality available lets you complete nearly all the work required to prepare a finished presentation.

Index

A

access
  blocking, 224–226
  limits on, workbook, 245, 292
  managing, introduction to, 63–64
  and password protection, 64, 67–68, 118, 246
  See also sharing files
Add Lists, Libraries, And Other Apps tile, 22
Advanced Search page, 59–60
Agenda list, 37
alerts
  setting up, 41–43
  for task list changes, 33
Alignment tab, for comments, 240
All Day Event field, 35
All Mark view, 216
All Of These Words field, 60
Alt Text tab, for comments, 241
Always Ask Where To Send option, 178
Animations tab, 99
annotations
  adding to coauthored presentation, 268–269
  deleting, 159
  Lync tools, 256
  in worksheets, 232, 237–241
  See also comments, notes, tags
Any Of These Words field, 60
Appear Away status, 148
apps. *See* Office Web Apps
archives, for messages, 124
Arrange command, 181
Asset Library, 29
Assigned To field, 31
Attendees list , 37
audio recordings, adding to OneNote, 182–183
author initials, hiding, 193

authority, 4
authors
  blocking, 224–226
  finding notes by, 193
  See also coauthoring
AutoText entry, in Quick Parts, 115
Availability Only option, 134–135
Available status, 148

B

background, setting for template, 102
Backstage view, PowerPoint, 263
backup notebooks, 202
Balloons option, 216
Basic Meeting Workspace template, 37
Be Right Back status, 148
Blank Meeting Workspace template, 37
blocking authors, 224–226
brainstorming sessions, pros and cons, 8–9
browser view options, 251–252
building blocks, 113–115
  control, 117
  in templates, 106–107
Busy status, 148

C

calendar
  managing, 136–137
  permissions, 136–137
  publishing online, 139–141
  sending by e-mail, 134–136
  sharing, 124, 138–139
  subscribing to, 284–285
Calendar app, 284–286
Category field, 35, 114
cells, making editable, 71–72, 252–253

About the Author

John Pierce was an editor and writer at Microsoft Corporation for twelve years. He is the author or coauthor of several books about Microsoft Office, most recently *MOS 2010 Study Guide for Microsoft Word Expert, Excel Expert, Access, and SharePoint* and *MOS Study Guide for Microsoft Office 365*. He currently works on a number of virtual teams involved in publishing content on the web, as e-books, and in print.

What do you think of this book?

We want to hear from you!

To participate in a brief online survey, please visit:

microsoft.com/learning/booksurvey

Tell us how well this book meets your needs—what works effectively, and what we can do better. Your feedback will help us continually improve our books and learning resources for you.

Thank you in advance for your input!